VALUES, VOICE AND VIRTUE

Matthew J. Goodwin is Professor of Politics at the University of
_____ ler
_____ , ... print and broadcast ...edia
including the *Sunday Times* and the BBC. Goodwin has advised more
than 200 organizations on political issues. He lives in London and
tweets @GoodwinMJ.

MATTHEW GOODWIN

Values, Voice and Virtue

The New British Politics

PENGUIN BOOKS

PENGUIN BOOKS

UK | USA | Canada | Ireland | Australia
India | New Zealand | South Africa

Penguin Books is part of the Penguin Random House group of companies
whose addresses can be found at global.penguinrandomhouse.com

First published in Penguin Books 2023
005

Set in 9.25/12.5pt Sabon LT Std
Typeset by Jouve (UK), Milton Keynes
Printed and bound in Great Britain by Clays Ltd, Elcograf S.p.A.

The authorized representative in the EEA is Penguin Random House Ireland,
Morrison Chambers, 32 Nassau Street, Dublin DO2 YH68

A CIP catalogue record for this book is available from the British Library

ISBN: 978-0-141-99909-8

List of Figures

Preface

This book is about the remarkable changes that have been sweeping through British politics. Over the last decade, Britain has been rocked by the rise of populism, the shock vote for Brexit, the collapse of the Labour Party, the stunning rise and then dramatic fall of Boris Johnson and the explosion of American style 'culture wars' over free speech, the legacy of Britain's empire, racism, gender wars and, ultimately, who we think we are as a country.

Much of this has overturned the old-fashioned and rather quaint idea of British politics as stable, boring, moderate, and consensual, held together by a 'civic culture' in which voters are happy to defer to their leaders in Westminster and the country steers clear of the emotional and divisive politics that has taken root in America and the rest of Europe. Instead, the new British politics is far more volatile, chaotic, divisive, and unpredictable, with rapidly rising numbers of voters openly rebelling against their leaders and searching for radical alternatives.

A majority of British people voted to leave the European Union (EU), so the joke goes, but ever since Brexit our politics has become far more European, more populist, emotional, polarised, unstable, and prone to the same political gridlock that has paralysed our neighbours, prompting *The Economist* in 2022 to rename the country 'Britaly'.

But while the rise of this new British politics continues to generate considerable debate it remains poorly understood. What has been driving the rise of populism in a country that used to be considered immune to it? Why did so many Brits vote for Brexit? How was Boris Johnson and the Conservative Party able to pull together a new and distinctive electoral coalition, and why did Liz Truss fail so spectacularly to keep it together? Why did the Labour Party collapse so dramatically at the last election, including in its northern, working-class and industrial Red Wall? And what do the answers to all these questions tell us about what is driving the new British politics and where it might be taking us in the years and decades ahead?

I decided to write this book because I wanted to offer a different explanation for why our politics has been upended. My argument is that this turbulence and turmoil is being pushed forward by three new drivers in politics, which have been a long time coming and still have a long way to run. They will shape not only what remains of the Conservative Party's time in office, under Rishi Sunak, and whether Labour and the left can truly recover, but the future of our politics and our country more generally. They will also speak to debates in global politics.

I am a university professor who has been exploring these issues for more than twenty years. Nearly a decade ago, I wrote a book, *Revolt on the Right*, written with Robert Ford, which warned that millions of voters were about to rebel against a liberal establishment which they felt had lost touch with the rest of the country.[1] Shortly afterwards, millions of voters shocked the establishment by suddenly propelling populist Nigel Farage, later an ally of Donald Trump, from the margins to the mainstream. Then, in 2016, the same drivers pushed millions more of them to cast a vote for Brexit, sending shockwaves around Britain and the wider world.

In my next book, *National Populism*, written with Roger Eatwell, I explained why, before Marine Le Pen won a record number of seats in France, before Viktor Orbán reached a new high in Hungary, and before national populists polled record support in the likes of Italy, Portugal, Spain and Sweden, similar tensions are driving similar revolts across the West.[2] Bringing together decades of research in the social sciences, we explained why this disruptive force has forged a strong connection with specific groups of voters and is now here to stay.

Four years on, *Values, Voice and Virtue* brings me back to my home country of Britain, where the political currents I first identified more than a decade ago have now gone mainstream. They not only powered the shocking rise of Nigel Farage's populist crusade and the historic vote for Brexit but went on to 'realign' the Conservative Party in the aftermath of that Brexit referendum, allowing it to tap into a new and distinctive coalition of voters.

How were a bunch of mavericks, outsiders, renegades and populists able to outflank the elite, even if some of them, such as Boris Johnson, clearly belong to the British elite? Which voters have rallied to them and why? Why have so many people in Britain today abandoned the political mainstream and why do many more feel so utterly disgruntled and disillusioned with the state of Britain? Where did Labour and the left go wrong? And what deeper trends, away from the headlines, are driving these remarkable changes?

This book is written for people on all sides of the debate; right-wingers, left-wingers, Remainers, Leavers, moderates, radicals. It will resonate not just in Brexit Britain but across the globe, in democracies that are struggling to contain similar revolts. And it openly challenges much of the conventional wisdom and misleading narratives that have taken hold of our debates about politics.

Whoever wins the next election – whether the Conservatives under the new leadership of Rishi Sunak or Labour under the new leadership of Sir Keir Starmer – what will become clear throughout this book is that the new drivers of politics will remain firmly in place for a very long time to come. Only those leaders and parties who respond to them will find success.

Before we embark on our journey, I would like to make two further points. Firstly, some of the issues we will explore are controversial, so it is essential that you can find the evidence for my claims. 'In God we trust,' said American engineer William Deming. 'All others must bring data.' The endnotes throughout this book will guide you to the evidence, usually drawn from large-scale, independent and reliable national surveys, such as the British Election Study and the British Social Attitudes surveys, or academic studies which have been reviewed by other academics. If you want to continue your intellectual journey then follow these notes; if you are not bothered then just ignore them and keep reading.

Secondly, I would like to thank a few people who have helped me along the way, either by working with me or allowing me to develop my arguments through articles and talks. They are Claire Ainsley, Noah Atkinson, Sarah Baxter, Kelly Beaver, Nigel Biggar, Vernon Bogdanor, Noah Carl, Sally Chatterton, Harold Clarke, Chloe Currens, Sir John Curtice, David Cutts, James Dennison, Roger Eatwell, Geoff Evans, David Goodhart, John Healey, Oliver Heath, Martin Ivens, Eric Kaufmann, Erik Larsen, Paul Marshall, Caitlin Milazzo, Ben Page, Joe Phillips, William Shawcross, Philippa Stroud, James Tilley, Susan Walton, Paul Whiteley and researchers at More in Common. I would like to thank my agent, Charlie Brotherstone, my research assistants Bill Bowkett and Lino Buckingham, Simon Winder at Penguin Random House, and the many people on Twitter (@GoodwinMJ) or Substack who have offered their thoughts, comments, and critiques (!) over the years.

Somebody once said there are two types of researchers; parachutists who survey the landscape from great heights and truffle hunters who immerse themselves only in a small piece of territory. While parachutists focus on the big picture at the cost of detail, truffle hunters focus on the detail but at the cost of the big picture.[3] This book is written by an unapologetic parachutist who is expecting criticism from truffle hunters. Nonetheless, I hope you find the view interesting. Lastly, this book is dedicated to my very patient wife, Fiona, and my daughter, Grace, who I love very much.

Matt Goodwin
London, November 2022

Introduction

British politics is coming apart. The symptoms of this crisis are all around: widespread disillusionment with politicians in Westminster, a growing sense of despair with the direction of the country, a fragmenting United Kingdom, a collapse of trust in institutions, and the emergence of a far more polarized or divided politics, with many people hunkering down and turning away from those who hold different beliefs.[1]

Remarkably, we now live in a country where more than half of people think 'none of the main parties represent my priorities and values', more than six in ten think 'Britain is broken', and nearly seven in ten think 'the experts in this country do not understand people like me'.[2] And over the last decade this crisis became impossible to ignore.

Suddenly, seemingly with no warning, the British establishment was rocked by three major revolts which almost nobody saw coming.

First came the meteoric rise of national populism, led by Nigel Farage, who blew apart many of the old myths about British society. Britain, it used to be said, is immune to the populist virus that has taken hold of other nations. For decades, scholars pointed to the country's moderate and deferential 'civic culture' as one reason why the British had not given rise to the more divisive, emotional and disruptive politics which has swept through Europe. But in the early 2010s all this was overturned when Nigel Farage, a beer-swilling, fag-holding populist, was suddenly propelled by millions of disillusioned voters from the margins to the mainstream.

Like other populists around the world, from Donald Trump in

America to Marine Le Pen in France, from Giorgia Meloni in Italy to Santiago Abascal in Spain, Farage resonated strongly with a large chunk of the country by promising to put the interests and the culture of the nation first, to speak for people who feel ignored, forgotten, even held in contempt by the elite, and by taking aim at that very elite in Westminster.[3]

Then, in 2016, came the second, much larger rebellion when 17.4 million people stunned the establishment all over again by voting for Brexit. In one fell swoop, they not only brought Britain's nearly fifty-year membership of the European Union (EU) to a crashing halt, demolishing the dreams of those who assumed the country would remain at the heart of Europe, but also shocked the wider world. Britain, which had first joined the European Community in 1973, now became the first major power to leave the club.

And then, three years later, in 2019, came the third rebellion, when after years of intense wrangling in Westminster about whether to respect the vote for Brexit, 14 million people returned to the ballot box to propel a renegade member of the elite, the Old Etonian and Oxford graduate Boris Johnson, into Number 10 Downing Street with the largest majority for any Conservative leader since Margaret Thatcher's final majority in 1987.

In the end, Johnson's controversial premiership only lasted two years and 348 days before he was forced to resign by his fellow Conservative MPs. A prime minister who liked to model himself on Winston Churchill only lasted the same number of days as Neville Chamberlain. Boris Johnson, so the joke went in Westminster, was the third prime minister to be brought down by Boris Johnson. After helping to bring down David Cameron, by campaigning for Brexit, and then helping to bring down Theresa May, by campaigning against her 'soft' vision of Brexit, Johnson then brought his own premiership to an end by presiding over a series of scandals in Number 10. Yet, like national populism and Brexit before him, Boris Johnson's emphatic majority in 2019, his successful invasion of the Labour Party's Red Wall, stretching across northern, working-class England, and his very distinctive electoral coalition were further symptoms of a deep malaise in the country, a yearning for change among millions of voters.

Underestimated and misunderstood, all three of these revolts shocked not only Britain but the world, tapping into global debates about a popular uprising against the elite. And their legacy remains with us today. They have overturned the old-fashioned view about the British as a moderate, consensual and deferential people. They have completely changed the direction of the country and a large part of the world order, for ever altering the relationship between Britain, the EU and other major powers, including America. They have cleared the way for a major and unprecedented overhaul of policy on the economy, global trade, immigration and foreign affairs. They reduced Labour and the left to four consecutive defeats, including their worst since 1935. And, as we will see, they overhauled the geography of British politics by mobilizing an entirely new electoral coalition, and changing the very meaning of left and right.

Why did this happen? There are many fashionable theories. Whether through Netflix documentaries, films, books or articles, we are routinely told that all these upheavals were driven by short-term factors in the here and now. Social media, shadowy big tech companies, misinformation, fake news, dark money, controversial campaigners, media barons, tabloid newspapers, Russia and what was written on the side of a big red bus are all frequently invoked.

But few of these explanations are convincing. What most of them share is a narrow obsession with campaigns, a failure to look beyond the promises, the personalities and the politics of the here and now, and a lack of interest in the deeper trends which have been tilting the axis of politics for many years, not just during the last election cycle.

Others have looked at politics through a longer-term lens, instead tracing these revolts to the legacy of Britain's old empire, to an outpouring of racism and to what we are routinely told is an 'institutionally racist' country – debates that re-emerged after the death of Queen Elizabeth II in 2022. Seen from this perspective, the upheavals of the last decade are not rooted in people's rational or coherent concerns about the country but an irrational outburst among bigots, racists and xenophobes who are no longer in control of their own emotions, who yearn to return to the days of empire or who simply did not know what they were voting for.

Yet nor are these accounts convincing. Few of these seductive narratives, as we will see, are supported by evidence on how modern Britain – including the British people's attitudes toward race, immigration and their national identity – have been evolving in recent years. In short, most of the theories that are offered to try and account for these political earthquakes are too narrow, politically biased or lacking in evidence to be taken seriously.

Many also reflect the human tendency for 'confirmation bias', whereby people cling to explanations which reinforce but do not challenge their existing beliefs. 'Every man [and woman],' wrote philosopher Bertrand Russell, 'wherever he goes, is encompassed by a cloud of comforting convictions, which move with him like flies on a summer day.'

Rather than throw light onto why so many people joined these revolts, most of these fashionable arguments represent little more than fairy tales which people who have found themselves outflanked in politics tell each other to try and explain away election or referendum results they do not like. When it comes to making sense of why politics is being transformed, and what we might do about it, they are hindering rather than helping us.

So, instead of clinging to fairy tales, in this book we will take a different approach. Rather than look at these revolts in isolation, or through a very narrow lens, we will look at them together and while drawing on a large pile of evidence. And when we do so, it will become clear that all these events are symptoms of something much bigger and far more profound: a deep-rooted and unfolding 'realignment' of politics which has been taking place not just in Brexit Britain but across the West.

The word 'realignment' refers to a decisive shift in the balance of power – a moment or period of time when a particular political party or a set of ideas become dominant over others, and end up reshaping their respective country in profound ways. Rather than being rooted in the here and now, these historic turning points take place when much longer-running demographic or electoral currents gradually push millions of people to switch sides at the ballot box, handing one party a new coalition of support which can last for years, if not decades, while making it difficult for other parties to recover.

This is what has been happening in British politics over the last decade. Many people, for entirely coherent and rational reasons, have been trying to realign the country's politics, and push back against a status-quo that has governed Britain for much of the last half century. While it is still too early to know whether this realignment will continue in the years ahead, whether Rishi Sunak will manage to reconnect with it or whether Keir Starmer will be able to address its drivers and swing the pendulum back toward Labour, what is clear is that it is already under way and has already had profound effects on politics and the country.

Whether reflected in the growing willingness of working-class voters in the Red Wall in the north of England to switch from Labour to the Conservatives, or prosperous liberal graduates in the southern shires switching from the Conservatives to Labour or the Liberal Democrats, this unfolding realignment is increasingly upending the old politics and transforming the country from below.

There have been realignments before.[4] Historians would point to the events of the 1840s, when Conservative prime minister Robert Peel sought to revoke the Corn Laws against the wishes of Conservative MPs. They would also point to the early 1900s, when Conservative protectionists went to war with their free-trade rivals. And they would point to the early years of the twentieth century, when Labour replaced the Liberals as the second major force in politics.

Readers from America would point to the realignment which began in 1932, bringing Franklin D. Roosevelt to power and ushering in a new consensus that ran until the 1960s. Or the realignment which began in 1980, which brought Ronald Reagan, the Republicans and a new conservative consensus to power. Some realignments turn out to be short-lived; others, such as the rise of Reaganism and Thatcherism, bring about truly transformative and long-lasting change, changing politics for ever.

The realignment that has been gradually unfolding over the last decade – finding its expression through national populism, Brexit and a very different brand of post-Brexit conservatism – is different from what has gone before. As we will see, it is rooted in a new set of drivers which have been pushing many voters to abandon their old allegiances and search for a new politics.

It is also more global than national, mirrored in similar trends which are sweeping through not just Brexit Britain but many other Western democracies: from the rise of the Trumpian Republicans, who have forged a stronger connection with white working-class voters and people without college degrees, to the breakthrough of national populists across Europe, like Giorgia Meloni in Italy, who are drawing their strongest support from the same groups – from people who feel they have been cut adrift by the elite. Many British pundits who routinely say the transformation of politics is 'just about Brexit' or Jeremy Corbyn ignore these global parallels.

All realignments generate reactions. And the one that has pushed through populism, Brexit and Boris Johnson is now producing a sharp backlash, reflected in rising support for Labour, the Liberal Democrats, the Greens, and the Scottish National Party among socially liberal graduates, middle-class urban professionals, young millennials and even younger zoomers from Generation-Z who feel repulsed by the rise of Nigel Farage, Brexit, Boris Johnson, and a more strongly pro-Brexit conservatism, and who are now yearning to push politics in a very different direction. We will explore this backlash throughout this book but our main focus will be on explaining what brought us to this point in the first place.

Why has this realignment been unfolding now? My argument, which I develop in the chapters ahead, is that it is being driven forward by millions of people who want to push back against the rise of a new dominant class – a 'new elite' – and a political revolution they have been imposing on the rest of the country for much of the last fifty years.

The new elite, as we will see in the next chapter, are not like the old elite who dominated British politics during the twentieth century. The old elite were united by their hereditary titles, wealth, family ties to the aristocracy and instinctively conservative values. The new elite, today, are utterly different. While they sometimes overlap with the old ruling class, the members of this new overclass are drawn far more from the rapidly expanding ranks of a new, professional, middle-class, urban and university-educated elite who have risen to positions of immense economic, political and cultural power.

This new elite is defined by very different things: their degrees from one of the most prestigious Oxbridge or Russell Group universities; their strong liberal cosmopolitan if not radically progressive cultural values; their increasingly loud and dominant voice in Britain's most important and influential institutions; and their growing sense of moral righteousness over other groups in British society.

It is the new elite, as we will see in Chapter 2, who have captured the benefits of a political revolution they have led and imposed on the rest of the country from the 1980s onward. The roots of today's more turbulent politics do not lie simply in the Brexit referendum, in promises to 'Take Back Control' or 'Get Brexit Done'. They lie instead in a deeply destabilizing political project which has been sweeping through Britain and other Western democracies for at least fifty years and is continuing to drive a huge wedge between different groups in society.

Inevitably, this revolution has taken on different forms in different countries. In Britain, it began on 4 May 1979 and continued to accelerate until the morning of 24 June 2016. It was, first and foremost, a political revolution that was committed to changing the country in mainly four ways – reshaping it around a far more disruptive, and divisive, model of 'hyper-globalization', an unprecedented new era of mass immigration, integrating the nation into supranational institutions such as the European Union and hollowing out its national democracy by handing power to a new, more insular, careerist and homogeneous political class in Westminster.

It is simply impossible to make sense of the new politics without making sense of how this revolution overturned and upended the country. The political scientist Walter Dean Burnham once said political realignments are a 'surrogate for revolution'.[5] They are driven by sharp clashes between different groups in society that are brought about by deeper changes in the economy, culture and society. They take place when the dominant ruling class has failed to recognize and adapt to a new set of divides in society. This is exactly what has been happening in Britain.

A revolution that was led by the new elite and which reshaped the country around their economic and cultural interests has, over the last decade, spawned a counter-revolution which found its expression through the rise of national populism, Brexit, Boris Johnson and post-Brexit conservatism, and which may yet continue to drive considerable change in the years and decades ahead.

Decades ago, it used to be argued that the main problem in Western societies was the incoherent and irrational masses; but today, it is the elites. Increasingly, over the last fifty years, many of the people who have assumed power in Britain have simply lost touch with much of the rest of the country in three key areas of our national life.

Firstly, they lost touch with the *values* which are held by many people. As a new minority elite arose to impose their liberal cosmopolitan and progressive world view on the rest of Britain, they cut many other people adrift, not just economically but culturally – from the new world view that now dominates the new 'mainstream'. The values of the new elite have simply never been shared by a much larger number of voters who neither recognize nor particularly like this new world view and how it has been changing the country.

As the new elite doubled down on the values of a university-educated minority in the cities and the university towns, millions of others came to the stark realization that their values were no longer recognized or respected by the people who now rule over them. In turn, they sought to reassert their values by rallying around populism, Brexit and Boris Johnson, and will continue to do so unless we find a better way of recognizing their beliefs.

Secondly, this growing rift, building for decades, has been reinforced by how the new elite have also taken control of Britain's political, media, creative, cultural and university institutions. While the university educated liberal minority have a loud and dominant voice in the national debate about who we are as a country, they simultaneously exclude the *voice* of many others who neither belong to this new ruling class nor share its values and beliefs.

Pushed out of the institutions, many people have spent years watching the transformation of Britain and its prevailing culture with a palpable sense they are now on the outside looking in – that the first word in 'representative democracy' no longer applies to them. Instead of feeling included in the national conversation, they feel excluded, if not completely silenced. In turn, many have flocked to populists and renegades to try and reassert their voice not just in Westminster but the prevailing culture. They will almost certainly continue to rebel in the years ahead unless our leaders and institutions find a better way of representing and recognizing their voice.

And, thirdly, these tensions are today being further reinforced by how the new elite no longer see some groups in Western societies as being as *virtuous*, or morally worthy, as others. Rather than treat all groups with the same degree of dignity, respect and moral worth, and bring the country together around unifying narratives, the new elite are increasingly embracing a world view that is hard-wired to push different groups apart, rather than pull them together.

They are reshaping institutions and the national conversation around a divisive new ideology of radical 'woke' progressivism that awards highly educated liberals and racial, sexual, and gender minorities a much greater sense of social status, honour, and respect than other groups. This has left many voters feeling that their values and voice have not only been cast aside but that they and their wider group are shamed and stigmatized as a morally inferior underclass, consisting of uneducated thickos, racists, authoritarians, gammons and Karens.

Today, when many voters, especially from the white working class and the non-graduate majority look at institutions such as the Labour Party and much else, they feel they are being looked down upon as morally inferior, if not illegitimate, members of the wider community. And this too has been pushing them from left to right, or simply to give up on politics altogether, and will continue to do so unless we can find a way of pushing back against this divisive ideology and returning to more unifying narratives that treat all groups in society with the same degree of respect.

Over the last decade, all three of these drivers – values, voice and virtue – have been pushing many people into a counter-revolution against the new elite. Already, it has sent a bunch of populists, mavericks and outsiders from the margins to the mainstream and pushed the country in a completely different direction. And by the time you reach the end of this book another point will have become clear – unless we all find a better way of addressing these new divides they will almost certainly continue to cause new political earthquakes in the years ahead as people search for leaders who will reassert their values, voice and sense of virtue against this new elite.

I
Rise of the New Elite

Over the last decade, many of the people who run Britain were confronted with the realization they do not know a large part of the country at all. Repeatedly, leading politicians, journalists, commentators and intellectuals were stunned by a succession of revolts they failed to see coming. In response, many turned inwards, blaming these upheavals on things which have nothing to do with them, which distracts us from exploring what has really led so many people to rebel against the status quo.

Routinely, over the last ten years, we have been told that the rise of national populism, Brexit, and Boris Johnson's election victory can all be chalked up to social media campaigns that were run by firms such as Cambridge Analytica, Dominic Cummings, simplistic promises to 'Take Back Control' and 'Get Brexit Done', or the remarkable unpopularity of Jeremy Corbyn, the radical left-winger who led Labour into the electoral abyss at the last general election in 2019.

The popularity of Netflix documentaries and dramas such as *The Great Hack* and *Brexit: The Uncivil War* reflects how these narratives resonate strongly among people who have struggled to make sense of these revolts. Instead of taking a step back to explore how deep-rooted and longer-running trends have been reshaping politics, many people have found it easier to rehearse the standard script by blaming Rupert Murdoch, big tech, dark money or a morally inferior underclass of racist, irrational and ignorant Little Englanders, who, we are told over and over again, did not know what they were voting for.

As I argued in my last book *National Populism*, people reduce complex movements to 'one type' of voter or 'one cause' because they want simple and straightforward explanations.[1] But when 5 million people rebelled against the establishment in 2015 by voting for Nigel Farage's party, when more than 17 million voted for Brexit, when 5 million switched to the Brexit Party three years later to try and ensure that vote was implemented, and when another 14 million propelled Boris Johnson and a different brand of post-Brexit conservatism into power in 2019, these simplistic stereotypes appear far from convincing.

Yet this has not stopped these narratives from morphing into conventional wisdom. One of the most popular focuses narrowly and exclusively on political campaigns and the people who run them. Typical was an article published in the *New Statesman* with the headline: 'How the Brexit campaign lied to us – and got away with it'. Rather than explore how deeper currents had pushed more than half the electorate to rebel against the status quo, its author, Helen Lewis, traced the rebellion to 'political advertising [that] is exempt from the regulation that would otherwise bar false claims and outrageous promises'.[2] Rather than see Brexit as a historic turning point in which millions of people sought to reassert their values and voice against a system which has excluded them for decades, some writers prefer to portray their fellow citizens as mindless, irrational, ignorant lemmings who are being pushed around from one election to the next by lies, misinformation and post-truth politics.

'We know that millions and millions of pounds were spent on Facebook ads in the 2016 Brexit referendum and in subsequent general elections,' argues journalist Peter Geoghegan, reflecting this obsession with social media and the supposed role of dark money, 'and that Facebook was the place in which hard-line messages have been pushed further and further.'[3] Many of these fashionable narratives, in turn, then spread like wildfire on social media platforms such as Twitter, which in both Britain and America are disproportionately dominated by left-leaning and more liberal university graduates.[4] Twitter is also where the media class congregate and so, unsurprisingly, these narratives then flourish in the wider debate.

The regulation of social media and how it is used by foreign powers to influence elections are certainly topics that demand serious attention. In a world where one in eight Americans believe in the QAnon conspiracy theory – which contends that a secretive clique of powerful Satanic paedophiles conspired against Donald Trump – few serious analysts would argue social media has no impact at all.[5] But, at the same time, ever since the Trump and Brexit revolts of 2016, many commentators, searching for an easy answer, have quickly awarded social media a level of attention that is wholly disproportionate to its actual impact.

One thing they ignore is that democracies across the West have been grappling with major populist revolts since at least the nineteenth century, long before the world was online. The roots of national populism, a distinctive ideology in its own right, can be traced back not just to the creation of Facebook in 2004, or Twitter in 2006, but to much older movements, such as the US People's Party, in the 1890s, which is widely seen as the first serious populist revolt.[6]

Similarly, in Europe, we forget that major populist revolts arrived in countries such as Italy in 1996, when the Northern League (now just the League) began to break through as a serious force; Austria in 1999, when the charismatic Jörg Haider, leader of the Freedom Party, brought his party its best ever result; or France in 2002, when Marine Le Pen's father, Jean-Marie, stunned the world by reaching the final round of the presidential election for the first time, where he was defeated by Jacques Chirac. The foundations of politics, in other words, were shaking long before anybody was on social media.

Popular accounts which begin and end with social media ignore not only these much older tremors but also a large pile of evidence which shows how the intensifying 'polarization' of Western politics began decades ago. As one recent study, published in 2020, at Stanford points out, the rise of a far more polarized politics of the sort we can see in America today can be traced to the 1980s – long before anybody was on Facebook and Twitter.[7] Among political scientists in Britain, too, there is a general consensus that many of the trends which set the stage for populism, Brexit and Boris Johnson's successful invasion of Labour's territory were visible decades ago.

The breakdown of the old, tribal bonds between voters and parties, the rise of a new set of cultural issues in politics such as mass immigration, a rising tide of disillusionment among working-class and non-graduate voters and a strengthening belief among voters that Left and Right are indistinguishable from one another can all be traced back to the 1980s and 1990s, if not earlier.[8]

Many of the seductive narratives that circulate widely among the elite also gloss over the fact that most people do not trust what they read on social media and do not see it as a reliable source of information. Contrary to the image, popular among elites, of the ignorant masses being pushed around by what they read while scrolling through Facebook and Twitter, research at the University of Cambridge finds that the British are among the *least* trusting of social media in the world. An overwhelming majority, 83 per cent, say they have 'little or no trust' in Facebook and Twitter. Just 1 per cent of the country trust social media 'a great deal'.[9]

Many of the people who have been the most likely to support these populist revolts, furthermore, have also been the *least* likely of all to use social media. After Boris Johnson's victory, in 2019, while more than half of voters on the left said their main source of news was online, only one in three voters on the right – who are more likely to rely on print and broadcast media for news and information – said the same. And in 2022, a major review of the impact of social media on politics – a 'meta-analysis' which reviews all the available studies – concluded that contrary to much that we are told there is actually 'little evidence that people learn about politics on social media'.[10]

Drawing a simple straight line from the offline transformation of politics to what voters are reading online is further undermined by evidence which suggests, strongly, that the impact of political campaigns, of spending money on elections, of political advertisements, is vastly exaggerated. There is no doubt campaigns can sway some undecided voters. But much of the evidence that has emerged in recent years points to the conclusion that their effect is rather small and short-lived, usually fading out after only a few weeks.[11]

Even if they do have some impact, they certainly cannot account for the sheer scale of the changes that are unfolding around us today. Remarkably, over the last sixty years in Britain, the share of 'swing voters' who switch their votes between parties has rocketed from

13 per cent in the 1960s to more than 60 per cent during the last decade. These 'volatile voters', in other words, have gone from representing a small minority to the majority.[12] We need more than social media and campaigns to explain why our politics has become so turbulent.

Another theory, popular among disillusioned liberal centrists, is that much of this churn and change can be pinned on Jeremy Corbyn – the radical left-winger who led the Labour Party between 2015 and 2020 and will go down in history as one of the most unsuccessful party leaders in British history. Seen through this lens, the unexpectedly strong levels of public support for Brexit in the Labour heartlands, the dramatic weakening of the Labour Party's relationship with the white working class and the party's complete collapse in 2019 all owed much to the remarkable unpopularity of Mr Corbyn.

There is no doubt he was uniquely unpopular. When Corbyn led Labour to its historic loss, in 2019, he was the most unpopular leader of the opposition on record.[13] Remarkably, shortly before Boris Johnson captured Red Wall seats such as Bassetlaw, which had been held by Labour since 1935, Bolsover (Labour since 1950) and Don Valley (Labour since 1922), three-quarters of the country thought Corbyn was doing a bad job as the leader of the Labour Party. His ratings were not just lower than Michael Foot's, another radical left leader who had led Labour into the abyss in 1983, they were also lower than Prince Andrew's, who was trying to defend his ties with a convicted paedophile.[14]

But focusing narrowly on Corbyn is also insufficient. For one thing, it cannot explain why Labour's relationship with the working class, as we will see, has been breaking down not just since 2015, when the radical left assumed control of the Labour Party, but for at least twenty years. A growing sense of apathy among working-class voters, a belief that politics makes no difference to their lives, and their willingness to defect to populists and the conservatives, were all visible in the 1990s. While the Corbynistas exacerbated the crisis, they certainly did not create it.

Like other myths that have taken hold, the British tendency to look only at what is taking place on these islands offers us a very limited view. It is only when we step back to look at the much wider landscape that it becomes clear that centre-left parties have fallen to record or near-record lows – not just in Britain but across the West. In fact, over the last forty years, average support for the centre-left across Europe, has slumped by nearly 10 points.[15]

In the last ten years alone, parties like Labour have tumbled to their lowest share of the vote in Germany since 1932, in Austria since 1911, in Sweden since 1908, in Switzerland since 1914, to a near-record low in Spain, and to a new low in the Czech Republic, Finland, France, Greece, Hungary, Italy, the Netherlands and Poland.

In France, in 2022, the French socialists, once a heavyweight, collapsed to a barely visible 1.7 per cent. And while some of these parties have staged a comeback, as in Germany, in 2021, even there Social Democrats remain on their third-lowest share of the vote since Germany returned to democracy after Adolf Hitler and the Nazis.

This is largely because, amid the unfolding realignment, centre-left parties are now under fire on two flanks simultaneously. This dilemma, the challenge of appealing to both a growing, more prosperous more liberal middle class on one side and a left-behind and more culturally conservative working class on the other, had first been noticed by academics in the 1980s. But ever since then this dilemma has been put on steroids, as the two sides have drifted even further apart.

On one side, the centre-left has been losing support among working-class and non-graduate voters to populists, conservatives or apathy, with many of their voters giving up on politics altogether, no longer really believing that politicians represent people like them. In her insightful study of how social democracy has been coming apart, Professor Linn Rennwald points out that, by the 2010s, the working class comprised an astonishing 42 per cent of the national populist vote in Germany, 44 per cent of Nigel Farage's vote in Britain, 48 per cent of support for Dutch populists Geert Wilders and Thierry Baudet, and 60 per cent of support for Marine Le Pen in France.[16] These workers did not always switch over from the left, but the strength of this blue-collar populism has deprived the left of many potential votes.

On the other side, meanwhile, many centre-left parties have also been losing ground among highly educated, middle-class, professional and strongly liberal graduates, as well as more recent generations of young millennials and even younger zoomers from Generation Z, who were born after 1996. Encouraged by more proportional electoral systems, these voters have often been switching instead to radical left, Green, or ultra-liberal parties, propelling Green parties in recent years to record results in Germany, Norway, Ireland, Switzerland, Belgium, Finland, Austria and the Netherlands or helping Joe Biden and the Democrats minimize their losses at the 2022 midterm elections in America.

This is not only further depriving the established left of potential votes but has plunged many political systems around the world into a far more fragmented and volatile politics – where larger numbers of parties are competing for the same number of votes and larger numbers of voters are more willing to switch their support. Not only in Britain, the challenge facing the centre-left is more structural than strategic; it is not just about leadership, Brexit, social media, or who said what during a campaign but, more fundamentally, is about how they have been losing touch with specific groups of voters over a much longer period of time, as we will explore in the pages ahead.

Another seductive myth for people who ignore these global winds traces these revolts to the lingering impact of Britain's old empire. The sudden popularity of three-word slogans such as 'Take Back Control', 'Brexit Means Brexit' and 'Get Brexit Done' has little to do with today's politics. Instead, they represent the latest outburst among a people who have never come to terms with losing an empire that once covered one-quarter of the earth's surface.

Speaking for more than a few people in the left-leaning intellectual elite, Professors Danny Dorling and Sally Tomlinson describe Brexit as 'perhaps the last gasp of this empire . . . a gasp of rancour which seems to have brought to the surface much resentment, hatred, and ill-informed debate'.[17] Instead of Brexit voters being driven by clear and coherent motives, they were ruthlessly exploited by nostalgic, upper-class, imperialist Tory elites who yearn to return to the days when Britain ruled the waves and people clasped hands while singing 'Rule Britannia!'

Professor Fintan O'Toole makes a similar argument, tracing the upheavals of the last decade to what he argues is the psychological legacy of empire. Because of their history, the British, or more specifically the English, so the thinking goes, were always hard-wired to oppose their status as merely one of twenty-eight member states of the European Union.

'In the imperial imagination', writes O'Toole, 'there are only two states: dominant and submissive, colonizer and colonized. This dualism lingers. If England is not an imperial power, it must be the only other thing it can be: a colony.'[18]

A similar argument has been made by journalist Sathnam Sanghera, in his book *Empireland*. 'It has admittedly become a cliché to think that Brexit is an exercise in empire nostalgia,' he writes, 'but clichés often exist for a reason.' As Britain's empire unravelled, so the argument goes, the British reluctantly joined with the rest of Europe, but soon felt they had been reduced to a colony, and so 'Brexiteers started pining, consciously and unconsciously, for some sort of rebirth of the empire.'[19]

While these arguments are interesting and fashionable, they fail to stand up to scrutiny. Aside from being firmly at odds with the evidence on why people voted to leave the EU, which we explore in Chapter 3, they say little if anything at all about why so many other former imperial powers have not followed the British out of the EU, whether by staging a Frexit, a Quitaly or an Espanope.

The Dutch, to take one example, have not only been more likely than the British to voice pride in their old empire but are also more positive about their EU membership – as are the Belgians, French, Italians and Spanish, all of whom had empires yet feel far more attached to the European Union than the British did.[20] Presumably, if imperial nostalgia is the driving force then other previously imperial powers would be staging similar rebellions while populists would be struggling in countries which did not have an empire, yet neither of these things are true. Furthermore, if the British or English are so obsessed with dominating others, then why did two-thirds vote to stay in the European Community at their first Brexit referendum, in 1975, when memories of empire were much fresher than at the second referendum on Europe, in 2016? None of these questions is answered.

Nor do these narratives engage seriously with historians who show that, while the loss of empire may have traumatized a small section of the elite, there is much less evidence to suggest it impacted on ordinary voters.[21] Indeed, throughout the entire postwar era, no electorally successful pro-empire party ever emerged. While the Conservatives downplayed empire, neither the fringe League of Empire Loyalists, founded in 1954, nor the far-right National Front in the 1970s, which absorbed many of the League's activists, ever won a seat in Westminster.

Yet, still, we are asked to believe that, suddenly, in 2016, a longing to return to the days of empire drove voters into the arms of the imperialist Brexiteers. Nor does this view of British politics sit comfortably with other evidence that has emerged since the Brexit referendum. In 2020, after Labour pledged to ensure 'historical injustice, colonialism and the role of British Empire is taught in the national curriculum', surveys found that only one in four people wished that Britain still had an empire. While this increases to around four in ten among Brexit voters, it remains a minority view. Furthermore, only one in three people today think Britain's empire is 'something to be proud of' – a view which, interestingly, is shared by 22 per cent of Britain's black and minority ethnic voters.[22] To suggest that imperial nostalgia, confined as it is to a small minority, powered the revolts of the last decade tells us more about the beliefs of the people who push this argument than what really motivated people to rebel.

Closely linked to this is another narrative which draws a simple, straight line from the upheavals of the last decade to what we are told has been an outpouring of racism and prejudice against minorities in an 'institutionally racist' country. 'The Brexit debate has made Britain more racist', wrote one commentator, in the *Washington Post*, speaking for many. 'The idea of "getting our country back", once considered a crass empire throwback, is now causing ripples of bigoted glee.'[23]

Countless other writers have made similar arguments, portraying Brexit Britain as overflowing with racism, xenophobia and bigotry. Yet, as we will explore in the chapters ahead, while elites are fond of portraying their fellow citizens as a morally inferior, racist underclass, the evidence tells a different story. As the most reliable and rigorous studies show, one curiosity in British politics is that populism, Brexit and Boris Johnson all cut through at the same time as overall levels of racial prejudice and intolerance of minorities have declined to their lowest levels on record. How people think about Britishness, about who is 'truly British', has also become far more inclusive.

While more than a few politicians, journalists, intellectuals and celebrities have rushed to deride much of the rest of the country as a racist hellhole, careful and detailed studies by academics have instead thrown light on what they call the 'populist paradox' – a remarkable and consistent *softening* of the British people's attitudes towards immigration, race, and their British national identity.[24]

When we step back from our heated debates to look at this evidence, as we will do, it becomes clear that even amidst these revolts Britain has become a much more tolerant, open, and welcoming society. Far from being held back by entrenched 'power structures' in what we are told is an institutionally racist society, the evidence shows that many people from minority backgrounds have been making remarkable progress in many areas of British life, even eclipsing their white counterparts in areas such as education and health. The argument that the revolts of the last decade simply reflect a country that is deeply racist and uncomfortable with the modern world, in short, appears far from convincing.

THE NEW ELITE

One of the arguments of this book, instead, is that if we are to truly make sense of what is transforming British politics then we need to spend less time on the misleading narratives that are promoted by the country's elite and spend more time looking at the people who belong to this elite. The transformation of our politics owes less to these fairy tales than to a much deeper and long-running divide in the country, a large and growing rift between a small and powerful 'new elite' and a much larger number of people who are rebelling against this new ruling class and the political project they have imposed on the country over the last fifty years.

Britain's new ruling class look and sound very different from the old elite who dominated the country during the twentieth century. Decades ago, the country was run by upper-class aristocrats, landowners and industrialists who were united by their hereditary titles, their wealth, and, importantly, their instinctively conservative values.

Those people clearly still exist. They can be found in the House of Lords, the *Sunday Times* Rich List, the private members clubs on London's Pall Mall and holding positions of influence in the Conservative Party. But in the early decades of the twenty-first century, the axis of power in Britain and many other democracies has been tilting away from them and towards a new ruling class.

The people who really run Britain and many other western democracies today, who wield enormous power, influence and control over the country and its institutions, come not from the old aristocracy or the old middle class but from a new middle-class graduate elite. And unlike the people who used to run the show, the members of this new elite are united by very different things.

Representing no more than one-quarter of Britain, and sometimes overlapping with the old elite, the new elite are held together by their university degrees from one of the prestigious Oxbridge or Russell Group universities, their financially secure if not prosperous professional and managerial jobs, their urban postcodes in London, the other big cities and the university towns, their parents and partners who belong to the same elite graduate class, their loud and dominant voice in the country's most important institutions and, above all, their strongly liberal cosmopolitan or radically progressive values.

If you want to make sense of the new elite then you need to make sense of the much deeper changes in British society which pushed them forward. 'To understand the man', Napoleon once said, 'you have to know what was happening in the world when he was twenty.' The new elite are the product of two seismic changes which transformed the country over the last seventy years. The first was the transition from an industrial to a post-industrial and knowledge-based economy; the second was the rapid rise of the universities, which expanded to supply this economy with a new, highly educated, highly skilled and culturally distinctive professional class. Together, these changes set the stage for the new elite who have not only risen to dominate Britain but have also lost touch with much of it.

Back in the 1960s, Britain's economy and society were dominated by white working-class men and people who had left school at the earliest opportunity, without any educational qualifications. More than half the workforce toiled in tough, blue-collar, manual jobs in heavy industries, nearly three in four had no qualifications whatsoever, and four in ten belonged to a trade union.[25] This meant that workers and people without degrees were so numerous that they dominated the economy, politics and society. It was impossible for Britain's leaders to win elections without recognizing and respecting them.

Fast forward to today, however, and the country looks completely different. As in other Western democracies, Britain has now transitioned into a post-industrial, knowledge-based economy which puts a premium on white-collar over blue-collar workers, more specialist technical training over manual labour and cognitive-analytical skills which are certified by the universities, though ideally one of the most prestigious Oxbridge and Russell Group universities.

As these changes unfolded, all the groups which dominated Britain during the post-war era – including the white working class and non-graduates – steadily became much less visible, much less influential and much less powerful. Increasingly, as we will see throughout this book, all the groups which used to dominate the country have found themselves being pushed aside by the new elite – economically, politically and culturally.

By the time of the Brexit referendum in 2016, only three in ten of Britain's workers were in working-class jobs, only one in three had no educational qualifications, only one in five belonged to a trade union – and most of them were in white-collar or public-sector jobs – and only one in ten rented their homes from the local council. Meanwhile, the share of people who owned their own home, who belonged to a growing and very powerful new middle class and who had graduated from university with a degree had exploded. All these broad trends reflect the rise of the new middle-class graduate elite.

Unlike Britain's old elite, the people in the new elite are defined by three things. The first is their professional or managerial jobs. Like their peers in other Western states, the new elite emerged to fill the

Figure 1: Decline of the Working Class, 1964–2019

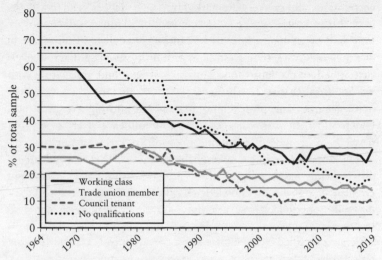

Source: British Election Studies 1964–1983; British Social Attitudes 1984–2012. Social class measured using Goldthorpe–Heath 5-category class schema. Figures are percentage share of total sample, except for class which excludes those who have never worked.

larger number of jobs in the more financially secure, prestigious and very powerful professional and managerial occupations.

Between the 1950s and the Brexit referendum, the share of jobs in the country that was provided by manufacturing collapsed from almost 30 per cent to just 9 per cent, while the share of jobs that was provided by the professional occupations – in science, education, health, technology, insurance and finance – surged more than three-fold to 31 per cent. Britain's public sector also expanded massively, to represent 16 per cent of all jobs, giving rise to a professional class across the NHS, government and other institutions.[26]

Crucially, unlike earlier years, many of these new professionals are women. Between 1971 and 2022, the employment rate for men fell from 91 per cent to 79 per cent, while the rate for women surged from 53 per cent to almost 73 per cent. Today, nearly one in three women in the workforce are in professional or managerial jobs and while they are more likely to work part-time they are, overall, more likely to occupy these positions, working as engineers, doctors, teachers, accountants and lawyers. Remarkably, nearly 80 per cent of all jobs in health and social work, and 70 per cent of all jobs in education, are now held by women, who are also pulling away from men in the rate at which they are getting good exam results at school, going to university, attending the most prestigious universities and graduating with 2:1 and first class degrees.[27]

Concentrated in professional, managerial and higher-status jobs, which allow them to wield considerable influence over society, the new elite is composed of Britain's doctors, architects, newspaper editors, journalists, politicians, publishers, think-tankers, broadcasters, civil servants and academics. They are sometimes called 'social and cultural specialists', or 'knowledge workers' – people who spend their days in jobs which are creative, autonomous, free from rigid

Figure 2: Rise of the Middle-class Graduate Elite, 1964–2019

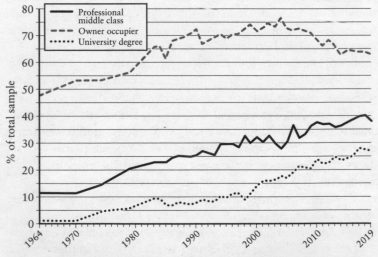

Source: British Election Studies 1964–1983; British Social Attitudes 1984–2012. Social class measured using Goldthorpe–Heath 5-category class schema. Figures are percentage share of total sample, except for class which excludes those who have never worked.

hierarchies, and which involve interacting with others, whether students or other like-minded professionals and managers, who often share their privileged backgrounds, elite degrees and liberal values.[28]

In America, Professor Richard Florida once referred to them as the 'creative class' – highly educated professionals in science, engineering, architecture, design, education, the arts, music, business, finance, law or healthcare, whose jobs involve solving complex problems that demand high levels of cognitive ability, independent judgement, university qualifications and encourage them to embrace a collective ethos which prioritizes creativity, individuality, difference, diversity and merit.[29]

Largely because of this, and unlike the old elite, the people who have joined the new overclass are also defined by a second characteristic – their elite education. They are the winners of the much broader shift towards a university-based meritocracy. Their degrees, typically from one of the most prestigious Oxbridge or Russell Group universities, have become a critically important marker not just of their higher education but, increasingly, their sense of social status, prestige and achievement. As Professor Rune Stubager has shown, across the West, today's university graduates have come to see their 'education-based identity' as a central aspect of who they are – as a form of 'group consciousness' that is similar but distinct from older forms of class consciousness in the twentieth century.[30]

For the new elite, their very identity as high-flying, highly accomplished graduates of elite institutions not only gives them a profoundly important and highly collective sense of unity but also shapes their values and political loyalties, as we will see. Their elite qualifications and elite beliefs have now become central to how they see themselves and distinguish themselves from the much larger number of non-graduates who surround them, who have a very different education and a different set of values. Increasingly, this is fuelling what academics call 'education-based polarization', with the university educated graduate minority drifting further and further apart from the new graduate majority.

Their sense of collective identity is also strengthened by their social networks, which are usually filled with other elite graduates from other elite universities. More often than not, people from the new graduate elite marry other members of the graduate elite. In 2022, Britain's highly educated graduates are among the most likely of all to marry within their own educational group, with 62 per cent of men and 53 per cent of women in the graduate class having partners who also belong to this class.[31]

Online, too, their Facebook and Twitter accounts tend to be filled with other elite graduates who spend their time consciously signalling their elite qualifications, backgrounds, experiences, lifestyles and political beliefs to one another, reinforcing this shared identity.

This is reinforcing the underlying rift in Britain and other Western democracies between people in the minority graduate class and the non-graduate majority, pushing these groups apart not only economically but also culturally and socially.

Much of this is shaping the third feature of the new elite, which also makes them distinct from the old elite – their liberal cosmopolitan if not radically progressive values. The growing education divide between the elite graduate class and the non-graduate majority is both economic and cultural. Economically, it is driving a wedge between, on one side, the relatively small, urban and university-educated new elite who have the right skills, the right qualifications and the right social networks – or 'cultural capital' – to adapt and thrive amid the new knowledge-based economy, and, on the other, a much larger number of non-graduates who lack the right skills, the right urban postcodes, the right qualifications and the right social networks to reap the same benefits.

Culturally, it is also pushing them apart, encouraging them to embrace very different values which lead them to see the country and the world in profoundly different ways. As many studies have now shown, liberal-minded people tend to 'self-select' into university education while the experience of studying at university and socializing alongside other students and staff has a strong influence on their values, further pushing them in a liberal direction.[32] One study, in 2022, drew on the prestigious British Cohort Study to show how people who went to university became more liberal than those who did not, becoming significantly more supportive of immigration, more economically liberal, and less supportive of traditionalist values.[33]

The 'liberalizing' effect of university education is, today, also reinforced by changes that have taken place within the universities themselves. Unlike the 1960s, when the ratio of left-wing academics to right-wing academics in Britain's universities was three to one, today it is closer to eight to one. In other words, while the number of university students has expanded, the range of perspectives they encounter on campus has narrowed. Meanwhile, more conservative students and academics are far more likely than their left-wing peers to experience discrimination on campus and to say they need to 'self-censor', or hide, their real views (see Chapter 4).[34]

Shaped by these experiences, the new middle-class graduate elite have simply become far more likely than their non-graduate counterparts to embrace a strongly liberal cosmopolitan or radically progressive view of the world. In Britain and across the West, the more financially secure new elite have been shown to put a much stronger emphasis than other voters on 'post-material' values, stressing the importance of self-expression, individualism, autonomy, choice, sexual freedom, creativity, secularism and diversity, while simultaneously feeling less wedded to traditional cultural norms, institutions and group-based loyalties which not only united the old elite but are still prioritized by the non graduate majority today.[35] They are, consistently, the most economically and socially liberal group in the country who, as Professors Geoffrey Evans and James Tilley show in their work, are also far more liberal than the old (typically non-graduate) middle class used to be.[36] In turn, graduates and non-graduates are developing different political loyalties, fuelling the realignment. Whereas graduates, as we will see, are moving leftwards in politics, to express their strongly liberal values by voting for left-wing or liberal parties, non-graduates are moving rightwards, largely in disgust at the choices that have been made by their degree-holding and far more liberal rulers.

Increasingly, then, over the last twenty years, the new elite have morphed into the British equivalent of what American writer David Brooks once called the 'BoBos' – Bourgeois Bohemians who combine their financial security and degrees from the elite universities with an ethos that prioritizes achievement, their intense desire to win approval from other elites and their bohemian disdain for established traditions, culture and ways of life, which they see as stuffy, stifling and old-fashioned, if not reactionary.[37]

This too separates them from the old elite, who, though often wealthy and disconnected from the rest of Britain, had often not gone to university and held more traditionalist values. Shaped by their backgrounds and the dominant culture at the time, most people in the old elite did feel a strong sense of duty, patriotism, attachment and obligation to the majority group, loyalty to the institutions, and an instinctive desire to defend and uphold Britain's national identity, culture and ways of life. But the new elite rarely feel any of these things; they are far more counter-cultural.

As much research since the shock votes for Brexit and Donald Trump in 2016 has shown, people in the elite graduate class – whom some academics call the 'Identity Liberals' – see the country in profoundly different ways from everybody else. Consistently, they feel much less attached than others to the group-based identities which have long held the country together, including a strong sense of commitment to the majority group and attachment to their national identity. Instead, the new elite are far more likely to view the world through an individualistic lens, prioritizing universal and individual rights over these collective, group-based attachments.

Because of this, they feel much less pride in the nation and are less likely to see their Britishness, and especially their English identity, as an important part of who they are. They are routinely the least likely to think the nation-state should prioritize its own interests, or to believe large multinational companies are undermining British companies and workers. They are also much less concerned than others with the need to protect and promote Britain's distinctive national identity, including its values, borders, traditions and culture, which they downplay in favour of more global themes, such as multiculturalism and diversity.[38]

This is why British thinker David Goodhart describes the new elite as the 'Anywheres' – highly educated, urban, interconnected elites who cluster together in the big cities, who feel less attached than others to their 'ascribed' identities, such as their membership of the British majority, their region or even the country, and who feel more strongly attached to their individual 'achieved' identities, such as their university degrees from the elite institutions and the professional achievements they list on their CVs or LinkedIn, which they routinely signal to other elites to try and win more status for themselves.[39]

Shaped by these values, the new elite have been the most strongly supportive of all the profound social and cultural changes which have swept through Britain and the West over the last half century and which they see as an extension of their liberal cosmopolitan or progressive values – much higher rates of immigration, multiculturalism, diversity, EU membership and globalization.[40] They are also the most supportive of protecting and promoting minority group rights, and a new generation of social movements which they see as reflecting their values; while 66 per cent of Britain's university degree-holders express strong support for Black Lives Matter, only 38 per cent of non-graduates do.[41]

When Britain officially left the European Union, in 2020, the think-tank More in Common threw more light on what makes the country's new ruling class, whom they call the Establishment Liberals, distinctive from other groups.[42] Representing only 12 per cent of Britain, they are financially secure if not wealthy graduate elites who are heavily concentrated in London and England's more prosperous south-east corner. They define themselves, foremost, as liberal cosmopolitan, pro-market, globally minded and strong supporters of the (pre-Brexit) status quo, which is why they are also strong supporters of rejoining the EU and think Brexit was a historic mistake.

Gathering their news from the BBC, *The Times* or Radio 4, they are far more likely than others to believe that rising diversity enriches Britain, that immigration, globalization and open markets are changing the country for the better, and that Britain should be even more strongly integrated into the global world. Because they have benefitted far more than other groups from these changes, both economically and culturally, the new elite are also the least concerned about rising inequality and the least anxious about the effects of rapid social, cultural and demographic change on the wider national community. They are also less likely than average to feel proud of Britain. Nonetheless, because their values have been mirrored in many of the changes which have been sweeping through and redefining Britain over the last fifty years, which we explore in the next chapter, they are also the most likely to say they trust the government and the institutions, and to feel they are included in the national conversation about who we are – they are nearly twice as likely as any other group in the country to feel their voice is represented, which reflects their total dominance over the commanding heights of politics, culture and society.

The new elite, as we will see in Chapter 5, not only hold these beliefs strongly but have also come to see them, like their elite education, as crucial markers of their social status, prestige and moral worth in wider society. Whereas the old elite used to distinguish themselves from the left-behind masses by signalling their wealth and luxury goods, the new elite distinguish themselves by signalling what Cambridge academic Rob Henderson calls 'luxury beliefs' – their strong commitment to liberal cosmopolitan and radically progressive beliefs, which reflect the values of the new elite but often negatively impact other groups.

Even if they are the least likely to be affected by these ideas, the new elite's passionate calls for more immigration, globalization and open borders and to rejoin the European Union, their claim that Western nations such as Britain are 'institutionally racist', and that white people should acknowledge their 'white privilege' or 'white guilt' because of things that happened decades, if not centuries ago, are all examples of their elite beliefs. Routinely, they signal these beliefs to other elites not only to try to garner more social status for themselves but to disassociate themselves from who they see as the morally inferior masses below, who have the 'wrong' education, the 'wrong' values, and the 'wrong' political loyalties.

In the years that have passed since the Brexit and Trump revolts in 2016, many people in the new elite have become even more strongly committed to these beliefs, which they consider central to their emerging liberal identity. Referred to in America as the 'Great Awokening', in reference to the rise of a more radical progressive 'woke' politics which a significant chunk of the new elite embrace, over the last six years highly educated white liberals have moved even more sharply to the left on cultural issues such as race, and identity.

Partly in reaction to these revolts on the right, the new elite have become even *more* supportive of increasing immigration and diversity, strengthening minority rights and ideas such as paying reparations to African Americans to compensate for the legacy of slavery.[43]

In Britain, between the Brexit referendum in 2016 and the fall of Boris Johnson in 2022, the share of typically university-educated Remainers who want immigration reduced collapsed by 20 points, to 23 per cent, while the share who want immigration *increased* jumped more than threefold, to 31 per cent.[44] In this way, some people in the new elite are replying to the rise of populism, Brexit, Boris Johnson and the continued era of Conservative Party dominance by doubling down on their liberal values by becoming even more liberal.

The new elite are also far more counter-cultural than the old elite used to be, more determined to challenge, criticize or even repudiate the established history, culture, identity and ways of life of the wider national community. Unlike the old elite, who generally felt attached to the institutions and symbols of British nationhood, from the monarchy to their national identity, the new elite are clearly more cynical about these things. Having often come of age during the 1960s and the 1970s, the older members of this new ruling class would have been shaped, during their formative years, by the first big wave of cultural liberalization which swept through Britain and the West.

Described by historian Arthur Marwick as the 'long sixties', which began in 1958 and lasted until 1974, this cultural revolution was, in his words, one of 'continuous, uninterrupted, and lasting consequences'.[45] The key milestones in this earlier revolution included the ending of national service in 1963 and of the death penalty in 1964, the arrival of the pill for women in 1964, the legalization of abortion in 1968 and of divorce in 1969, and the rise of 'New Left' social movements, such as the Gay and Women's Liberation Fronts, and a stronger focus on anti-discrimination, as reflected in Rock Against Racism. Shaped by their education and counter-cultural ethos, early members of the new elite came to embrace political campaigns which reflected their emerging values, which stressed global human rights, social justice, racial, sexual, and gender equality, multiculturalism, environmentalism and anti-discrimination.

But some also embraced what American intellectual Daniel Bell described at the time as a new 'adversary culture', a far more critical stance towards the established narratives, institutions, history, myths and memories of Western states. Rather than uphold the old ways of life, which the new elite saw as oppressive and old-fashioned, the new, post-1960s university elite became openly anti-traditionalist, focused on dismantling or 'deconstructing' the established ways of life which had long held Western nations together.

This was reinforced by what became known as the 'cultural turn' on the left of politics, where many thinkers and social movements, disillusioned by the failure of the Soviet Union, lost interest in the old class-based loyalties and the white working-class who had shown little interest in overthrowing capitalism. Instead, they began to embrace a far more radical if not authoritarian brand of progressivism which not only included demands for racial, sexual, and gender equality, minority rights and anti-discrimination, but also advocated curtailing free speech in the pursuit of these goals and was openly hostile towards the West's established identities, authorities and culture.

Increasingly, the new elite abandoned the traditionalist values which had united the old middle-class and replaced them with a far more assertive social and cultural liberalism which became a new kind of class consciousness, giving an otherwise highly individualistic elite a cultural, not just economic, sense of solidarity, which was reinforced by their elite education. Today, this has morphed into the mainstreaming of debates about radical progressive or 'woke' politics, whereby a clearly visible section of the new elite believe Western nations such as Britain are institutionally racist, see their British identity and history as a source of shame, feel much less pride than others in the nation, and feel much less attached to their national identity and the wider national group.

Representing somewhere around 13 per cent of the British population (though researchers at Kings College London put the figure at a much higher 23 per cent), these radical progressives are a smaller group within the new elite. They belong to this new ruling class because they too are among the most highly educated people in Britain, holding undergraduate if not postgraduate degrees, are financially secure if not wealthy, are concentrated in London, other cities or university towns and gather their news from the *Guardian*, Channel 4 or podcasts. And, like other and more moderate members of the new elite, radical progressives are disproportionately represented in the most important and influential institutions in society, wielding considerable influence over politics, culture, media and the universities, as we will see in Chapter 4.[46]

Described by philosopher John Gray as 'hyper-liberals', Britain's radical progressives are even more passionately supportive of immigration, diversity and minority rights, which they routinely prioritize above the majority. This is why they are also the most strongly supportive of groups such as Black Lives Matter – which 100 per cent of them support – and are sceptical if not hostile towards the identity, history, and culture of the majority group.[47] Leaning strongly to the left in politics, they are the most likely to believe that people's outcomes in life are defined more by social forces than by individual responsibility. They are strongly motivated by the pursuit of social justice; they are the most likely to think racism is a major problem in British society and that the country is structurally or institutionally racist, and to describe their own identity as highly political. In turn, they are, by far, the most likely to regularly promote their political beliefs on social media, such as Twitter. In fact, they are six times more likely than any other group in the country to do so.[48]

Referred to by the researchers who study them as highly critical, strongly opinionated, frustrated, radically cosmopolitan and environmentally conscious, radical progressives are the least likely of all to feel attached to the majority group and the nation. They are the most likely group to think rights for minorities have not gone far enough, the most likely to feel ashamed of their British identity and the country, the least patriotic, the least nostalgic about the past and the most likely to say their British identity is not an important part of who they are.

Instead, they are overwhelmingly focused on what they see as the marginalization of minorities based on their race, gender and sexuality, and on the urgent need to entrench a more assertive 'anti-racism' and celebration of diversity within institutions such as schools and universities. They are also the most likely to stress the need to address historic injustices, such as the legacy of Britain's empire and slavery. They simply do not believe Britain or other Western nations can move on unless they stop to address what they see as historic mistakes.

In fact, so strongly do they feel about these issues that some have suggested that radical progressives are not even liberal at all. In his book *Liberalism and Its Discontents*, Francis Fukuyama warns that while liberal progressives began their campaign decades ago with a very legitimate critique about the failing of liberal societies to include all groups on an equal basis, in more recent years they have embraced an *illiberal* critique of liberalism's core principles. Rather than working within the framework of a truly liberal society, radical progressives are now undermining liberalism on three fronts: they elevate the group over the individual, reducing citizens to mere members of fixed identity groups that are defined by race, sex and gender; they are openly sceptical of, if not hostile towards, the scientific method, objective knowledge and free speech, which have long guided the search for truth in liberal societies but which progressives subordinate behind people's 'lived experience'; and they are no longer just critical but cynical of the established identities, history and culture which have long held Western liberal societies together. Instead they demand the 'deconstruction' of what they argue are hidden power structures in society which disproportionately benefit the old elite.

While it might be tempting to dismiss these ideas as belonging to a fringe minority, they have now become strongly embedded in many of Britain's institutions, reflecting the growing dominance of the new elite over these institutions. Yet, at the same time, as we will see in this book, progressives are often firmly at odds with the values and the views that are held by much of the rest of the country, which is now playing an important role in driving people from left to right in politics.

In the pages ahead, we will explore this new elite in a lot more detail. The key point for now is that over the last sixty years Britain has been transformed from a country where the working class, people without degrees and a more conservative ruling class were dominant to one where, today, these groups have been pushed aside by the new graduate elite who are united by their elite education, meritocratic ethos, metropolitan tastes and, more than anything, their liberal cosmopolitan if not radically progressive beliefs. They have not only risen to become the most powerful group in the middle class, they have also now fully replaced the old elite in many of the institutions. And, over the last forty years, they have moved to consolidate their power in several important ways.

ELITE CONSOLIDATION

The rise of the new elite has stoked a strong backlash among voters who share neither their agenda nor outlook. But while this new ruling class dismiss this backlash as an outpouring of racism, ignorance or imperial nostalgia, in reality it marks a rational response to how the new elite have consolidated their power, coalescing into a closely connected, insular and self-serving ruling class who have turned their back on many people, no longer representing or respecting their views.

This has unfolded in three areas of British life at the same time: in education, in geography and in politics. In education, the new elite have been the main beneficiaries of a university-based meritocracy, which has come to see having a university degree, preferably from the most prestigious Oxbridge or Russell Group universities, as the only way of leading a successful and respected life. They have also used this system to reproduce their class and entrench their power.

Whether reflected in Tony Blair's pledge, in 1999, to send half of Britain's school leavers into university, or, in 2022, his pledge to send seven in ten school leavers into the universities, the new elite have doubled down on themselves. Whereas in the immediate postwar years, Britain's university system was organized around no more than thirty small and very elitist institutions, by 2019 the country had 165 higher education institutions, which between them counted some 2.4 million students and half a million members of staff. Between the 1960s and the 2010s, the number of people who were enrolling in university each year rocketed from 18,000 to more than 350,000.[49]

These trends are even more dramatic when they are broken down by generation. By the time of the Brexit referendum, in 2016, whereas nearly half of Britain's pensioners had left school without any educational qualifications, only one in twenty of the country's under-35s had done the same; and whereas only one in ten pensioners had a degree, almost four in ten young Britons had one.[50] Yet these changes have not benefitted everybody equally.

Over the last fifty years, consistently, it has been children of the new elite who reaped the benefits of this university meritocracy. During the first big wave of university expansion, between the 1960s and the 1990s, the probability of children from the new elite being accepted into one of Britain's most prestigious universities was consistently higher than it was for children who came from other backgrounds.[51] Between the eras of Margaret Thatcher and Tony Blair, while 35 per cent of students from families in the new elite were given places in the most prestigious Oxbridge or Russell Group universities, only 13 per cent of students from working-class families were given the same.[52]

The children of the new elite, consistently, have also been far more likely than others to make it into the most elite universities and to graduate with an upper second- or first-class degree – even after taking into account their prior educational performance.[53] In his study of global trends, academic Moris Triventi finds that British children who have parents in the graduate class have been among the most likely of all children in Europe to graduate from the best universities, underlining this powerful, in-built advantage for the country's new ruling class.[54]

One powerful way of showing how the deck has been rigged firmly in their favour is to consider what happened instead to children from the left-behind white working-class. They have been completely cut adrift. While the new elite rushed to signal their liberal progressive values, debating dubious concepts such as white privilege and the patriarchy (see Chapter 5), white working-class *boys* have consistently been the least likely to get strong exam results at school, to progress to university and to attend elite universities.[55]

In 2021, just 13 per cent of white working-class boys went to university compared to 27 per cent of black Caribbean boys, 42 per cent of Pakistani boys, 51 per cent of black African boys and 66 per cent of Chinese boys. Typically, only children from Gypsy, Roma and Irish Traveller families perform worse than left-behind white working-class boys.[56]

Furthermore, contrary to the popular trope that Britain's education system is institutionally or structurally biased against minorities, in 2022, for the very first time, every other ethnic group outperformed the white working class, with both black Caribbean and black African students pulling away from their more disadvantaged white peers.[57]

The dominance of the new elite and their descendants has also been encouraged by the universities, which, led by the same elite, have routinely failed to devote the same amount of effort to helping children from the left behind as to aid their own descendants.[58] One study, published in 2019, found that of more than 800 university enrolment targets, only eleven mentioned children from the white working class and only one in eight universities had targets for them.[59]

One symbol of this imbalance arrived in 2018, when the rapper Stormzy was praised for providing scholarships for black British students to attend the University of Cambridge. Yet, at the same time, private schools rejected Professor Sir Bryan Thwaite's offer of similar scholarships for white working-class children to attend some of Britain's most elite private schools on the basis that it might be considered racial discrimination. In a system that has long been hard-wired to favour the new elite and their values, some children have simply not been fashionable enough for a hashtag or a target.

Beyond education, the new elite have also consolidated their power through geography, by dominating Britain's large metropolitan cities, university towns and the prosperous commuter belt in England's southern shires. Remarkably, today, one-quarter of all graduates in the country, more than half of the most elite Oxbridge graduates, and nearly 40 per cent of graduates with a first- or second-class degree from the elite Russell Group universities move to London within six months of graduating, reflecting how the capital hoovers up the best and the brightest from across the country.[60]

It also underlines how the new elite dominate the most prosperous and powerful areas of the country. Of the sixty constituencies in

British politics which have the largest share of graduates, more than half (thirty-six) are in London while another twelve are in the surrounding commuter belt in south-east England. The new elite, in other words, disproportionately enjoy all the benefits which come with living and working at the very epicentre of Britain's economic, political and cultural power.

Typically, they are concentrated in places such as Battersea, Chelsea, the City of London, Kensington, Richmond, Wimbledon, Hornsey and Wood Green, Putney and Tooting, while outside London, they dominate the likes of St Albans, Cambridge, Oxford, Esher, Bath, Bristol West, Henley, Manchester Withington, Brighton, Sheffield, Leeds, Walton, Hitchin, Harpenden, Guildford, Winchester, Reading and Maidenhead.

None of this is unique to Britain. Across the West, the deeper education divide between the graduate class and everybody else is now rapidly being compounded by this geographical divide between the big cities and everywhere else. Increasingly, while small, medium, post-industrial and coastal towns are drifting into long-term decline, watching the 'best and brightest' leave for the bright lights, the megacities and high-tech towns are hoovering up new generations of the graduate class, global elites and also immigrants, who are flocking into the cities and their surrounding periphery.

Holding the right postcodes in the right metropolitan areas, the new elite and their descendants have long lived on the right side of some of the sharpest regional inequalities in the Western world, benefitting far more than others from property that has increased the most in value and neighbourhoods with the highest 'gross value added' or 'GVA per head' – a key measure of the value of goods and services. Of the ten areas with the highest GVA per head all but one is in London; of the top fifty all but thirteen are in London or the new elite's south-east enclaves.[61] This is why crude debates about the 'north versus the south' miss the point. It makes far more sense to focus instead on the rise of what academics call 'highly segregated urban elite zones' in major cities – very high-income, very highly educated, very high-value and very interconnected neighbourhoods where the new elite withdraw and hunker down, turning away from others.

Contrary to all their talk about openness, diversity and tolerance, the new elite, as sociologist Mike Savage has shown, not only dominate these urban elite zones but are also among the most 'socially exclusive' group in Britain; they are the most likely to spend time in the company of other members of the new elite who work in the same jobs, have the same values and know few people from other parts of British society.

'This is evidence of a degree of closure and exclusiveness at the top of the social structure,' writes Savage, 'indicating that forms of economic capital intersect closely with social networks and social capital to produce a pulling-apart from the rest at the highest levels of the social hierarchy.'[62] The closure and exclusion which characterize the new elite is also visible online, where, in Britain and America, highly educated liberals have been shown to be far more likely than other groups to interact with, or follow, only people who exhibit the same values and beliefs as themselves.[63]

Meanwhile, workers and non-graduates are pushed to the very margins of the big cities or left in the declining small towns, where they are forced to compete with immigrants for housing, jobs, wages and recognition while finding themselves berated by the new elite for their allegedly racist, intolerant and ignorant views. One person who has documented this bleak state of affairs is French geographer Christophe Guilluy who, in his book *Twilight of the Elites*, argues that this intensifying rift between the West's big, diverse, metropolitan cities and the surrounding periphery has now become a major new fault line in the new politics; while the populists, conservatives, and revolts such as the Yellow Vests attract most of their support from the periphery and small towns, the new elite in the big cities are drifting further leftwards, losing touch with the areas that surround them.[64]

In this way, the urban new elite and the non-graduate majority are drifting apart, living alongside neighbours and in areas that hold very different world views. Over the last twenty years, as research since the Brexit vote has shown, Britain's densely populated, metropolitan centres of the knowledge and creative economy have drifted away from other areas not only but also culturally, becoming the epicentre of cosmopolitan and progressive views. Beginning in the early 2000s, if not earlier, the urban areas dominated by the new elite have become far more positive about rising immigration, diversity, the European Union and giving more opportunities to ethnic and sexual minorities, while other areas have generally remained much less enthusiastic about these things and far more traditionalist.[65]

In 2022, the British Social Attitudes survey found that Londoners were far more pro-welfare and socially liberal than people in other parts of the country, even after controlling for differences in their level of education, age, and income. While around one third of Londoners, 34 per cent, are classified as liberal, this compares to only one in five people, or 21 per cent, across England overall; and while close to half of London's graduates, 45 per cent, are liberal only one in three graduates across the rest of England share their liberal outlook.[66] This reflects the fact that cities have larger numbers of graduates and professionals working in them and also that people who hold liberal values tend to self-select into them. In turn, people who live in big and diverse cities then interact with other social liberals, which further cements their world view. While not even one in three of Britain's less well-educated voters say they have friends from different countries, this rockets to nearly three-quarters of people among the new graduate elite who congregate in the cities.[67]

In their study of sixty-six countries around the world, Davide Luca and his colleagues find that the world's large, urban cities are far more liberal cosmopolitan in their values, tastes and lifestyles; they are far more supportive of abortion, homosexuality, casual sex, prostitution, divorce, gender equality and immigration.[68] Yet while the new elite cheer these trends, their heavy concentration in the big cities and the university towns is also one reason why they were outflanked over the last decade, as we will see.

Aside from education and geography, the consolidation of the new elite is also being reinforced by a third factor: politics. Increasingly, in Britain and across the West, as we will see in Chapter 4, the new elite now disproportionately dominate not just the centre of Britain's economic power but also political power – they dominate the most important and influential institutions, from political parties through to media, cultural institutions, creative industries and the universities.

In turn, they use their disproportionate power in the institutions to magnify their voice and their values, imposing their world view on the rest of the country.

This is fuelling a rising tide of anger among many people who feel powerless, as though they no longer have a voice. While the new elite dominate the institutions, they have also moved to exclude the voice of groups that do not share their values and which are now glaringly under-represented in media, politics, the creative industries and more. The exclusion of these voices has further encouraged many people to rally behind leaders and populists who are promising to reassert their voice, not just in politics but across society.

When, in 2021, David Brooks returned to explore what had happened to the Bobos in his home country of America, he reflected on what he had got wrong in his original study. 'I got a lot wrong about the bobos,' he recalls. 'I didn't anticipate how aggressively we would move to assert our cultural dominance, the way we would seek to impose elite values through speech and thought codes. I underestimated the way the creative class would successfully raise barriers around itself to protect its economic privilege ... And I underestimated our intolerance of ideological diversity.'[69]

He has a point. Despite talking a great deal about openness, tolerance and diversity, in politics today the new elite are the most likely to try to ring-fence their position by turning away from people who hold values and beliefs they disagree with. Consistently, in Britain, they have been more likely than Brexit voters or Conservatives to block or unfriend voices they disagree with on social media, to perceive their political rivals as selfish, closed-minded, hypocritical and dishonest, to say they find it hard to stay friends with somebody who holds different political views and to say they would feel uncomfortable if one of their relatives married somebody who votes for the Conservative Party or supported Brexit.[70]

While only 11 per cent of Brexit-voting parents would feel upset if their child married somebody who had voted to remain in the European Union, 39 per cent of Remain-voting parents would feel upset if their child married a Brexiteer; and while only 13 per cent of Conservative-voting parents would feel upset if their child married a

Labour voter, 34 per cent of Labour parents would feel upset if their child married a Tory. When, in 2021, voters were asked how they felt about people with different opinions, progressives were the most negative. They gave Brexiteers and people who held different views about Black Lives Matter or trans rights the lowest score of all.[71] Similar findings have emerged in other countries where it is often the new elite who are the most politically intolerant of all.[72]

As we will see in the pages ahead, this intolerance of people who hold different beliefs – alongside their elite degrees, privileged backgrounds, distinctive values and dominance over the most influential institutions – has become another important marker of the new elite, and one that is playing into the unfolding realignment of British politics, leaving many people with a sense that the new ruling class does not just disagree with them but does not even like them.

After a decade of political turbulence and turmoil, therefore, Britain in the 2020s is in the grip of a new ruling class, the new middle-class graduate elite. Held together by their elite education, their strongly liberal or radical progressive beliefs, their postcodes in the cities and university towns, and, as we will see, their dominance over the commanding heights of British society, the new elite have become the new overclass. Economically, they hold the right degrees from the right universities; culturally, they hold the right beliefs to garner status, esteem and moral worth; and, politically, they not only dominate the institutions but also, as we will see in the next chapter, have been on the right side of a political revolution which over the last fifty years has profoundly transformed the country, reshaped it around their interests and excluded millions of others.

2

Revolution

The new elite have not only risen to dominate the country, they have also reshaped it in their image. Over the last half century, they imposed on the rest of the country a political revolution which has completely changed Britain. Beginning in 1979 and then accelerating until 2016, this deeply transformative and highly destabilizing project overhauled Britain in three ways. It opened the economy to a new and very disruptive model of hyper-globalization. It opened the country's borders to a new and unprecedented era of mass immigration. And it opened up and hollowed out its national democracy, handing much greater power, influence and control to supranational institutions.

All three of these changes, all of them profound, not only transformed Britain's economy, culture and ways of life but reveal the extent to which the country is now firmly in the hands of a new ruling class who think very differently from much of the rest of the country. And the decisions they made have had profound political consequences, setting the stage for an almighty backlash.

The political revolution was led by two deeply transformative administrations – one on the right, the other on the left – which dominated Britain for nearly half a century. Beginning in 1979, eighteen years of uninterrupted Conservative Party rule were then, from 1997, followed by thirteen years of uninterrupted New Labour rule. On the right, Margaret Thatcher ushered in a very different brand of conservatism which was rooted in a radical economic liberalism; on the left, Tony Blair embraced much of this economic legacy while ushering in a radical cultural liberalism.

Both projects had different ideological roots, and their supporters will object to them being placed side by side. But the key point is that by the time they were finished Britain had been completely rebuilt around a new and narrow orthodoxy of economic and social liberalism which reflected the outlook of the new elite. Left and right converged on the same political territory, becoming indistinguishable.

HYPER-GLOBALIZATION

The most important change, by far, was the rise of what economist Dani Rodrik calls 'hyper-globalization' – a new economic model which drove a wedge down the country, pushing different groups apart. Through much of the postwar era, Britain had basked in the so-called 'golden age' of capitalism, enjoying relatively strong growth, rising wages and increased equality of income and wealth. By the 1970s, however, this had come to a crashing halt as the country was engulfed by a severe financial crisis, rampant unemployment, rocketing inflation, a big and 'overloaded' state that was struggling to fulfil its growing number of roles, and severe industrial unrest between the government and very powerful trade unions.[1] Britain looked like a failed state. A great power had been reduced to a three-day working week, piles of rotting rubbish, unburied corpses, a humiliating loan from the International Monetary Fund (IMF) and, during the Winter of Discontent in 1978–9, more than 2,000 strikes. It was the 'sick man of Europe', falling well behind most other major powers.

This is why, at the country's first referendum on Europe, in 1975, 67 per cent of people followed the advice of their leaders, voting, for economic reasons, to endorse their new membership of the European Community, which would later evolve into the European Union. 'For twenty-five years', said Conservative Ted Heath at the time, 'we've been looking for something to get us going again. Now here it is.'[2]

National decline often clears the way for radical political experiments. And one such experiment arrived, in 1979, when Margaret Thatcher ushered in a more radical 'neoliberal' conservatism. Shaped by thinkers on the New Right who were associated with the University of Chicago and the Austrian School, this very different brand of conservatism was strongly critical of the role of the state in the economy and saw unbridled free markets as the main driver of growth. Some of their concerns were entirely justified. In Britain and across the West the state had become too bloated, controlling and inefficient. Thatcher also had a point when she argued that the old economic model, which sought a compromise between workers and business, had become unsustainable. The expansion of welfare had also stripped away incentives for people to take control of their own lives while the left's long march through the institutions, she warned, had cultivated a culture of immorality, envy and resentment.[3]

Instead, Thatcher gave the British people what they had never had: a potent cocktail of radical economic liberalism combined with traditional appeals to family values, individual responsibility, strong defence and a promise to put the nation first, whether during war with Argentina over the Falkland Islands, or increasingly fraught negotiations with the European Community, symbolized by her phrase 'I want my money back!' Far more importantly, Thatcher also ushered in the new era of hyper-globalization – a transformational project to open national economies to global trade, liberalize finance and deepen Britain's economic integration with other states.[4]

In both Britain and America, the rise of hyper-globalization marked a decisive and permanent shift in favour of financial markets over nations, enabled by a concerted effort to remove the costs of trade and capital flows. It pushed the power of globalization beyond national democracy, which, until now, had regulated, stabilized, and legitimized financial markets. Globalization became the end, notes Rodrik, national economies became the means.

This had profound consequences. The needs of markets were now prioritized above the needs of the nation. Traditional industries which could not compete in the global economy were shut down or privatized, while London's financial services were deregulated. This was exemplified by the 'Big Bang' in 1986, which abolished capital controls, slashed red tape and transformed London into a truly global hub that would now spend less time managing the national economy and more time managing the capital of people who lived in other parts of the world. The decisions that were taken at this time also set the stage for a series of major and very costly financial crises – the Swedish banking crisis and the Mexican currency crisis in the early 1990s, major financial crises in Asia, Russia and Argentina in the late 1990s and early 2000s, and the Great Financial Crash in 2008.

In fact, under Thatcher, Britain's economic boundaries were erased so much that it no longer made sense to talk about a national economy at all. 'The United Kingdom was, to an extent not known before, owned by foreigners,' writes David Edgerton in his book *The Rise and Fall of the British Nation*, 'the big City institutions, the service companies, the infrastructure operators, the car makers, even the chocolate makers were now owned abroad.'[5]

While Thatcherites celebrated all this as heralding a return to the buccaneering free trade spirit of the Edwardian era, this was misleading. Unlike that earlier era, many of Britain's assets were simply sold off. The British no longer owned large chunks of their own economy. While the new generation of neoliberal Thatcherite Tories talked about building a new world order, their one-nation predecessors, who had seen themselves as not just the liberators of markets but custodians of the nation, warned their successors they were selling off the family silver.

'The sale of assets', complained former prime minister Harold Macmillan, 'is common with individuals and states when they run into financial difficulties. First, all the Georgian silver goes, and then all that nice furniture that used to be in the saloon. Then the Canalettos go.'[6] It was a reminder of the philosophical difference between one-nation and neoliberal conservatism – a difference that would reappear in the later divide between Boris Johnson and Liz Truss.

Margaret Thatcher's supporters claimed that their experiment did, in the end, make Britain far more competitive and prosperous. And this is certainly true. Her critics, of which there are many, routinely forget just how miserable and inefficient Britain was before she entered Number 10 Downing Street. Between 1980 and 1990, inflation declined from 13 to 8 per cent, and the number of days that were lost because of strikes and disputes collapsed from nearly 30 million to 1.9 million in 1990. Before Thatcher, Britain's economy had lagged behind the economies of most other major powers; after Thatcher, it overtook them while a booming service sector, mainly driven by spectacular growth in the City of London, did bring some people, especially families in the middle class, higher incomes.[7]

But there is also no denying the fact that her experiment came with enormous costs which remain clearly visible today and played a key role in setting the stage for the political revolts of the 2010s. While Britain did become a richer country, it also became a more unequal one. Contrary to what many New Right economists argued at the time, that the arrival of hyper-globalization and the unleashing of free markets would inevitably lift all boats, the evidence that has emerged in the years since their experiment tells a very different story.

'Britain', concluded Oxford's Professor Anthony Heath, after comparing rates of inequality across the world's most advanced democracies, 'showed the largest increase in inequality after 1980, going from being one of the most equal economies in the 1970s to one of the most unequal by the 1990s.'[8] Only in America did the rate of inequality soar higher. In 2020, similarly, Britain's Office for National Statistics pointed out that whatever measure of inequality one used, they all increased sharply during the Thatcher years before widening even further during the New Labour governments of Tony Blair and Gordon Brown, who accepted much of this legacy, and then only falling slightly back after the Global Financial Crash, amid a prolonged economic squeeze.[9]

As this suggests, hyper-globalization was not just a child of the neoliberal right, it was also raised and nurtured by the left. Contrary to the myth it was imposed on Britain by ruthless neoliberal capitalists, detailed research by Professor Rawi Abdelal has shown how the rise and implementation of hyper-globalization was overseen as much by left-leaning technocrats in international institutions such as the European Union, the OECD and the IMF, including many former prominent French socialists such as Jacques Delors and Pascal Lamy.[10]

In Britain, too, the loudest cheerleaders often came not from the right but the left, such as Peter Mandelson, who symbolized the mood when, in 1999, he told Silicon Valley executives that New Labour was 'intensely relaxed about people getting filthy rich'.[11] As Professor Colin Hay showed at the time, in the most detailed study of New Labour's transformation, by the late 1990s the left and right had essentially become indistinguishable. Across a wide range of policy areas – trade unions, employment, education, welfare, industrial strategy, privatization and the deregulation of London's financial services – Labour and the Conservatives looked identical. 'Labour', concluded Hay, 'ceased effectively to be a social democratic party, committed as it had by then become to a pervasive neo-liberal economic orthodoxy and to a basic acceptance of the legacy of the Thatcher years.'[12]

The same point was made by US statesman Henry Kissinger in a letter to Margaret Thatcher shortly after Tony Blair came to power, in 1997. 'I never thought I'd congratulate you on a Labour victory in the British elections,' he wrote, 'but I cannot imagine anything that would confirm your revolution more than Blair's program. It seems to me well to the right of the Conservative government that preceded yours.' Thatcher did not take long to reply. 'I think your analysis is the correct one but to make one's political opponent electable and then elected was not quite the strategy I had in mind!'[13]

While New Labour certainly did more to help some of the people who were being left behind by the new consensus, including pensioners and families who had slid into poverty, they only tinkered round the edges. It was under Blair, after all, that the top 1 per cent in Britain saw their strongest income growth of all and inequality reached new heights. When New Labour came to power, in 1997, promising things can only get better, the average pay of Britain's CEOs was forty-seven times higher than the pay of the average worker; by the time Blair and Alistair Campbell were campaigning against Brexit nearly twenty years later it had rocketed to 145 times higher.[14] Much of this increase took place under New Labour.

The revolutionaries who were now reshaping Britain in their image also tended to be dogmatic and dismissive of any opposition. Anybody who dared question how hyper-globalization was changing the country were instantly derided by the new elite as the 'closed-minded' or 'nostalgic' ones who yearned to return to the 1950s, and who were routinely contrasted with the 'open', 'tech-savvy', 'university-educated', 'mobile' and 'winners of globalization'.

This was a common tactic not only in Britain but across the West. The new elite have become experts in cloaking their politics in appeals to 'openness', 'tolerance' or 'diversity' while at the same time berating anybody who challenges the direction of travel. By portraying their political opponents as an assortment of fascists, racists and closed-minded reactionaries, the new elite seek to shut down the conversation and exclude them altogether.

In Britain, this was famously demonstrated, in 2005, when Tony Blair dismissed all those who wanted to debate how hyper-globalization was changing the country by saying 'you might as well debate whether autumn should follow summer'. In the era of globalization, he continued, 'there is no mystery about what works: an open, liberal economy, prepared constantly to change to remain competitive. The new world rewards those who are open to it.'[15]

But this was not true. The rewards were not evenly distributed. They went to the new elite who were concentrated in the big cities and the university towns, or to people who were not even British at all. The winners included not just the new elite but a new plutocracy in London, composed of international, jet-setting elites, Russian oligarchs, and non-domiciled 'High-Net Worths' who might have had a home in London but felt just as at home in New York, Paris or Heathrow Terminal 5, on their way to another global city.

London, to all intents and purposes, was transformed into a tax-haven for international investors who had lots of money but no sense of obligation to the wider national community. By the 2010s, this became visible to everybody when the Panama Papers revealed the extent to which 'Londongrad' had become, in the words of Oliver Bullough, 'Butler to the World' – a safe house of sorts for an assortment of oligarchs, gangsters and kleptocrats.[16]

One symbol of this, in 2021, was the finding that even amid a national housing crisis at least 250,000 residential properties in England and Wales are registered to people overseas, often in tax havens such as Jersey, Guernsey, the Isle of Man and the British Virgin Islands.[17] As Lawrence Summers, secretary of the treasury under Bill Clinton and an early advocate of hyper-globalization, later conceded, one problem with the model is that, as this underlines, it encourages 'the development of stateless elites whose allegiance is to global economic success and their own prosperity rather than the interests of the nation where they are headquartered'.[18]

Hyper-globalization – which also comes with its own moral code which valorizes urban graduates, financiers and large corporations – also transformed the country's economic geography. London and the surrounding commuter belt in south-east England were put on steroids while people who lived beyond the bright lights of the cities, Oxbridge and the university towns, who lived in the small coastal and industrial towns were cut adrift, relegated to second class status.

Britain's economy was even more strongly wrapped around London and its far more volatile financial services, which would later bring about the worst financial crisis since the Great Depression, and a strong pound, which weakened other parts of the real economy. In turn, industries which had once brought a sense of purpose, meaning and collective identity to people's lives – coalmining, shipbuilding and steel – collapsed.

Remarkably, while Britain was once a manufacturing workshop of the world, it now began to import more goods than it exported, with the dire effects later memorialized in films such as *The Full Monty*, *Brassed Off* and *This Is England*. While the decline of these industries was a long time coming, between the 1970s and the 2010s the share of jobs in manufacturing collapsed from one-third to one in ten.[19] While London boomed, the rest of the country experienced one of the sharpest declines in manufacturing in the developed world. Britain didn't make things any more, while in Westminster there was no plan for what would come next, no plan for how to compensate the losers of hyper-globalization.

This exacerbated the country's already sharp and widening geographical inequalities. As Professors Philip McCann and Raquel Ortega-Argilés point out, because of the deliberate political choice to double down on London and its wider hinterland economy, while at the same time eschewing any real sense of responsibility to the rest of the country, Britain's regional inequalities were left to sharpen, unabated, for forty years.[20]

Remarkably, by the 2010s, many people in Britain were living amid the sharpest rates of interregional inequality in the industrialized world, with the new elite enjoying the spoils at one end and much of the rest of the country languishing at the other. Studies found that at least half the population were living 'in regions whose prosperity is no better than the poorer parts of former East Germany and poorer than the US states of Mississippi and West Virginia'.[21]

Workers, non-graduates and pensioners who found themselves living on the wrong side of hyper-globalization suffered many other problems. Their average living standards have been no better than what is seen in impoverished US states such as Alabama. Their quality of healthcare has been compared to that in eastern Europe. And their hollowed-out communities suffer from unusually large numbers of people living alone, on lower-than-average earnings, with worse outcomes in health and education, a shorter life expectancy, lower levels of civic engagement and social mobility.[22]

Unsurprisingly, given all this, as Britain entered the 2020s, not even one-third (31 per cent) of people in England's north-east felt optimistic about their life prospects, compared to 78 per cent of Londoners and 74 per cent of people in the far more prosperous south-east.[23]

None of this was unique to Britain. Across the West, economists have now produced a large pile of evidence which directly undermines the narrative that was promoted by Blair and the new graduate elite – that hyper-globalization would lift all boats. This was simply wrong and ignored what was really happening in many working-class communities. As detailed reviews by economists such as David Dorn, Peter Levell and David Autor make clear, these choices had profoundly negative effects on labour markets, particularly in areas which had long relied on jobs and industries that compete with imports.[24] 'These studies show', summarized one review in 2021, 'that regions that were heavily affected by trade – and workers and industries most directly competing with China and Mexico – suffered significant and long-term income losses.'[25]

While the new elite pulled ahead of everybody else, the country's workers and non-graduates were left to deal with what economists call 'distributional' or 'adjustment' costs – namely, higher rates of joblessness, lower wages, a lower share of national income and a rising burden of unsecured debt. Even under the centre-left administrations of Bill Clinton and Barack Obama, areas in America which had been more fully exposed to hyper-globalization suffered profoundly negative effects – a loss of manufacturing jobs, a decline in earnings, increased mortality, child poverty and larger numbers of people defecting to Donald Trump, whose America First philosophy and rampant criticism of China, free trade and globalism struck a chord among many of these left-behind workers.[26] At the 2022 midterms, six years after Trumps initial victory, exit polls suggested the Republicans won 55 per cent of non-college educated voters, and 72 per cent of white non-graduate men, more than they won in 2016.

In Britain, to make matters worse, in the aftermath of the Global Financial Crash many of the same areas were then subjected to the most severe spending cuts in the country, presided over by a new generation of neoliberal conservatives, led by David Cameron and George Osborne. Though some parts of London were hit hard by austerity, it was in the north and the Midlands – Newcastle, Birmingham, Oldham, Middlesbrough, Nottingham, Doncaster and the Liverpool–Leeds corridor – where people who had already suffered the most negative effects of hyperglobalization were left to deal with spending cuts of more than 25 per cent. These cuts, as the research shows, were especially severe in the industrial towns while 'a swathe of "middle England" in the south central part of the country experienced the smallest spending cuts'.[27]

Unsurprisingly, by the 2020s, many people felt utterly disillusioned with how their economy and the wider country had been transformed. Two-thirds felt the economy has been rigged 'to advantage the rich and the powerful', while almost the same share said 'Britain's political and economic elites do not care about hard-working people'.[28]

But it would be a mistake to think hyper-globalization is just about the economy, because it is not. Its effects have been just as much to do with culture. One crucial point conservatives downplay if not ignore is how this model not only hollowed out the economy but weakened many of the cultural guardrails in society which had once brought a sense of stability and purpose to people's lives – including strong families and communities.

In recent years, the erosion of these guardrails has been reflected in higher rates of suicide, alcohol and drug addiction, family breakdown and depression, which have been the most troubling symptoms of the new elite's failed revolution. They have also been far more visible in areas of the country that were simply cast aside by the new elite.

Home to 16 million people, England's industrial towns were left to deal not only with these problems but enormous numbers of people being pushed onto welfare benefits, who now had little dignity, meaning or purpose in their lives. By the time of the Brexit referendum, thirty-eight of the fifty districts with the highest rates of unemployment were in England's industrial heartlands, where almost 1 million people now rely on benefits from the state.[29]

Much the same has taken place in America, where working-class men, living in areas that were battered by hyper-globalization, have been the most likely to fall into idleness and joblessness and suffer from so-called 'deaths of despair', or 'slow motion suicides' from drug and alcohol abuse, HIV/AIDS and increased homicides.[30]

While these trends have been less pronounced in Britain, it is no coincidence that people from the same working-class communities that are rarely on the radar of the new elite have consistently been more likely to spend more of their lives in poor health and to die sooner. Over the last decade, men in the *least* deprived areas in England were living a decade longer (to 83.5 years) than men in the 10 per cent *most* deprived (to 74.1 years). Today, average life expectancy for men is eight years lower in areas such as Blackpool, Middlesbrough, Manchester and Liverpool than it is in areas where the new elite live, such as Chelsea.[31]

While the underlying causes are complex, including harsh winters and flu outbreaks, one major review by Public Health England draws a straight line from these bleak outcomes, including a recent surge of drug overdoses from heroin and cocaine, to the country's much stronger economic and geographical inequalities which were stoked by this London-centric project.[32]

Britain's deaths of despair have been on a sharp upward trend, mainly affecting middle-aged men who live alone in working-class communities. In 2021, drug-related deaths across England and Wales reached their highest level since records began, in 1993. Men accounted for more than two-thirds of these deaths, the highest rates recorded among 40- to 49-year-olds.[33]

Nor is it any coincidence that as the revolution swept through British society, undermining or disregarding many of the things which used to hold the British people together, the country is now home to some of the highest rates of family breakdown in the advanced world. Here too, economists have shown how hyper-globalization not only cost people jobs and wages but has also, to quote one study, increased 'the fraction of mothers who are unwed, the fraction of children in single-headed households, and the fraction of children living in poverty'.[34]

In Britain, the marriage rate among opposite-sex couples recently plummeted to the lowest level since records began – in 1862. The number of children born to couples who are not married – and who in turn are more likely to suffer disproportionately from worse mental health outcomes, depression, alcoholism and drug abuse – has rock-eted from just 8 per cent in 1971 to almost 50 per cent in 2019. So too has the number of single-parent families in Britain, which by 2019 had grown to more than 3 million. By the end of the 2020s, Britain is forecast to have one of the largest numbers of single-parent families in the advanced world.[35]

Once again, some groups have been hit much harder than others. Consistently, people in the new elite who preach elite beliefs – who argue the loudest for looser cultural norms, sexual freedom, individual choice, permissive lifestyles and alternative family structures – are the most likely to get married, stay married and have children while they are mar-ried. They are the least likely to practise what they preach. While they routinely tell others to challenge or disregard the institution of family they are, by far, the most loyal to it.

While the rate of divorce increased sharply over the last fifty years, it levelled off and reversed among the most highly educated but con-tinued to rise among the less well educated. Highly educated, degree-holding women in the new elite are the most likely of all to have a child while they are married and the least likely to give birth while they are not living with a partner or cohabiting with one. While nearly 70 per cent of births to highly educated women happen within a marriage, only 17 per cent of births to the least well-educated women do. The latter are far more likely to give birth while not even living with a partner at all.[36]

Children of the new elite, in other words, have profoundly

different experiences of family life than children in the non-graduate majority; their upbringing is far more secure, stable and conducive to doing better later in life. While 72 per cent of children whose mothers belong to the graduate class live with both their parents, only 43 per cent of children whose mother has less than a GCSE-level education can say the same.[37]

And, once again, the largest number of single-parent families are found in the former industrial regions which were hit hard by the revolution and pushed aside by the new elite. 'Being born to married parents', concludes one of the most detailed reports, by the Institute for Fiscal Studies, 'is more prominent in the South East and London, regions that have benefitted most from the recent decades of economic growth and the fallout of globalisation.'[38]

Against this backdrop, it is unsurprising that the political revolts of the last decade found their strongest support in Britain's small, medium, industrial and coastal towns which, consistently, were left on the wrong side of the new elite's revolution. Support for Brexit, which many voters saw as an opportunity to push back against the new elite, was significantly higher in communities which were more exposed than others to intense import competition from China and eastern Europe. Calls to 'Take Back Control' resonated especially strongly in communities which, over the last twenty years, had been left to grapple with long-term economic *and* social decline – deteriorating housing markets, higher rates of unemployment, higher rates of family and community decline, and much higher rates of inward migration and demographic change as their local economies were reshaped around cheap labour.[39]

Ordinarily, all this might have been expected to attract the attention of the ruling class. But, as economist Paul Collier points out, these disastrous new effects coincided with a new elite who appear less interested in upholding the strong sense of obligation to others, national belonging and ethical purpose which had characterized Britain's leaders in years gone by.[40] Whether left or right, Britain's rulers are now focused on pushing through a revolution which reflects their values, interests and priorities but shows little interest in everybody else.

DE-POLITICIZATION

The effects of hyper-globalization might have been more limited if the British people could still influence a second major area: the decisions affecting their daily lives. But as the national economy was overturned so too was their national democracy, leaving many people who did not belong to the new ruling class feeling completely and utterly powerless.

Between the 1980s and the 2010s, meaningful choice in British politics disappeared, while power and influence were pushed beyond the borders of national democracy to distant and less accountable institutions. Politics was stripped out of politics; it was depoliticized.

One of the most remarkable aspects of the revolution was the extent to which it united left and right. Unlike the old politics, when there existed meaningful differences, by the end of the twentieth century the major parties had converged on the same territory, offering people the same economic and cultural liberalism. A single way of talking and thinking about Britain descended across not just politics but also the national culture and wider society.

The Labour Party played a particularly important role in entrenching this consensus. Historically, Labour had combined a strong left-wing stance on the economy with what would now be seen as a right-wing stance on culture. It combined strong calls to redistribute resources with strong appeals to social patriotism. Labour leaders were not afraid to say they loved the country, respected its institutions and, overall, saw the best in Britain.

Shaped by the cultural conservatism of the time, many Labour politicians, from Clement Attlee to Peter Shore and Tony Benn, were also instinctively sceptical about how things such as globalization, EU membership and immigration might impact on British workers. Instinctively, they put the national economy and the national community first.

But from the 1990s, things changed. The rise of New Labour reflected the rise of a new wave of more globally minded social democrats who drifted to the centre on economics, embracing the New Right legacy of the 1980s, while also installing a more distant, technocratic and homogeneous politics. This was the Third Way, which

charted a new course between the old right, which was anti-state and pro-market, and the old left, which was pro-state but anti-market.

Seemingly overnight, New Labour became the strongest supporter of the revolution, embracing not just hyper-globalization but EU membership and, from 2004, the opening of Britain's borders to a completely new era of mass immigration. In fact, centre-left social democracy moved so far from its original position that, in the words of one study, it had 'more in common with its main competitors than with its own positions roughly three decades earlier'.[41]

Though it was not recognized at the time, the arrival of this new orthodoxy was about to have profound effects. Not least, it stoked a palpable sense among millions of people in the country that there was no longer any meaningful difference between left and right which, in turn, weakened the old class-based loyalties which had once guided British politics.

At the height of Thatcherism, more than 80 per cent of British people said they could see a great deal of difference between Labour and the Conservatives. But from then on, this figure crashed – to 55 per cent in 1992, 33 per cent in 1997, 27 per cent in 2001, and to just 22 per cent in 2005. On the eve of Brexit, which many people saw as a rare opportunity to vote for an alternative to this new, dreary orthodoxy, fewer than three in ten people said they could tell left and right apart.[42]

Serious choice, serious debate, serious politics left Westminster. Instead, when many people looked out at their political institutions they saw an identikit governing class, composed of careerist politicians who shared the same backgrounds and values (see Chapter 4). While many of these politicians would later rush to blame the rise of populism, Brexit and Boris Johnson on everybody else, in reality the path for these revolts had been cleared long ago by the glaring lack of meaningful choice in Westminster.

One person who noticed this at the time was Professor Colin Crouch, who, in his book *Post-Democracy*, argued that political 'debate' in Britain and the West had now been reduced to a tightly controlled spectacle. Politics was no longer about genuine engagement between citizens and politicians; it was merely a game managed by rival teams of professionals, spin doctors, focus group consultants and pollsters, who were expert in the techniques of persuasion and minimizing the role of the masses in democracy.

Politicians only ever debated a small number of issues which had been carefully pre-selected for discussion and which did not risk cutting across, and certainly did not challenge, the new liberal consensus. Any policies which signalled a genuine break from this pro-EU, pro-globalization, pro-immigration consensus were simply never entertained.

Instead, in Britain and across the West policies were increasingly decided behind closed doors, through the interaction between political, corporate and financial elites who were more interested in representing the interests of the ruling class, big business and other global elites. In these post-democratic societies, argued Crouch, where democracies are dominated by small circles of interlocking elites, democracy merely becomes a shell of its former self.[43]

Britain's transition into this new and depressing era of depoliticized, or even post-democratic, politics was further reinforced by other changes. Shortly before the vote for Brexit, Professor Anthony King asked a simple but crucial question: who governs Britain? He answered by pointing not to citizens, voters or elected politicians but to a growing number of global institutions, financiers, unelected regulators, independent agencies, and large multinationals that were now wielding enormous influence over the country.[44]

Britain's political system, he pointed out, had been pushed into the new era of 'governance', in which genuine political power and influence had been transferred away from the people to a complex web of organizations and agencies which sat firmly outside the borders of national democracy and were certainly not accountable to voters.

'Throughout the 1980s and 1990s', summarized Professor Michael Moran, in another study of how Britain's political system had been transformed, 'the state was reconfigured so as to create a defensive barrier of regulatory bodies that stood between policy makers and popular expectations. Bodies as different as the Monetary Policy Committee, the National Institute for Clinical Excellence and the separate utilities regulators converted sensitive issues of popular demand and distributional struggle into a technocratic vocabulary that erected a high barrier to democratic intervention.'[45] Democracy was now rapidly making way for a far more distant and remote technocracy.

One small example of this was how, by the 2000s, £1 in every £3 the government was spending on public services went to independent providers, such as Carillion, which later collapsed with £2 billion of debt in 2018, or Interserve, which also collapsed. Public services from hospitals to schools were pushed out in an ad hoc fashion to private firms but with few mechanisms that people could use to hold them to account or assess whether they were value for money. Many such schemes suffered chronic problems and wasted hundreds of millions of pounds.[46]

More fundamentally, political power and accountability were pushed upwards, away from citizens, to a growing array of international institutions, markets and transnational organizations whose reach extended well beyond the nation-state. This too was part of a global trend which reflected the liberal cosmopolitan outlook of the new elite.

In Britain and elsewhere, key milestones in this new era included the signing of the Maastricht Treaty in 1993, which strengthened the European Union, the launch of the World Trade Organization, which made it harder for countries to shield themselves from international trade competition, the North American Free Trade Agreement (NAFTA), the arrival of the 'Euro' single currency in 1999 and the eastward expansion of the EU into former communist states.

Aside from further diluting the influence of voters, these changes reflected the new elite's growing appetite for a new world order in which democracy would, eventually, be superseded by transnational governance – a new system, led by highly educated expert technocrats, drawn from the new elite, who saw domestic politics and the masses as an unnecessary hindrance.

Alan Greenspan, former chair of the US Federal Reserve, expressed the basic idea in 2007, when asked who he would support in the presidential election: '[we] are fortunate that, thanks to globalization, policy decisions in the US have been largely replaced by global market forces. National security aside, it hardly makes any difference who will be the next president. The world is governed by market forces.'[47] Jean-Claude Juncker, president of the European Commission, voiced a similar idea when he pointed to how citizens were now only playing a secondary role. 'We decree something, then float it and wait some time to see what happens. If no clamour occurs and no big fuss follows, because most people do not grasp what has been decided, we continue – step by step, until the point of no return is reached.'[48]

Juncker was referring to another ostensibly democratic organization which was gaining more and more power and had support from both the left and right in British politics: the European Union. Despite frequently making Eurosceptic noises, it was the Conservative Party which had overseen the most important steps in Britain's integration into the EU. It was the right, not the left, which led the country into the European Community in 1973, who oversaw the Single European Act in 1986, which removed barriers to the free movement of goods, services, money and people and introduced qualified majority voting, whereby individual nations could be overruled in key areas of policy, such as trade, social and environmental policy. And it was the Conservatives who, under John Major, signed the Maastricht Treaty, paving the way not just for Britain's continuing economic integration with the EU but its political, social and monetary integration, too, including shared citizenship, a shared flag and a shared anthem.

From here on, nation-states were transformed into EU member states, while national citizens were transformed into EU nationals. Everybody who lived in the EU would be free to live and work in other EU member-states, blurring the boundaries between nations.

These changes, too, were then embraced by New Labour, which reversed its previous scepticism of European integration to become – as with hyper-globalization – the most enthusiastic supporter of another key pillar of the revolution. Despite having called for an early Brexit, in 1983, by the 1990s the Labour Party, which was now in the hands of the new elite, fully embraced the pro-EU cosmopolitan mood. 'I have a bold aim,' declared Blair, in 1999. 'That over the next few years Britain resolves once and for all its ambivalence towards Europe. I want to end the uncertainty, the lack of confidence, the Europhobia.'[49] Both left and right were now singing the same song.

New Labour became so committed to EU integration that Blair even campaigned for a referendum on joining the Euro single currency, before his chancellor, Gordon Brown, ruled it out, and before the Eurozone imploded into a major sovereign debt crisis.[50]

New Labour also threw its weight behind the enlargement of the

European Union, signed the Maastricht Treaty's Social Chapter (which John Major avoided), agreed to extend qualified majority voting over other areas of policy, talked about putting the EU Constitutional Treaty to a referendum and then quietly signed the Lisbon Treaty, extending the EU's reach over many other areas of British life, including trade.[51]

Though Conservatives turned up the volume on their Euro-scepticism – campaigning under William Hague, Iain Duncan Smith and Michael Howard to 'Keep the Pound' and reform Britain's relationship with the EU – they always fell short of calling to leave the club, unwilling to tackle the new consensus in the new politics.

Such was the scale of this consensus that when the Brexit referendum arrived, in 2016, no less than 96 per cent of Labour MPs, 75 per cent of all MPs, 80 per cent of David Cameron's Cabinet, and a majority of Conservative MPs campaigned to remain in the EU.[52] Only a very small number of Britain's politicians were willing to challenge the new orthodoxy, which pushed opposition to EU membership outside the mainstream and handed the populist outsider, Nigel Farage, a major issue of his own.

The new elite's strong and passionate support for Britain's EU membership might have been less problematic had there not been a glaring 'democratic deficit' at the heart of the organization. To be democratic, organizations need to fulfil three criteria; they need to give people the right to participate by casting a vote; they need to give them the right to be represented; and they need to give them the right to organize meaningful opposition and compete for control of the executive. While the EU was certainly *procedurally* democratic, allowing people to vote every five years and be represented in the European Parliament, it was never *substantively* democratic because its core executive remained out of reach for voters. The most senior positions in the European Commission have been decided not through open, democratic elections but behind closed doors, which violates one of the founding principles of democracy – namely, that citizens must be able to participate in executive decisions through open competition. When it came to fundamental issues that were having a real impact on people's lives, such as trade and immigration, policies at the EU level had often been determined by elites over whom voters had very little influence.

While national politicians never admitted it, the blunt reality was that remaining in the EU seriously constrained what they could offer voters at national elections. While the countries that were members of the EU were national, the policies that were being delivered by the EU were supra-national in scope. Often, they trumped domestic laws, which meant politicians were unable to offer people a genuine alternative from what was decided at the EU level because such an alternative was no longer possible. Whether economic policy, environmental policy, energy policy or migration policy, many laws were 'locked in' at the EU level, making it difficult if not impossible for individual governments to overturn them.

In turn, national governments often used EU membership to lock their successors into policies which had been decided at the EU level and, therefore, could not be changed or reversed unless a majority of EU states agreed, which was unlikely to happen. In this way, the only policies that were allowed were policies that had been pre-approved by the new elite and their counterparts in other EU member states.

'As the commitments deriving from EU membership increase,' explain scholars Kyriaki Nanou and Han Dorussen, 'governments become more constrained in terms of the policies they can implement . . . As parties adjust their policy platforms to adopt positions in line with EU legislation, they offer less choice to voters.'[53]

This was powerfully symbolized by David Cameron's failed attempt, ahead of the Brexit referendum, to renegotiate Britain's EU membership. Despite proclaiming to voters that the relationship could be fundamentally reformed, Cameron's hopes soon collided with reality. Aside from securing an assurance that the EU's overriding goal of 'ever closer union' no longer applied to Britain, on most other issues, notably immigration, he was unable to secure serious reforms because opposition from other EU member states made such reforms impossible. As Cambridge professor Helen Thompson pointed out: 'When he [Cameron] returned home he had to ask British voters to Remain, having just put on an overt demonstration of how little influence the UK could exercise in a Union whose founding text he had disowned.'[54]

It was a powerful example of how Britain's leaders could no longer seriously influence many of the big issues of the day and certainly not in a way that voters thought they could. Policies at the EU level were often deliberately insulated from the masses and the inconvenience of national elections, which partly explains why the slogan 'Take Back Control' resonated so strongly in Britain, a country that for centuries has put a strong emphasis on the critical importance of accountable and representative government. In the world of the EU, as academic Peter Mair pointed out, key decisions were often not taken by voters but by 'political elites with a more or less free hand', by a new ruling class that was 'reluctant to have their hands tied by the constraints of popular democracy'.[55] Rather than being genuinely democratic, other experts conceded that the EU had evolved into an 'enlightened despotism'.[56] While it consulted the European Parliament every now and then, it ultimately sought to marginalize the masses.

As Britain's national democracy was hollowed out, then, it became increasingly clear that the country's leaders were no longer deriving their sense of authority and legitimacy from their vertical relationship with the voters below – the people who had elected them – but from their horizontal relationship with other global elites, whether in the EU, the universities, think tanks or Davos.[57] This widening gulf, this huge void between the elites and the masses, was best summarized by one of Blair's ministers, Lord Falconer: 'What governs our approach', he said, 'is a clear desire to place power where it should be: increasingly not with politicians, but with those best fitted in different ways to deploy it.' Falconer went on: 'This depoliticising of key decision making is a vital element in bringing power closer to the people.'[58]

MASS IMMIGRATION

The growing gulf between politicians and the people was then further reflected in a third major area of policy: the onset of mass immigration. While the left followed the right on economics, when it came to culture and identity it charted a completely different course. Whereas Thatcher had combined radical economic liberalism with an appeal to traditional family values, from the 1990s, New Labour kept the former but replaced the latter with a far more radical cultural liberalism.

The liberal consensus of the new elite was now complete and firing on all cylinders.

This too marked a radical break from the past. Historically, in Britain and across the West, cultural liberalism had only ever played a secondary role in centre-left social democracy, with most parties remaining focused on building a welfare state, strengthening collective bargaining and redistribution.[59] But because of the embrace of hyper-globalization, which demanded cheap migrant labour to serve large corporations, and the rise of the new elite who are driven far more strongly by their liberal cosmopolitan values, by the time Britain entered the twenty-first century things had changed. Its ruling class was completely committed to a policy that would have seismic political effects and do more than anything else to drive support for populism, Brexit, Boris Johnson and the realignment of politics: mass immigration.

Throughout the twentieth century, more people had left Britain than had migrated into it. But during the New Labour years, between 1997 and 2010, this was completely turned on its head. In less than a decade, as shown in Figure 3, the British were subjected to a scale of immigration that was unique in their history. In only a few short years, the new elite redefined Britain as a country of continuous, large-scale immigration.

Between 1991 and 1995, before New Labour came to power, the annual average level of net migration into Britain – meaning, the number of people entering minus the number of people leaving – had been a moderate and manageable 37,000 each year. By the time New Labour left office, in 2010, it had rocketed past 250,000 and, between 2015 and 2019, because of the changes introduced, was soon averaging 266,000 each year.[60] Between 2011 and 2021, the Office for National Statistics estimates net migration added 2 million people to England and Wales. Britain simply experienced one of the sharpest increases in immigration in the Western world.

Because of these changes, during the first two decades of the twenty-first century, Britain's immigrant population more than doubled to more than 9 million. By the early 2020s, the overall share of the population that was foreign-born had surged to 14 per cent. In 2022, the census confirmed that 10 million people resident in England and Wales

Figure 3: Estimated Average Net Migration to the UK, 1901–2011

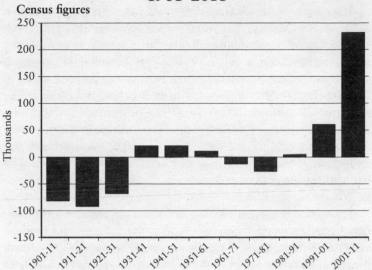

Census figures

Source: ONS Annual Abstract of Statistics (various editions); *Long Term International Migration Estimates*, 2nd series (LTIM calendar year); https://researchbriefings.files.parliament.uk/documents/ SN06077.pdf. *Note:* There was no census in 1941.

had been born abroad, up from 7.5 million in 2011. The most common countries of birth are India, Poland, Pakistan and Romania.

Many urban areas, as a result, have experienced what sociologist Steve Vertovec call 'hyper-diversity' – a rapid increase in the number of ethnic groups, religions, languages, customs and cultural practices.[61] By 2019, this was further reflected in the fact that a record of more than one in four births in England and Wales are now to women who were themselves born outside of Britain – in Poland, Pakistan, Romania, Bangladesh and Nigeria.[62]

These shifts have completely changed the driver of Britain's population growth. In the past, it had been 'natural change', namely the difference between births and deaths, while immigration played a secondary role. But during the first two decades of the twenty-first century, as Britain's fertility rate dropped below the 'replacement rate' of 2.1, declining sharply after 2012, immigration and higher fertility rates among young migrants have made immigration the main driver of population growth. By 2022, more than half the total population increase in England and Wales in the past 10 years is because of net migration

And this will now continue to redefine the country in the years ahead, not least because of the liberalization of immigration from outside of the European Union that was introduced by Boris Johnson and the Conservative Party in the aftermath of Brexit, and continued by Liz Truss. Over the next decade, the Office for National Statistics forecasts that another 5.6 million people will migrate into the country while about 3.4 million will leave Britain. By 2041, if current immigration levels continue, Britain's population will increase from around 67 to 72 million – equivalent to about five new Birminghams.[63]

Whereas in the aftermath of the Brexit referendum there was a sharp decline in immigration from across the EU, since then, the number of people arriving in Britain from outside the European Union has increased sharply. Close to 1 million visas were issued in 2021, comprising a combination of workers, international students, refugees from Hong Kong and family members of existing migrants, reflecting a continuation of these record migration levels. At the same time, the number of people arriving in Britain illegally, on small boats in the English channel, hit a record high of nearly 40,000 in 2022, including 12,000 Albanians.

The initial onset of mass immigration reflected specific choices that were made by New Labour, and which have since played a key role in driving voters away from the party (see Chapter 3). New Labour's more liberal approach to immigration not only reflected the extent to which the new elite dominate the party but a deliberate attempt to impose their liberal cosmopolitan and progressive values on the rest of the country.

'I remember coming away from some discussions', recalled Andrew Neather, one of Blair's former advisers, 'with the clear sense that the policy was intended – even if this wasn't its main purpose – to rub the Right's nose in diversity and render their arguments out of date. That seemed to be to be a manoeuvre too far.'[64]

While the relaxation of immigration controls reflected what Neather described as 'a deliberate policy' to 'open up the UK to mass migration', New Labour was also deeply reluctant to discuss the move publicly for fear it would alienate the party's working-class and more traditionalist voters. It was another example of how the decisions that were affecting people's lives were being kept as far away from them as possible, as Neather continues:

> The PIU's [Tony Blair's Performance and Innovation Unit] were legendarily tedious within Whitehall but their big immigration report was surrounded by an unusual air of both anticipation and secrecy. Drafts were handed out in summer 2000 only with extreme reluctance: there was a paranoia about it reaching the media . . . Ministers were very nervous about the whole thing . . . there was a reluctance elsewhere in government to discuss what increased immigration would mean, above all for Labour's core white working-class vote. This shone through even in the published report: the 'social outcomes' it talks about are solely those for immigrants . . . In part, they probably realised the conservatism of their core voters: while ministers might have been passionately in favour of a more diverse society, it wasn't necessarily a debate they wanted to have in working men's clubs in Sheffield or Sunderland.[65]

A key moment arrived in 2004, when Blair decided not to follow other leaders in the EU by imposing transitional controls on immigration from inside the EU. Instead, he opened the door to unlimited free movement. It was a watershed moment, even if many people did not recognize it at the time. The decision stoked considerable public concern, which not only created ample space for populism but would later become a core driver of Brexit, leaving Tony Blair as much an unintentional architect of the vote to leave the EU as David Cameron, the Conservative prime minister who introduced the referendum on EU membership to begin with.[66]

While people's growing anxiety about how immigration was changing Britain was often blamed on bigotry, many voters were influenced by their real-world experiences. One symbol of what many people outside the cities were experiencing arrived when popular retailer Sports Direct opened a factory for 3,500 workers on the site of an old mining pit in northern England. The company, recalled the local Labour MP, 'set out to mine an apparently endless seam of Eastern European workers who were willing to move to North Derbyshire, live six to a house, and work in conditions most UK workers would consider oppressive and underpaid'.[67]

Furthermore, contrary to the trope that was often heard in London, that the growing backlash to immigration was being pushed by people who had no experience of immigration, studies published since the Brexit referendum – including my own research – find that this pushback to the new elite was strongest in areas which experienced a sudden and sharp increase in immigration over a very short period of time – many of which were based outside the big cities and university towns.

The popular claim that immigration would only be a net positive for the economy and the country was also undermined by research. One review of this evidence, published in 2022 by the reputable and independent University of Oxford's Migration Observatory, concludes: 'Studies examining the fiscal impact of migrants have produced different results, although in all cases, the impacts have been estimated at less than +1 per cent or -1 per cent of GDP.'[68] In other words, the estimated economic effects of opening the country to millions more people have been small.

Nor were these concerns only about the economy. As Professor Lauren McLaren and Mark Johnson showed in a major study of British public attitudes, the wave of concern that followed New Labour's decision and powered the rise of populism was often driven far more strongly by people's worries about how, in their eyes, these changes were damaging not just Britain's finances but its distinctive national identity and national culture.

'Britons are clearly worried about the symbolic threats of immigrants,' they concluded, after crunching the data, 'the threat of religions that are perceived to emphasise non-British values and a terminal community other than that of Britain, and the threat to shared customs and way of life.'[69] Unfortunately, in some areas these concerns were further inflamed by the failure of governments, whether on the left or the right, to focus on integrating new and old arrivals.

In some ways, the story of integration into Britain has been a remarkable success story, with many people from minority ethnic backgrounds powering ahead in many areas of our national life, as we will see in Chapter 5. But, at the same time, over the last twenty years a series of independent reports have pointed to the glaring lack of integration in many areas of Britain, variously warning that people from different ethnic or religious groups are leading 'parallel lives' or 'sleepwalking to segregation'. The Casey Review, published in 2016, went further, warning that Britain was experiencing 'high levels of social and economic isolation in some places and cultural and religious practices in communities that are not only holding some of our citizens back but run contrary to British values and sometimes our laws'.[70]

These concerns have more recently been underlined in books such as Ed Husain's *Among the Mosques*, for which he turned up unannounced at some of Britain's 20,000 mosques.[71] Most Muslims he met felt strongly attached to Britain and proud of their British identity. But, in some areas, he found clear evidence of 'communalism' and *caliphism*, namely, cultural and social attitudes that were influenced by a sense of separatism and a desire to be governed more by a rigid interpretation of sharia law than state law – an outlook that was arguably visible during disturbances between young Muslims and Hindus in Leicester in 2022.[72]

'In parts of Glasgow, Blackburn, Bradford, Manchester, Rochdale, Dewsbury, Birmingham and east London', writes Husain, 'a Muslim can spend months with no contact whatsoever with mainstream 'white' Britain. From banks to hospital staff to taxis to grocery stores to websites and dating apps, a parallel Muslim-only environment has emerged for those who want it.'[73]

His claims are supported by surveys which suggest that while close to nine in ten British Muslims feel attached to Britain, nearly one in five – equivalent to 700,000 Muslims – would prefer to lead a separate Islamic life as far as possible, or in a fully separate Islamic area.[74]

People's concerns about mass immigration and its effects on the country have also been stoked by a perceived lack of accountability and control. Even if Britain's leaders had wanted to slow the pace of change by curbing the number of people entering the country, when it came to immigration from inside the European Union there was little, if anything, they could do. So long as Britain remained in the single market it was subject to the free movement of EU nationals. For this reason, most of the people who felt concerned about immigration also agreed with the statement 'I feel I cannot do anything to improve the situation'.[75]

These feelings of powerlessness were also stoked by people's realization that, like it or not, they were having to deal with the effects of crises that were erupting elsewhere in the EU. Their scepticism of European integration was not only shaped by the glaring democratic deficit at the heart of the European Union but also by how, from 2008, the eruption of a major sovereign debt crisis within the Eurozone had led many, mainly young EU nationals from countries such as Italy and Spain to migrate to Britain for work. The post-2014 refugee crisis further amplified this growing sense among many British voters that neither their political leaders in Westminster nor EU officials in Brussels and Strasbourg were in control.

The result was a total collapse of public confidence in Britain's leaders and the system. While Britain's civil servants initially forecast that 13,000 people would arrive, the number soon soared into the hundreds of thousands and eventually reached 3.7 million.[76] Nor was this profound loss of public confidence helped by a string of unnecessary errors and blunders. In 2012, the Office for National Statistics revealed that the population of England and Wales was almost half a million higher than what had initially been forecast, which they traced to the 'underestimation of long-term immigration from central and eastern Europe in the middle part of the decade'.[77] Then, seven years later, in 2019, the number of immigrants thought to have arrived over the previous decade was revised upwards, by 25,000 each year, while the number of EU migrants who were thought to have arrived between 2011 and 2016 was also increased.

And then, in 2021, it was revealed that throughout the previous decade net migration had been 93,000 higher each year than what people had been told.[78] Unsurprisingly, large majorities of people blamed both the Labour and Conservative parties for having lost control of an issue they cared deeply about. When, shortly before Brexit, people were asked who they trusted to manage the issue the most popular answer was 'none of them', or Nigel Farage, who, alongside EU membership, was now handed another major issue in British politics, which he would ruthlessly exploit.[79] Trust had left the building. It was an ideal habitat for populists.

In this way, and as the independent British Election Study would later conclude, Tony Blair's decision to throw open Britain's borders and rebuild the economy around cheap migrant labour became one of the most consequential decisions in Britain's recent political history. 'This decision set in train a process', they write, 'that raised the salience of immigration and led to the entanglement of the EU and immigration issues. A key issue was the inability of the government – any government – to respond to rising public concern'.[80]

In the short term, the effects of Blair's decision were concealed by his election victories in 2001 and 2005, which further convinced the new elite to double down on the revolution. But, beneath the surface, these changes were dramatically weakening Labour's relationship with its traditional working-class voters and, as we will see, would soon push many of them to search for far more radical political alternatives.

One person who tried to win them over, from 2010, was the liberal conservative David Cameron who promised to reduce net migration 'from the hundreds of thousands to the tens of thousands'. But, in the end, because of the inability of British politicians to change these decisions, he too presided over the highest rates of immigration that had ever been seen. Cameron's loss of control, much like Blair's and Brown's, was symbolized by his doomed attempt to renegotiate the widely unpopular policy of free movement ahead of the Brexit referendum. As in other areas, he was forced to return home with only minor changes, reinforcing the growing sense among voters that nobody was in control.[81]

In fact, many Conservative voters had long felt dubious about the extent to which, if at all, Cameron really did want to push back against the revolution. Ever since becoming leader, he had talked continuously about wanting to steer his party away from its image as the 'nasty party', to stop 'banging on about Europe' and to shift attention away from the traditionalist voters who were abandoning his party for Nigel Farage, and whom he derided as 'fruitcakes, loonies, and closet racists'.[82]

Much like Blair, Cameron and his self-styled 'progressive conservatives' were driven by their desire to reassure the new elite in the big cities and the university towns that they too were entirely comfortable with cosmopolitan and progressive Britain. Like their counterparts in New Labour, who had often gone to the same schools and the same universities, Cameron's Conservatives worked overtime to reassure the new elite that they could switch from New Labour to the New Tories, safe in the knowledge the revolution would continue.

Some of this was also shaped by electoral pragmatism. Because of the toxic legacy of Thatcherism, pre-Brexit conservatism had never been electorally competitive in the Labour heartlands, which often had massive Labour majorities. Even in 2015, when Cameron finally won his own majority in the House of Commons, in many of the seats that would later switch to Boris Johnson only four years later – Bolsover, Redcar and even Blair's own seat of Sedgefield – the Conservatives trailed well behind Labour. While Cameron struggled to relate to the lives and values of these voters, he also had few electoral incentives to try to win them over.

For much of the country, the rise of this liberal conservatism was yet another reminder of the extent to which left and right were now completely united behind the revolution. When, in 1997, Britain's Conservative prime minister John Major had conceded to Tony Blair, he reminded his successor that one reason why conservatism had been so devastatingly effective was because it had forced a socialist party to abandon socialism. But when Gordon Brown conceded to David Cameron thirteen years later, he might have said something similar – that one reason why New Labour was so devastatingly effective was because it had forced the Conservative Party to abandon conservatism.

While New Labour had embraced the economic legacy of the New Right, the Conservatives had embraced the cultural liberalism of the New Left. And this new consensus shared by the new elite, would cut much of the country adrift.

3
Values

Revolutions divide societies. While they are cheered on by their most passionate supporters, who often only represent a small minority, many others feel aghast at what is unfolding around them, alarmed by both the pace and scale of change.

It has been the same in Britain. While the revolution that was unleashed over the last fifty years was celebrated by the new elite, it simultaneously stoked a rising tide of anger among a much larger number of people who could sense they were no longer on Westminster's radar. Disillusioned and disgruntled, over the last decade the forgotten masses have been staging a counter-revolution, rallying around national populism, Brexit, Boris Johnson and a very different brand of post-Brexit conservatism to try to swing the pendulum away from the new elite and back towards people like themselves.

While each of these revolts is seen through the prism of Britain's relationship with Europe – with their calls to 'Take Back Control' and 'Get Brexit Done' – in reality they symbolize a much broader attempt by millions of people to push back against not just Brussels and Strasbourg but also the new elite who stopped listening to them long ago.

None of this was supposed to happen. Routinely, the new elite told themselves that the demographic trends that are sweeping through Britain and the West would inevitably cement their dominance and bring them large and unassailable majorities. For years, journalists, pollsters and academics argued that it was only a matter of time until the 'Londonization' of Britain would hand the new elite uninterrupted political power. The people who vote for populists, so the thinking goes, will soon die out and be replaced by a new cosmopolitan alliance, comprising the new graduate elite, the rapidly rising number of minority ethnic voters, young millennials and even younger zoomers from Generation-Z, who were born after 1996.

Whether this argument was made by American Democrat pollster Stan Greenberg, shortly before the rise of Donald Trump, or British journalist Jeremy Cliffe, shortly before Brexit, it has appealed strongly to a new elite who have long fallen into one of the oldest and most misleading narratives in politics – demography is destiny.[1]

'Even if not a single person has changed their mind since the [Brexit] referendum', wrote columnist Polly Toynbee, in 2019, shortly before the post-Brexit Tories won their largest majority in Westminster for more than thirty years, 'the demographic shift alone will have done the heavy lifting. Enough old leavers will have died and enough young remainers will have come on to the electoral register to turn the dial on what the country thinks about Brexit.'[2] This tendency to see politics as a conveyer belt on which conservatives fall off and liberals stay on reflects how progressives see the world. Rather than see politics and human nature as what they are – unpredictable, chaotic, messy, and volatile – the new elite believe they are on a linear path towards 'progress', that history will only ever bend in their direction.

But neither election results nor the evidence supports this seductive narrative. In Britain, despite the country rapidly becoming more ethnically, culturally, religiously and sexually diverse, and giving rise to a larger graduate class, ever since the late 1990s it has been the right not the left which has seen its share of the vote increase at every general election. Instead of winning large and unassailable majorities, Labour and the left have been handed four consecutive defeats, including most recently their heaviest since 1935.

In global politics, too, many trends undermine this narrative. In Europe, national populists continue to enjoy some of their strongest results on record, with the likes of Marine Le Pen attracting their support from young men and women and significant numbers of LGBT voters who worry that their rights are under threat from the spread of Islam. In America, at the last presidential election in 2020 Donald Trump lost the White House but still walked away with support from one in three Latino and Hispanic voters and close to one in eight African Americans, most of whom have not gone to university. Most minorities did not vote for Trump, but record numbers of them did, reflecting how seductive narratives about angry old white men are wide of the mark. Many of these voters have since told researchers that they feel taken for granted by the left and alienated by the rise of radical 'woke' progressives, including calls to 'defund the police', a luxury belief for the new elite that mainly impacts on low-income, working-class communities where they do not live.[3]

Why, then, were the new elite outflanked? And why did populism, Brexit and Boris Johnson manage to cut through? The answer is that, like their counterparts across the West, the new elite failed to recognize and respond to the rise of three powerful new divides in our politics. The most important, by far, is what we will explore in this chapter – a growing rift among the British people over their *cultural values*, over how they think Britain ought to be.

THE COSMOPOLITAN-
TRADITIONALIST DIVIDE

Contrary to what you might have heard, these new divides in politics were not only stoked by ruthless populists and right-wing culture warriors; they are the direct result of the seismic changes that were overseen by the new elite and which we explored in the last chapter. The counter-revolution that has gathered pace over the last decade has drawn the bulk of its strength from people's deep-rooted anxieties about the effects of hyper-globalization, EU membership, mass immigration and the hollowing out of their national democracy.

As the revolution swept through society, it increasingly polarized different groups of voters not just along the old lines of their class, wealth, income and how they think about the economy but also along the new lines of their level of education, age and geography, all of which shape how they think about their identity. Politics, in short, has moved from the old transactional debates about what we have to the far more existential debates about who we are.

This shift was a long time coming. Across the West, political scientists who have tracked this change now share a broad consensus that the foundations of politics began to change in profound, possibly permanent ways in the 1980s. Whereas throughout the twentieth century political battles had been fought between the economic left and the economic right, dividing those who wanted to use the state to redistribute resources from those who wanted to have a smaller state and let the free market play a bigger role, in today's politics, where new cultural debates over immigration, identity and diversity have surged up the agenda, the battle lines have changed in important ways.

Now, they are shaped just as much, if not more so, by a new rift between cosmopolitans and traditionalists, between those whose values instinctively support the new elite and the revolution and those who, instead, feel far more strongly attached to the nation, the majority group, and who desperately want to find leaders who will preserve their distinctive national identity, culture and ways of life.

Politics, in other words, has become 'two-dimensional', shaped not only by the old left and right economic divide but now also by the cosmopolitan and traditionalist divide. And the single most important determinant of where people sit in this debate is their level of education. On one side stand the new graduate elite and their allies who benefitted most from the revolution and embrace its guiding cosmopolitan and progressive ethos. The people who belong to this cosmopolitan alliance include the new graduate elite, the young millennials, and the even younger zoomers, born after 1996, who are far more likely to have passed through the universities and have known nothing other than the revolution. Moving leftwards in politics, they accept the revolution or want it to go much faster. But, contrary to the misleading narrative that demography is destiny, these groups, for reasons that we will see, are still a long way from being able to command complete power in the country.

On the other side stands a new alliance of mainly non-graduate voters who have lost out from the revolution and who today worry that their values and their vision of an ideal Britain are being pushed aside by the new elite. While the people who have joined this traditionalist alliance come from different classes and financial backgrounds and often voted for different parties in the past – with some very wealthy – they have been pushed together by their shared sense that the revolution has gone way too far and too fast, and the new elite are no longer serving the interests of the wider country.

Comprising people from the working class, the non-graduate majority, and older generations who can remember Britain before the revolution, traditionalists have been trying to reassert their values, pushing forward entirely new parties, such as the UK Independence Party and the Brexit Party, supporting Boris Johnson as they tried to reshape the post-Brexit Conservative Party along the way, and transforming Britain's political geography, enabling the Conservatives to successfully invade Labour's Red Wall.

Clearly, there will always be outliers, people who do not sit neatly in either camp, such as the one-quarter of Britain's graduates and one in three black and minority ethnic voters who voted for Brexit, the one in five 18–24-year-olds who voted for Boris Johnson and the four in ten who left school after their GCSEs but who still support Labour and the left. There will also be people who identify with aspects of both world views, holding cosmopolitan views on some questions and traditionalist views on others. But, broadly speaking, these are the exceptions. The cosmopolitan–traditionalist divide is now central to British politics and, as we will see, extends well beyond Brexit.

If the new elite, as we saw in Chapter 1, are united by a very distinctive world view, then so too are the traditionalists who outnumber them. While members of the new elite are fond of telling themselves they represent the majority, this is simply not true. Britain is becoming a more liberal country but even in 2022, according to the British Social Attitudes survey, still only 22 per cent of the country could be classified as strongly liberal, while a much larger number, close to 40 per cent, were classified as traditionalist (with the rest falling in neither camp).[4] Though on many issues, as we will see, the share of traditionalists is much higher.

These numbers help to explain why, whether they are on the right or left, Britain's traditionalists have spent recent decades feeling increasingly alarmed by the pace and scale of the revolution and how the new elite no longer seem to recognize or even respect people who hold different values. While right-wing and left-wing traditionalists think very differently about the economy, with Conservative traditionalists leaning right and Labour traditionalists leaning left, when it comes to questions about culture and identity they are in complete agreement – they think the new elite have made a series of catastrophic mistakes and can no longer be trusted to run the country.

As their name implies, they want to reassert a more traditional vision of British identity, culture and ways of life; they want to slow, not stop, the pace at which the country is being transformed. Resentful of the new elite and what they see as their self-serving agenda, over the last decade traditionalists have been searching for leaders who will put the interests of the nation and the majority first – not the new elite, global corporations, the EU or minorities.

Traditionalists do not only want to stay out of the European Union, make Brexit a success and control immigration; they also want to live in a more ordered and stable society which is characterized by slow rather than fast change, not one which they feel is being continually redefined by the new elite as a country of constant flux, change and instability. While the new elite dislike hierarchies, want to prioritize the free and equal interaction of people and support those who do not conform to conventional ways of life – such as racial, sexual and gender minorities – traditionalists want to live in a society where these hierarchies are upheld and respected, and where people are encouraged to conform with established ways of life, so as to uphold the unity of the national community.

Traditionalists, as the country's most reliable surveys make clear, want to see a tougher stance on law and order, want people to show greater respect for British values, want to live in a society where children are taught obedience and to respect authority, where criminals are given stiffer sentences and the death penalty is not necessarily off limits. Support for leaving the EU was endorsed by 70 per cent of people who support reintroducing capital punishment but by only 20 per cent of people who do not.[5]

And while people might like to think these are the views of a small fringe, today about half the country support reintroducing the death penalty while around two-thirds would like to see criminals given much tougher sentences.[6]

Traditionalists would also like to spend as much time defending and promoting Britain's distinctive identity, culture and history as the new elite spend championing more globalist or universal themes, such as multiculturalism and diversity. This is why, in their book on the same rift in America, Professors Marc Hetherington and Jonathan Weiler describe the two sides as representing the *fixed* and the *fluid*: whereas cosmopolitans favour a fluid society, characterized by rapidly changing norms, diversity and novelty, traditionalists lean towards a fixed society, where change is slower.[7]

Many of the voters who rallied around national populism, Brexit and the post-Brexit Conservative Party are instinctively wary of the kind of rapid change which defined the revolution and upended Britain. Unlike the new elite, they see this as disorder, loss and as posing a threat to the group-based identities which they feel more strongly attached to than the country's graduates. They prefer the familiar and the predictable to the unfamiliar and unpredictable, and want their leaders to prioritize evolutionary rather than revolutionary change. This is why they feel instinctively uncomfortable with the sheer pace at which everything from statues to sexual and gender identities, and interpretations of history, is being revised or overturned.

Traditionalists are not opposed to immigration *per se* but they do want less of it – something both Labour and the Conservatives have, so far, failed to deliver. While they have become more positive about immigration since the Brexit referendum, they still remain deeply sceptical about how it is changing Britain and the sheer numbers of immigrants.

When, in 2022, voters were asked whether immigration over the past ten years had been good or bad for Britain, half of the traditionalists who rallied behind Brexit felt it has been 'mostly bad' while only 10 per cent felt it has been 'mostly good' (another 34 per cent said both good and bad). They are more inclined to believe that the government prioritizes minorities over the majority and are the least likely to think that movements like Black Lives Matter (BLM) are a 'force for good'.[8]

While lazy caricatures portray traditionalists as a homogeneous group of voters who all think and look the same, they are quite diverse. In their study of the different tribes of voters in British politics, published in 2021, the think tank More in Common identify several groups which broadly align with this traditionalist world view.[9]

They include Backbone Conservatives, who represent 15 per cent of the country; they are nostalgic, patriotic and confident about Britain's future now that the country has left the EU. Concentrated in England's villages and small towns, they are older, wealthier and white. They are strongly supportive of Brexit, feel the most negatively about immigration, see their British or English identity as a central part of who they are and are the proudest of Britain's history, heritage, traditions and symbols of nationhood.

They are joined by Disengaged Traditionalists, who represent another 18 per cent of the country and share these views. Coming from the working class, the Midlands and England's smaller post-industrial towns, they have lower-than-average levels of education and earnings and stress self-reliance and individual responsibility, though they are the least likely to vote. They also want to live in a well-ordered and stable society and feel a strong sense of pride in British history. But they are more likely than all others to think British identity is rapidly disappearing, to feel negatively about immigration and to voice their hostility towards metropolitan graduate elites in London and England's more prosperous south-east.

Both these groups have also been joined by a third tribe, called Loyal Nationals, who represent another 17 per cent. Concentrated in small or medium-sized towns in Yorkshire, the north-east and Wales, these working-class voters put even stronger emphasis on the sense of security and belonging that come from being in a nation with a strong identity and shared values. They feel strongly attached to the British majority, though they fear they will soon be a minority, and are fiercely proud of the country, its history and achievements.

Like other traditionalists, they feel besieged and under threat from the forces that are swirling around them – high levels of immigration, the record numbers of asylum-seekers who are crossing the Channel, rising diversity and political correctness, which they fear are undermining Britain's cohesion and unity. Feeling like strangers in their own country, they are united by a sense of loss, anxiety and frustration at having their views excluded by the new elite in London, who, in their eyes, look down on them and their group.

Routinely, ever since Brexit, we have been told that these voters are irrational and did not know what they were voting for. Instead of holding clear and coherent motives, they were motivated by blind rage, lashing out incoherently against the ruling class, immigrants and minorities. But the evidence that has emerged since the Brexit referendum tells a different and far more nuanced story – they knew exactly what they wanted. It is just not what the new elite want.

EUROPE, DIVERSITY, IDENTITY

Traditionalists think very differently from the new elite and other groups in society when it comes to three key areas of national life: Britain's relationship with the European Union, immigration and rising diversity, and what makes somebody British. Contrary to those who argue that people's views about these issues have simply been shaped by events in the recent past, by what took place during a referendum or election campaign or what they read online, traditionalists and cosmopolitans have actually been drifting apart from one another since the 1980s, as the revolution and its effects unfolded.

On EU membership, it was the new elite who lost touch with much of the rest of the country. While some commentators like to argue the Brexit rebellion was single-handedly orchestrated by Dominic Cummings, the reality is that it had been building for decades. As the reliable and independent National Centre for Social Research has shown, long before David Cameron even called the referendum, from as early as 2004, more than half the country either wanted to leave the EU or seriously reduce the amount of power the EU had. Then, from 2012, as the Eurozone was plunged into a sovereign debt crisis, the figure surged above 60 per cent as a large majority of voters embraced more Eurosceptic views, setting the stage for Brexit.[10]

Those who argue that Brexit was caused by a manipulative and misleading campaign also gloss over the fact that, at least since the 1990s, the British had consistently been the most Eurosceptic of all people in the European Union. For forty years, they were always among the least likely to think being in the EU was a good thing, the least trusting of EU institutions in Brussels and Strasbourg, the least likely to say they felt

'European', the most likely to send anti-EU politicians to represent them in Brussels and the most likely to say they would vote to leave the club if they were given a chance.[11] If anything, the most striking aspect of the referendum was how Remain managed to mobilize 48 per cent, not how Leave managed to mobilize 52 per cent.

But these views, as shown in Figure 4, were not spread evenly across British society; they were strongest among the very groups that had been left behind by the revolution and pushed aside by the new elite. It was the working class, non-graduates and pensioners who became the most supportive of Brexit and far more so over time. While the new elite supported the status quo or wanted an even closer relationship with the EU – including a significant number who wanted to build a 'single European state' – most traditionalists wanted to weaken this relationship if not end it completely.

By the mid-2010s, the time of the Brexit referendum, the divide between them was the largest on record; while almost half the working class wanted to leave, only 30 per cent of the professional middle

Figure 4: Support for Leaving the EU, 1993–2019

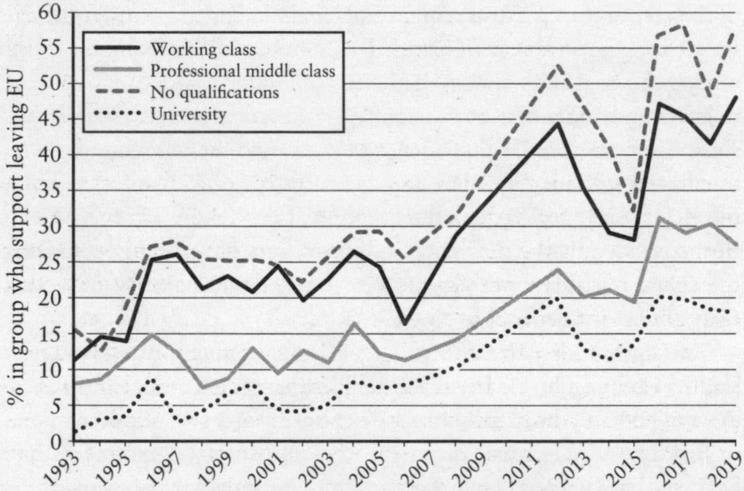

Source: British Social Attitudes survey data 1993–2019.

class wanted to follow them; while nearly 60 per cent of non-graduates favoured Brexit, only 20 per cent of graduates wanted the same.

This huge gulf between the graduate class and everybody else then became the sharpest of all at the referendum – and much sharper than the other divides over income and class. While eight in ten people who had left school at the earliest opportunity voted for Brexit, only one-quarter of people who graduated from university joined them.[12]

Brexit not only propelled the underlying rift between cosmopolitans and traditionalists to the forefront of politics but also strengthened it in several ways. So fraught was Britain's debate over Brexit that it ended up wrapping these groups in entirely new political identities; while the new elite and their allies became Remainers, traditionalists became Leavers. Nor were these new identities short-lived. Even in 2021, five years after the referendum, people felt so strongly attached to them that while only 57 per cent of the country identified as a Labour or Conservative voter, 86 per cent still identified as a Remainer or Leaver.[13]

These new identities also reflected the growing polarization of British politics around the Brexit question. Like Americans, in the years since the vote for Brexit the British have taken on all the characteristics of what scholars call 'affective polarization', a tendency among people on either side of a debate to like and trust people on their own side while disliking and distrusting their opponents.

Whereas Remainers came to see Leavers as hypocritical, selfish and closed-minded, while describing their fellow Remainers as honest, intelligent and open-minded, Leavers came to see Remainers in similar terms while feeling more attached to their fellow Leave voters.[14] But, consistently, the new elite and Remainers have been more likely to express hostility towards their opponents than vice versa, reflecting the political intolerance of the new elite.

And Brexit also strengthened this divide through another factor: political geography. As the result of the referendum revealed, the two groups not only hold different values but live in very different parts of Britain. Of the fifty areas where Remain was strongest, more than half were in London while the rest were in university towns such as Brighton, Bristol, Cambridge, Edinburgh, Manchester and Liverpool.

Yet while votes for Remain stacked high in the cities and university towns, the votes for Leave were scattered more evenly across the country, representing a majority in more than six in ten constituencies. Though it was not appreciated at the time, this would soon hand a major advantage to the growing counter-revolution against the new elite, helping Theresa May and Boris Johnson mount a more serious offensive against Labour and the left.[15]

Why did so many people vote for Brexit? While the new elite have since argued that voters were duped by shadowy figures and could not possibly have known what they were voting for, all the evidence that has emerged since the referendum tells a different story. Consistently, their two core motives were to restore Britain's national sovereignty and to regain control over immigration which, ideally, they wanted to see being not just controlled but lowered.

According to YouGov, the two key motives were 'to strike a better balance between Britain's right to act independently, and the appropriate level of co-operation with other countries' and to 'help us deal better with the issue of immigration'. Conservative pollster Lord Ashcroft found the same two motives were key: people wanted 'decisions about the UK to be taken in the UK' and 'to regain control over immigration'.[16]

The same story has been confirmed by the rigorous, reliable, and independent British Election Study. 'The clear picture portrayed by these analyses', they write, 'is that Leavers are concerned primarily about sovereignty and immigration. In fact, reading responses shows that many respondents mention both sovereignty and immigration together, showing that these two issues were closely linked in the minds of British voters.'[17] And when the University of Oxford's Centre for Social Investigation asked Leavers to rank their top priorities, they selected: (1) 'to regain control over immigration from the EU'; (2) 'I didn't want the EU to have any role in UK law-making'; (3) 'I didn't want the UK sending more money to the EU'; and, in a distant fourth, 'I wanted to teach British politicians a lesson'.[18] Brexiteers did hold clear and coherent concerns; they were just not the same concerns driving the new elite.

They were also far more united than their rivals. Such was their disillusionment with the revolution that once it became clear there was an alternative to the dreary consensus in Westminster – by pushing through Brexit and rallying around Boris Johnson – most of these voters flocked to it. Between 2015 and 2019, the share of Leavers who switched from left to right at elections rocketed by 30 points, to reach 74 per cent. Yet it was a very different story on the other side of the spectrum; while anti-Brexit parties won more than half the popular vote in 2019, fewer than half of Britain's Remainers rallied behind Labour, while the rest were divided between the Liberal Democrats, the Greens, the SNP, Plaid Cymru and the Conservative Party, with a significant one in four backing Boris Johnson's call to 'Get Brexit Done'.[19] This is how the counter-revolution outflanked the new elite. By doubling down on the rise of this new, broad and cross-class alliance of traditionalists, Boris Johnson, in 2019, was able to ruthlessly exploit these divisions among his opponents and win one of the largest majorities in his party's history.

But the counter-revolution he tapped into wasn't just about Brexit. The growing cultural divide between Britain's traditionalists and cosmopolitans has also been visible on another far more contentious issue: the decision to transform Britain into a country of mass immigration. Here, too, the new elite simply lost touch with much of the rest of the country and this has had profound consequences

It is certainly true that, in recent years, the British people's attitudes towards immigration have been changing in important ways. Overall, and again contrary to much that is written about Brexit Britain, the country has become more positive about immigrants and their actual or perceived contribution to British society. Over the last decade, between 2011 and 2022, the share of British people who think immigrants are having a positive impact on the economy has increased from 21 per cent to 50 per cent, while the share who think immigrants enrich Britain's cultural life has likewise increased, from 26 per cent to 48 per cent.[20]

But, at the same time, it is also true that throughout much of the last forty years a large majority of people have consistently wanted to reduce the overall amount of immigration into the country. Consistently, between the 1980s and the 2010s, three-quarters of people wanted their leaders to reduce immigration, while around the same share saw it as more of a problem than an opportunity. In fact, this view has been so widespread that it became what academics call a 'valence issue', an issue most people consider important and on which they hold the same view. Like wanting a strong and growing economy, or a functioning National Health Service, most people in recent years simply wanted much less immigration than the new elite.

Traditionalists, furthermore, have been especially likely to think this way. Britain's non-graduates, workers, and older voters have consistently been far more likely than their graduate, professional middle-class and younger counterparts to want to reduce immigration. Once again, the divide between educational groups has been the most striking. In recent years, while nearly three-quarters of people who have no educational qualifications wanted immigration reduced, not even one-third of the new elite felt the same way.

And this enormous gulf remained on full display in 2022, six years after the vote for Brexit and even as the country, overall, became more positive about migration. While more than two-thirds of liberal cosmopolitans who rallied around Remain, or 68 per cent, felt that immigrants who come to Britain from other countries have a positive impact on the economy, only one-quarter of the traditionalists who rallied around Brexit agreed; and while almost two-thirds of Remainers, 65 per cent, feel that immigrants enrich British culture, only one in five Brexiteers, 22 per cent, agreed with them.

Throughout the last decade, as with EU membership, the divide between these groups on the immigration issue became the largest on record, which created even more space for the counter-revolution against the new elite to break through. Wanting to lower immigration has consistently been one of the most powerful drivers of public support for all the revolts that erupted, propelling millions of people into the arms of Nigel Farage, Brexit, and then Boris Johnson. Eight in ten of the people who voted for Johnson in 2019 wanted less, not more, immigration into Britain – something both Johnson and his successor, Liz Truss, would fail to deliver, as we discuss in the final chapter.[21]

Figure 5: Perception of the Economic and Cultural Impacts of Migration, by Attitude Towards Brexit

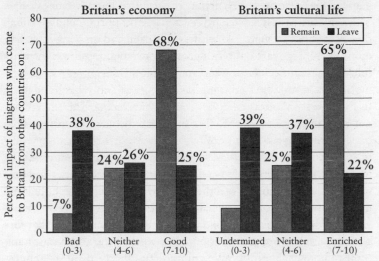

Source: 'Culture wars: keeping the Brexit divide alive?', *British Social Attitudes* survey, https://www.bsa.natchen.ac.uk/media/39478/bsa39_culture-wars.pdf.

This is not to say traditionalists want immigration reduced to zero, however. Another misleading trope is that the people who voted for these revolts are closed-minded racists who want to throw immigrants out of the country. 'If you voted Leave', noted the BBC, in a segment called 'Things not to say to someone who voted Brexit', 'you may well have been called a racist.'[22] We will explore the decline of racism in British society in Chapter 5; suffice to say for now that the story is far more complex than these crude stereotypes would have you believe.

The reality over the last decade, as Professor Simon Hix and his colleagues have shown, is that the vast majority of people wanted immigration reduced, ideally from 330,000 each year to a more sustainable and manageable 133,000. Yet while Remainers, on average, wanted immigration reduced to 59 per cent of its current level, Leavers wanted it reduced to 25 per cent. In other words, most traditionalists want slower, not zero, immigration – a point that is often missed in many of the crude portrayals about who they are and what they want.[23]

In the United States, similarly, ever since the rise of Donald Trump, researchers have found that while some of his voters were certainly motivated by a dislike of other groups, or 'racial resentment', many others, as Matthew Grossman and Daniel Thaler point out, were motivated by a desire to defend their traditional culture and identity from rapid social, cultural and demographic change. This, they point out, is distinct from charges of racism which the new elite often use to try to stigmatize conservatives.[24]

Nor are people's concerns over immigration just about numbers, money or policy. The widening gulf between traditionalists and cosmopolitans, as research since the Brexit vote shows, is anchored in a much deeper rift over how they feel about identity and diversity more generally. In Britain and beyond, the new elite not only hold far more positive views about immigration but a world view and a set of cultural values which lead them to embrace rapidly rising rates of ethnic, cultural, religious (and gender) diversity in all of its forms.

Routinely, they express far more positive feelings towards minorities, are far more supportive of using the state to protect and promote minority rights and, as we noted in Chapter 1, feel much less strongly attached to the majority group and the group-based identities which traditionalists cherish. Ever since the Brexit and Trump revolts, highly educated liberal cosmopolitans and radical progressives have also come to see the political fight *for* immigration, minority group rights, rising diversity and a more assertive anti-racism as a central aspect of their very identity, of who they are.

This sharp divide in how the country's cosmopolitans and traditionalists think about diversity and minority rights was underlined by the British Social Attitudes survey, in 2022. Whereas 69 per cent of liberal cosmopolitans think equal opportunities for women 'have not gone far enough', only 37 per cent of traditionalists agree; whereas 71 per cent of cosmopolitans feel the same way about rights for black and Asian people, only 27 per cent of traditionalists agree. Whereas more than half of cosmopolitans, 56 per cent, feel rights for transgender people have not gone far enough, not even one in five traditionalists, only 17 per cent, agree with them. And while close to half, 44 per cent, of liberal cosmopolitans think transgender people should be able to have the sex recorded on their birth certificate changed, only one-quarter, or 24 per cent, of traditionalists, agree.

Liberal cosmopolitans have also become far more sensitive than other voters to accusations of racism, are motivated by a strong internal desire to behave in non-racist ways, feel angry with themselves if they do think in racist or prejudiced ways and want to live their lives in accordance with these 'anti-racism' norms, which have also become an important part of who they think they are.[25]

Traditionalists, however, are less motivated by these things. They are not just opposed to mass immigration but feel a deeper anxiety

Figure 6: Attitudes to Equal Opportunities for Minority Groups, by Position on Liberal–Traditionalist Scale

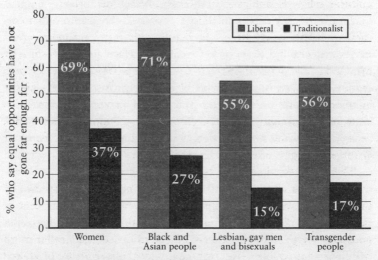

Unweighted base 1052 (Liberal), 1121 (Traditionalist).
Source: Based on data in 'Culture wars: keeping the Brexit divide alive?', *British Social Attitudes* survey, https://www.bsa.natchen.ac.uk/media/39478/bsa39_culture-wars.pdf.

about Britain's transition into a 'hyper-diverse' society and what this means for the country and their identity. While they too dissociate themselves from overt expressions of racism and prejudice, they feel far more threatened by the sheer speed and scale of this demographic change and, in turn, tend to backlash politically.

While they certainly want less immigration, they also share a cluster of other views about diversity and how it is changing Britain; they are more likely to think widespread immigration and diversity are undermining the economy and culture; they are more likely to think Britain will begin to lose its very identity if more Muslims, Europeans and other migrants arrive and settle; they are more likely to think the government should stop advocating policies which encourage minorities to remain distinct from the wider community; and they are more likely to believe that the government is taking better care of minorities than of the British majority, views which are about much more than the level of immigration or how it is or is not impacting on the country's gross domestic product (GDP).[26]

This deeper fault line over identity and diversity is partly reflected in how these groups think about an issue which will become a major touchstone of this debate in the years ahead – the rapid growth of Islam in British society. Recent forecasts by the independent and credible Pew Research Center suggest that while the share of Muslims in Britain was 6.3 per cent in 2016, by 2050 it will rise to 9.3 per cent (with no future immigration), 16.7 per cent (with medium levels of immigration) or more than 17 per cent (with high immigration, similar to current levels).[27] In the years ahead, these profound changes will be especially visible in areas such as Birmingham, Bradford, London, Greater Manchester, Leicester and their surrounding areas, and may turbocharge these concerns about the pace of change.

In the years ahead, the role and increasing presence of Islam in British society will likely become a new flashpoint between traditionalists and cosmopolitans. While a large majority of British people openly worry that the country 'will begin to lose its identity if more Muslims come to live in Britain' only a very small number of graduates, typically about one-third, feel the same way. While only 30 per cent of typically university-educated Remainers believe 'there is a fundamental clash between Islam and the values of British society', this figure rockets to 64 per cent among Leavers.[28]

Apart from Europe, immigration, and diversity, this deep-rooted divide over values can also be seen in a third area of our national life: what it means to be British. Liberal cosmopolitans and traditionalists hold very different conceptions about Britishness, about what it means to come from this place we call home.

When people talk about national identity they often distinguish between what is called a 'civic' identity, which centres on people's acceptance of political and legal institutions, and an 'ethnic' identity, focused on things such as a shared language, traditions and ancestry, that is, whether people were born in Britain. But this very crude divide is unhelpful, not least because it encourages people in the new elite to portray many of the people who surround them as aggressive, if not dangerous, ethnic nationalists who view their British identity through the lens of race and ethnicity.

But very few people view Britishness in this way. Contrary to much that has been written since the Brexit vote, Britain has now evolved into a country where most people – whether cosmopolitan or traditionalist – see their Britishness through a far more inclusive lens. While the radical progressives who dominate the institutions, and American journalists who write on Brexit Britain, are fond of portraying the country as a racist hellhole, the evidence tells a very different story. When it comes to how the British think about their Britishness, they have become noticeably more open and inclusive, much as they have, overall, when it comes to immigration.

Today, just 3 per cent of people think that to be considered 'truly British' somebody has to be white, which is down from 10 per cent in 2006. Most Conservatives (93 per cent) and most non-graduates (90 per cent) similarly reject the suggestion that to be truly British you have to be white.[29] This softening of the British people's attitudes about their national identity has also been found by the National Centre for Social Research, which points out that almost nobody in Britain today holds an 'ethnic-only' view of British identity.[30] When most people think about what is important to being British, two-thirds now stress a combination of civic and ethnic aspects, prioritizing the importance of speaking English, having British citizenship, respecting British institutions, feeling British, having lived one's life in Britain and, to a lesser extent, being born in Britain.

In recent years, in other words, the British have been steadily moving away from more 'ethnocentric' aspects of their national identity. Between the mid-1990s and the early 2020s, the share of Brits who feel that being born in Britain is important 'for being truly British' has fallen from 76 per cent to 45 per cent while, since the early 2000s, the share who feel the same way about sharing British ancestry is down from 46 per cent to 37 per cent.

Yet while the country has, overall, adopted a more inclusive definition of Britishness, of who we are, there are still some big differences beneath the surface. Unlike the new elite, traditionalists are far more likely to hold a 'thicker' conception of what it means to be British and to stress the more distinctive features of this identity. While more than two-thirds of traditionalists, 67 per cent, think being born in Britain is important for 'being truly British', only 19 per cent of cosmopolitans agree; while almost six in ten traditionalists, 59 per cent, think British ancestry is important for being truly British, only 11 per cent of cosmopolitans agree; while more than eight in ten traditionalists, 81 per cent, think that 'feeling British' is important for being truly British, less than half of cosmopolitans agree; and while almost two-thirds of traditionalists, 65 per cent, think of themselves as 'very strongly British', only one in five, or 22 per cent, of cosmopolitans feel the same way. These differences are both large and consistent.

Traditionalists are also the most likely to feel strongly attached to the British majority group, which they see as another important symbol of their identity, to voice pride in the nation and to see Britain as superior to other nations around the world. In 2021, when people were asked whether they agreed with the statement 'I would rather be a citizen of Britain than of any country on earth', 72 per cent of the traditionalists who rallied behind Brexit agreed but only 41 per cent of cosmopolitans who rallied behind remaining in the EU felt the same way.[31]

Those who lean towards a more traditionalist world view are also

Figure 7: National Sentiment, by Position on Liberal–Traditionalist Scale

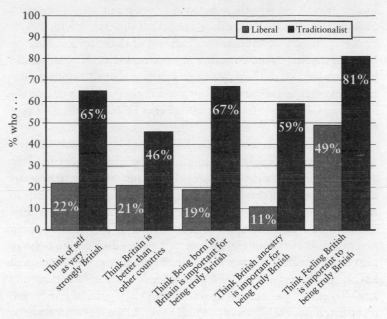

Unweighted base 1052 (Liberal), 1121 (Traditionalist).
Source: Based on data in 'Culture wars: keeping the Brexit divide alive?', *British Social Attitudes* survey, https://www.bsa.natcen.ac.uk/media/39478/bsa39_culture-wars.pdf.

more likely to feel attached to Britain's Christian heritage.[32] Christianity has, overall, become a much weaker part of Britain's national identity. Since the 1980s, the share of people who identify as Christian has slumped by nearly 30 points, to 38 per cent, while, today, more than half the country have no religion at all. These trends are especially striking when broken down by generation: while more than one in three of the oldest Britons still identify with the Church of England, and about the same share of traditionalists view this Christian faith as important to Britishness, today only 1 per cent of young zoomers from Generation Z identify with the Church of England and only very small numbers of them consider Christianity as important to who they are.[33]

The new elite, in sharp contrast, hold a very different vision of Britishness. They are the most likely to think anybody can be British so long as they adopt this identity, follow the rules and respect Britain's institutions. They are less likely to think that to be considered British somebody must have lived in Britain for most of their life, must have been born in Britain and must share British traditions. They are simply much less wedded to these thicker ties of nationhood.[34] Unlike traditionalists, they are also far more inclined to think that minorities should remain distinct from the wider community, to voice their support for government efforts to encourage minorities to remain separate and to feel less concerned about the need to protect the distinctive British values, culture and ways of life which traditionalists cherish.[35]

People who see Britishness through this much thinner, 'civic-only' lens – who put less emphasis on the importance of sharing British traditions, customs, and historic ties – remain a minority, but their number is growing: from 23 per cent of the country in the 1990s to more than 30 per cent today. These civic nationalists are made up of the country's rising number of university graduates, millennials and zoomers.[36] They want to redefine Britishness and Englishness around a celebration of more global liberal themes, such as immigration and diversity, which they prioritize. And as we will see below, many of these younger Britons also generally feel much less wedded to the thicker ties of nationhood.

But while their efforts to redefine British identity in this way might chime with other elites around the globe, they simultaneously alienate traditionalists, who worry that the distinctive aspects of their identity, culture and ways of life are being sacrificed on the altar of liberal cosmopolitanism. Increasingly, traditionalists worry that the new ruling class no longer has much of an interest in the unique and deep-rooted aspects of their national identity and is, instead, far more interested in subordinating Britishness to their liberal cosmopolitan values. As academic Francis Fukuyama points out, to say a country is welcoming of others may well be true, but it cannot be the basis of an entire national identity, because if the only thing holding a people together is that they welcome others then it is like saying they have no identity of their own.[37]

Figure 8: National Sentiment, by Age-group

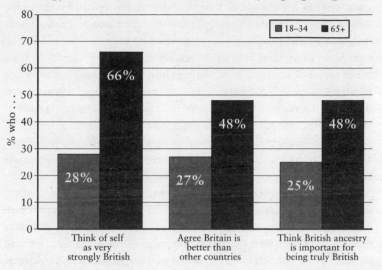

Unweighted base 698 (Liberal), 828 (Traditionalist).
Source: Based on data in 'Culture wars: keeping the Brexit divide alive?', *British Social Attitudes* survey, https://www.bsa.natchen.ac.uk/media/39478/bsa39_culture-wars.pdf.

In today's era of mass immigration, these fears about the erosion of national identity are often further stoked by how, as Professor Eric Kaufmann points out, members of the new elite devote much of their time to promoting what he calls 'asymmetrical multiculturalism'. While the new elite passionately support if not celebrate the unique identity, history and culture of minorities, they simultaneously criticize the majority for celebrating their distinctive identity or urge them, instead, to reshape their national identity around the international celebration of diversity.[38] When voters sense this contradiction, when they feel that the ruling class is no longer interested in celebrating their distinct identity, there emerges a huge opening for leaders who promise to reassert it.

For these reasons, it is no coincidence that as the new elite's much thinner vision of Britishness has become more prominent in politics and the institutions, rising numbers of voters have flocked away from them to support movements which do promise to reassert a fuller sense of who we are – which campaign to restore British traditions, customs, and ways of life. One of the strongest drivers of the Brexit vote, as Sir John Curtice points out, was a desire not just to leave the European Union but defend a distinctive national identity.[39] 'The Leave victory', concluded another major study of the vote, 'was not about objective demographics alone. Matters of identity were equally, if not more strongly, associated with the Leave vote – particularly feelings of national identity and sense of change over time.'[40]

This growing rift between cosmopolitans and traditionalists, then, has been on the rise for decades and is rooted in fundamental differences in how these groups think about Britain's relationship with the EU, mass immigration, diversity, and their British identity. And all these attitudes map neatly onto the Remain versus Leave divide which erupted at the Brexit referendum in 2016. Whereas Britain's Remainers are much more likely than the country's Leavers to think positively about rejoining the EU, and the effects of immigration and diversity, and to hold a thinner vision of Britishness, Leavers are much more adamant that they want to stay out of the EU, are far more sceptical about the effects of immigration and diversity, and are more likely to adopt a 'thicker' conception of who we are.

Far from being resolved by the country officially leaving the EU, therefore, the cultural chasm between these groups, which is rooted foremost in their very different values, looks set to persist for the foreseeable future and will likely continue to have political effects.

WHY LABOUR LOST

This underlying rift over values also helps to explain how and why the Labour Party ran into difficulty in recent years. Over the last two decades, these cross-cutting disputes over Europe, immigration and identity increasingly drove a wedge between working-class and non-graduate Labour traditionalists on the one hand, who often lean left on the economy and right on culture, and middle-class, professional, degree-holding Labour cosmopolitans on the other, who often combine their centrist views on the economy with their very strongly cosmopolitan views on culture and identity.

Academics often refer to these working-class traditionalists as 'cross-pressured'.[41] Their pro-redistribution and anti-immigration values simply do not fit neatly on Britain's traditional 'left versus right' grid. In the old politics, when debates were about the economy, public services, and the welfare state, this tension was less visible and less consequential; but in the new politics where debates about identity, culture and belonging have surged forward and cut across the old divides this tension has become far more visible and politically consequential especially for the Labour Party.

When it comes to economics, many of the Labour traditionalists who abandoned the party for Nigel Farage, Brexit and then Boris Johnson are often far more supportive of economically interventionist and big-government policies than the Conservative MPs and 'liberal Leavers' they have been voting for. Few of these cross-pressured former Labour voters in the Red Wall dream of building a low-regulation, low-tax, small-state, high-migration and neoliberal Davos-on-Thames, of the sort that was promoted by Liz Truss and her government in 2022. Indeed the complete failure of the Truss project reflects how marginal this vision of Brexit was in the wider country.

But when it comes to culture and identity, these voters are often much closer to the Conservatives and populists than Labour. While they think Britain's economy is rigged to favour the elite, they want immigration reduced. While they think there is one law for the rich and another for the poor, they support Brexit. And while they are sceptical of big business, which they think exploits workers, they want tougher sentences for criminals and a tougher approach on law and order.

What led them to prioritize their cultural concerns over economics were not just the changes sweeping through British society but New Labour's embrace of the revolution and the rise of a far more liberal cosmopolitan if not radically progressive activist class inside the party. For many voters, these changes made it abundantly clear that Labour was now in the hands of a new ruling class who celebrate all the things they find deeply alarming, who appear uninterested in their values and even want to impose 'politically correct' speech codes to silence any dissent.

Increasingly, this drove a wedge through Labour's electorate, pushing these voters apart and creating even more space for the counter-revolution to break through. By the late 2010s, while only 20 per cent of Labour's middle-class, university-educated cosmopolitans thought Britain had accepted too many immigrants, 90 per cent of Labour's traditionalists felt this way; while only one in five Labour cosmopolitans felt that being born in Britain is important to being British, more than half of Labour traditionalists felt this way; while only 16 per cent of Labour cosmopolitans think 'the will of the majority should always prevail, even over the right of minorities', more than half of Labour traditionalists hold this view; and while 51 per cent of Labour cosmopolitans think minorities should adapt to British traditions, 85 per cent of Labour traditionalists hold this view.[42]

These different camps within the Labour tent also held completely opposing views on Brexit; while 86 per cent of Labour cosmopolitans wanted to remain in the EU, 70 per cent of Labour traditionalists wanted to leave. The latter felt especially disillusioned with Labour's decision, in 2019, to switch to campaigning for a second referendum at which prominent Labour politicians, including Keir Starmer and Emily Thornberry, made it clear they would vote to remain, thereby, in the eyes of many voters, overturning the 2016 vote for Brexit.[43] Looking at the people who left Labour to vote for Boris Johnson in 2019, almost three-quarters voted for Brexit while about the same share of the Labour voters who instead switched to the Liberal Democrats or the Greens voted Remain. Amid the Brexit fallout, the underlying cultural rift between Britain's cosmopolitans and traditionalists now cut directly across Labour's base, weakening the party and further helping populists and conservatives to break through.[44]

Unsurprisingly, given the direction of British politics and society over the last fifty years, the groups that left Labour have also felt very differently about the extent to which they are recognized and respected in politics. Labour traditionalists, who, as we will see in the next chapter, have been pushed out of the party, are also far more likely to think that politicians do not care what people like them think, they have no say in what government does and that politicians only look out for their own interests rather than the people who elect them.[45]

This sense of powerlessness, of no longer having a voice in politics, further encouraged them to abandon Labour and search for a more radical alternative.

Their strong sense of disillusionment with the Labour Party has also been exacerbated by the growing visibility of a more specific group within the Labour electorate, who we met in Chapter 1: highly educated, financially secure, urban and very radical progressives.

Progressives not only hold the cosmopolitan outlook of the new elite but promote, often aggressively, a far more radical set of ideas that are simply not shared by the rest of the country. Britain's progressives, who wield disproportionate influence in the Labour Party, the media and other institutions, and are the most visible on social media, hold values that are very different from those of the average voter, including the people who have been steadily abandoning the Labour Party in recent years.

Compared to others in society, radical progressives are, by far, the most likely to reject the suggestion that British society is changing too fast and to express their very strong support for immigration and rising diversity, which, like the new elite, they often see as central to their identity: while only 43 per cent of all British voters think immigration changed Britain for the better, 85 per cent of progressives do.[46] They are also far more likely to want to prioritize the interests of minorities over the majority and to think the expansion of rights for women, ethnic minorities and trans people has 'not gone far enough'; while only 7 per cent of traditionalists think rights for trans people have not gone far enough, 71 per cent of progressives hold this view. The gap between progressives and the rest of the country on many of these issues is simply enormous.[47]

They are also far more likely than others to feel ashamed of Britain and its past and are the least likely of all to feel nostalgic about how Britain used to be. More often than not, progressives see their British identity as a source of embarrassment; while eight in ten traditionalists and a majority of all voters feel proud of Britain, only one-quarter of progressives do; while more than six in ten traditionalists would like Britain 'the way it used to be', less than one in twenty progressives agree; and while nearly nine in ten traditionalists think that 'too many people in the UK run our country down', only one in ten progressives agree.[48]

In short, progressives are radical because their values and view of the world are often completely detached from those of the average voter.

They are also, consistently, the most likely to believe that Britain is a racist country, and that racism is a major problem in the country. Despite evidence that Britain is becoming a much less racist and more open society, as we have already seen and will explore further in Chapter 5, radical progressives believe the very opposite. When people are asked to what extent they feel racism is present in British society, only one-third of all voters feel there is a 'great deal' of racism, which falls to one in five Leavers and Conservatives. But nearly half of Labour and Remain voters, among whom progressives congregate, think this way, underlining how they are often hardwired to see Britain as a racist society.[49]

Britain's radical progressives are also far more concerned than other voters with what they consider to be an urgent need to address historic injustices.[50] Consider the following two statements: 'We cannot move forward as a nation if we do not acknowledge the mistakes during the period of the British Empire,' or, alternatively, 'There is no point in going over the rights and wrongs of our history. We need to move forward and focus on our future.' Whereas 84 per cent of progressives think Britain cannot move on unless it deals with past mistakes, only 41 per cent of all voters in the country share this view; and while 60 per cent of all voters say there is little point endlessly going over the rights or wrongs of what happened years ago, only 16 per cent of progressives agree.[51]

They also have very distinctive and radical views on sex and gender, they are far more likely than much of the rest of the country to want to promote more fluid gender identities. While only 31 per cent of all people feel it is appropriate for children to be taught about trans issues in primary school, the figure is almost double, at 61 per cent, among progressives. While only 33 per cent of all people think it is appropriate for primary schools to tell children that some people are gay, it is more than double, at 68 per cent, among progressives. And while only 46 per cent of all British people think 'a transgender woman is a woman', this surges to 71 per cent among progressives, who are often adrift from other voters.[52] On all these debates about sex and gender, traditionalists are far more likely to think that somebody's identity is fixed, that gender reassignment is unnatural and to reject the suggestion that trans women should join women-only sporting events. [53]

Crucially, progressives are also the most likely of all groups to favour restrictions on people's speech as a means of promoting their values and, in their eyes, protecting minorities. They often stress the need to limit speech or revise symbols and national history to avoid causing harm to minorities. But this puts them in direct conflict with traditionalists, who instead stress the importance of freedom of speech and feel more attached to these symbols of nationhood – whether statues, historical figures or traditional interpretations of British history. While traditionalists are absolutely convinced that political correctness has 'gone too far', progressives are the only group who do not think this.[54] They are far more comfortable than others with restricting freedom of speech in the pursuit of their goals – they are the most likely to support the 'no-platforming' of speakers who hold controversial views, the most likely to think Britain 'needs to change the way people talk' about people from different backgrounds and the only group who prioritize restricting speech they consider offensive in universities, over exposing students to views they find offensive.[55]

The problem with this deeply moralistic and dogmatic approach to politics is that it can often trigger a sharp backlash from traditionalists, who feel their speech, and in turn their values, are being pushed out of the public square or, even worse, are stigmatized as socially unacceptable (see Chapter 5). In their study of what they call the 'ironic effects of anti-prejudice', academic Lisa Legault and her colleagues find that pressuring people to comply with speech codes and 'anti-racism' programmes produces a sharp negative reaction that is worse than doing nothing at all. 'This research reveals', they write, 'that these types of messages not only do not work, but also can produce the opposite of their intended effects.'[56]

More generally there is now a growing mass of research which suggests that requiring people to take mandatory 'anti-racism' training in schools, universities and the workplace – much of which is based on so-called 'implicit racism' measures which have been shown to be flawed – can backfire, either by having no impact at all or, worse, encouraging people to become more prejudiced.[57] According to one major review of diversity and anti-racism training, published in the well-regarded journal the *Annual Review of Psychology* in 2022, despite governments spending millions if not billions each year on these programmes, it found many had no impact or stoked a negative reaction.

'This state of affairs is concerning,' summarized the study's co-authors, Patricia Devine and Tory Ash, 'particularly in light of the enthusiasm for, and monetary investment in, DT [Diversity Training]. Implementation of DT has clearly outpaced the available evidence that such programs are effective in achieving their goals.'[58]

Similarly, research on support for Donald Trump found that when people perceived that their speech was restricted by politically correct elites, they became significantly more supportive of him. After priming moderate Americans to think about 'politically correct' attempts to restrict what people can say, social psychologist Lucian Conway and his colleagues found higher support for Trump – even after taking their ideology into account. 'They suggest', said the researchers, summarizing their findings, 'that instead of producing the niceness that they are intended to produce, these norms instead might lead to more nasty political discourse in the long-term.'[59]

More recent research, in 2021, examined what happens when people are taught about the concept of white privilege, which is also promoted by radical progressives. When psychologist Erin Cooley and her team explored the impact of this idea, which is now taught in schools and universities, they found that highly educated white liberals became *less* sympathetic towards economically marginalized whites. 'White privilege lessons', they note, 'may increase beliefs that poor White people have failed to take advantage of their racial privilege – leading to negative social evaluations.'[60]

Radical progressives often believe they are making the world a better place, and many are driven by good and noble intentions. But, at the same time, when it comes to many issues that really matter to voters, they often hold values that put them in a world of their own, promoting ideas which exacerbate the underlying rift over values, which risk causing a much greater political backlash among the much larger number of traditionalists, or actively encouraging these voters to abandon the Labour Party and the left to join the counter-revolution.

As Britain passed through the eras of Margaret Thatcher, John Major, Tony Blair and Gordon Brown, therefore, the country was increasingly in the hands of a university-educated minority who had not only reaped the benefits of the revolution but held very distinctive values. They were far more likely to think that the revolution had changed Britain for the better – that immigration, hyper-globalization, diversity and EU membership have all been positive for the country. And they were increasingly subscribing to a much thinner vision of Britishness, feeling less attached to the majority group and less concerned about the perceived need to protect Britain's distinctive identity, culture and history. Traditionalists, meanwhile, had become far more sceptical about the effects of these profound social and cultural changes, felt more strongly attached to the majority group and the nation-state and saw these things, alongside a thicker sense of Britishness, as central aspects of who they are.

By the 2010s, the picture was clear. On one side stood the new elite and their cosmopolitan allies who embraced a diverse, global and fast-changing Britain, who were less bothered about group attachments and who increasingly saw their British identity through the prism of multiculturalism and diversity; on the other, stood an emerging alliance of traditionalists who had not only lost out from the revolution but felt they were now being pushed aside culturally by the new values that were dominating the mainstream. While one side has come to see themselves as the vanguard of the revolution, viewing Britain's former EU membership, immigration, rights for racial, sexual and gender minorities and a more assertive anti-racism as symbols of their values, the other has come to see themselves as the true defenders of Britain's distinctive identity, traditions, culture and ways of life, which, today, they worry are at risk of being lost for ever.

4
Voice

The new elite have not only imposed their values on the rest of society, they have also taken control of Britain's most important and influential institutions, wielding a disproportionately large amount of power over politics, the national debate and the prevailing culture. Instead of representing the wider country, many of these institutions have instead been reshaped around the interests, the tastes, the lifestyles and the political priorities of the new elite, while millions of others have found their voice excluded.

One person who has vented his frustration with the growing power of the new elite is a man called Keith Craig, who, in the aftermath of Brexit, sent a letter to the *Financial Times*.[1] 'Your pages overflow with predictions of disaster brought on by the Brexit/Trump axis,' he wrote, taking aim at the new elite. 'Leaving aside the depressing and repetitive pointlessness of this mass guesswork, its underlying assumption – that things were better when People Like Us [PLU] were in charge – is at best dubious, at worst delusional.'

Under the new elite, he continued,

> we have two failed wars [in Iraq and Afghanistan] and the Middle East in flames, China expansionist, Europe enfeebled, America ineffective and Russia resurgent. At home, we have banking crises, stagnant median incomes, uncontrolled borders, record indebtedness, profiteering by the 'professional' classes and general social polarisation. This is the Eden from which the rude and licentious electorates have expelled us? Face it. We FT readers had our decades in charge, and we blew it for everyone but us.

The letter went viral. It resonated powerfully with many people in Britain today who have long felt frustrated with how the new graduate elite now dominate almost all the political, media, creative, cultural and educational institutions. Despite routinely preaching about the wonders of 'openness', 'diversity' and 'democracy', in reality the new elite have ensured that many of these institutions are not particularly open, diverse or democratic at all. Even after the revolts of the last decade, they overwhelmingly represent the values and the voice of the new elite, leaving much of the rest of the country with a palpable sense their voice is no longer heard at all and certainly isn't respected.

This has been especially visible in the world of politics, though it is by no means confined to Westminster. The idea behind representative democracy is that all groups should be treated fairly and given an equal voice. They should have descriptive representation, with their group given a seat at the table, and substantive representation, with their values represented in the policy-making process. Both are critically important because they send a signal to the wider community about who is, and who is not, respected. But, in recent years, many people have come to realize they have neither of these things.

DEMOCRATIC PLURALISM

No democracy, including Britain's, has ever lived up to the ideal of representative democracy. Some groups, notably women and minorities, were historically excluded while many institutions have always been dominated by a narrow elite. But it is also true that there was a time in our history, not so long ago, when the political system did make room for a wider range of voices than the very homogeneous and self-serving ones which dominate today. There was a time when people who neither came from the new elite nor shared its values were much better integrated into our national and political life.

Between the Second World War and the 1970s, Britain and other democracies in the West were characterized by what American writer Michael Lind calls the era of 'democratic pluralism' – a time when workers, non-graduates and others who did not belong to the elite were recognized and represented in the corridors of power. 'Democratic pluralism in North America and Europe,' he writes, 'an alternative to the extremes of free market liberalism, socialism, and state corporatism, compelled the representatives of national overclasses to share power and bargain with lesser elites who acted as power brokers for working-class communities in the three realms of the economy, government, and culture.'[2]

This bargaining power came from the much stronger trade unions at the time. In Britain, between the 1890s and the 1950s, the number of people who belonged to one of the 200 unions that were affiliated with the Trades Union Congress surged from 1.5 million to more than 9 million, representing more than 40 per cent of Britain's workforce.[3] But it also came from politics, where the major parties were genuinely 'mass parties', with large memberships and much stronger roots in civil society than they have today.

In the 1950s, Labour and the Conservatives had nearly 4 million members, compared to only 700,000 today.[4] The much stronger relationship between the parties and the people was also reinforced by how Labour, in particular, was rooted in a tradition of community-based trade unionism, mutual and cooperative societies, working men's clubs and sporting societies.[5] There was also a sprawling network of some 4,000 working men's clubs across Britain which, until the 1970s, had 4 million members. On the right, meanwhile, the Young Conservatives, known as the 'best marriage bureau in the country', played a similar role, bringing together 160,000 members across 2,500 branches.[6] All this helped reinforce the bond between Westminster and the wider country.

Britain's representative democracy was certainly not perfect, but it was wider and deeper than it is today. This was reflected in a degree of political loyalty that is remarkable by today's standards. In the 1950s, nine in every ten voters felt attached to the big parties while nearly half of them felt strongly attached.[7] When people went to the ballot box, as they did when Sir Winston Churchill defeated his old rival, Clement Attlee, in 1951, an astonishing 97 per cent of them voted for either the Labour Party or the Conservative Party. The two parties were utterly dominant and inspired considerable support in the country.

Many people were still cynical about politics. Even in the shadow of the British people's 'finest hour', their triumph over Nazi Germany, the share who felt that their leaders in Westminster were 'out merely for themselves' or 'for their party', at nearly 60 per cent, was much higher than the share who felt that their leaders were out 'to do their best for Britain', at 36 per cent. Yet, even still, these figures were much healthier than they have been in recent years when almost 80 per cent think that their leaders are only looking after themselves or their party and just 10 per cent think they are working for the interests of Britain.[8]

Because of the strength of the trade unions, political parties and associations that connected people to politics, the era of democratic pluralism was also a time when most people did feel their voice was heard in the corridors of power. This was not just about blind loyalty, deference or how the parties were organized; it also had much to do with how Britain's politicians at the time often shared the backgrounds, experiences and values of the people they had been elected to represent.

On the left of politics, throughout the twentieth century, the Labour Party was not just for workers but was filled with workers. While there was a highly educated elite – Clement Attlee and Harold Wilson both went to Oxford – this was a time when, overall, the graduate class comprised only 5–10 per cent of Britain. And these voices were also balanced out. In his study of Britain's political class, published in 1963, historian Wilhelm Guttsman points out that almost half of Labour's MPs at this time looked like the people who elected them. They were 'rank and file workers' who had not gone to university.[9] Graduates outnumbered non-graduates on the right but non-graduates outnumbered graduates on the left, which brought a diverse range of voices into politics.

Leading Labour lights included people such as Manny Shinwell, who educated himself in a public library before working as an apprentice tailor, Ernest Bevin who had worked as a labourer and lorry driver, Herbert Morrison who had left school to become an errand boy, Nye Bevan, a self-taught trade unionist from a mining family, and many others – Tom Williams, Jack Lawson, George Hall and Joseph Westwood – who had all started their careers down the mines. Labour still had its share of upper-class socialists, such as Clement Attlee, who had gone to a private school before Oxford. But this was a time when these elite voices were balanced out by people who came from far more humble origins.

Their presence ensured not only that the masses had a voice but that their interests were reflected in the policies coming out of Westminster. It is no coincidence that in Britain and other Western democracies the era of democratic pluralism coincided with the rise of the welfare state and the National Health Service (NHS), the New Deal in America and similar social settlements across Europe, all of which represented a serious reply to the needs of the wider majority and supported the post-war boom that would follow.

This voice was also, to some extent, reflected in national culture. It was a time when, as Michael Lind notes, the influence of the Church and Christian faith remained strong, there was a far more culturally conservative political elite on both the left and right, and civil society groups scrutinized the educational establishment and cultural industries to ensure they did not offend traditionalist values. In the media, too, many journalists, like politicians, often came from outside the elite graduate class, working their way up through local and regional media and often remaining strongly rooted in the communities they came from. While there certainly was an interconnected network of upper-class elites – which Henry Fairlie first defined in 1955 as 'the Establishment' – most of the people who belonged to it had also served in one or both of the world wars and so felt a strong sense of loyalty and obligation to people who came from different backgrounds, regions and classes. While the old elite was certainly privileged and wealthy, when it came to questions about culture, identity and belonging they often shared the instinctive conservatism of most of the voters who surrounded them.

Things were certainly not perfect. Nothing in the post-war years was. Women were almost completely absent from the House of Commons, while the old elite dominated the institutions. There were also worrying signs of what was to come. In 1956, Labour's Clement Attlee pointed to the rise of a new breed of 'professional politician' who appeared more interested in living *off* politics than living *for* public service. 'Nowadays', he complained, 'there are quite a lot of chaps who are in the House because the idea of sitting in Westminster and helping to govern the country appeals to them.'[10] But, on the whole, this was a time when politics looked more like a broad church than the fringe cult it has become today – when people could look at Westminster and see people who looked and sounded like them.

TECHNOCRATIC LIBERALISM

Today, that era no longer exists. Over the last thirty years, as the revolution has gathered pace, the new graduate elite have not only imposed their liberal cosmopolitan and progressive values on the rest of the country; but they have completely taken over the institutions.

One symbol of this revolution, what academic Christopher Lasch once called the 'Revolt of the Elites', arrived a few years ago, when the people of Ingleton, a small village in northern England, held their summer fair. Everything about the day was quintessentially British. Homemade cakes and bacon butties were on sale in the village hall, people were drinking tea in the cricket pavilion, and children were enjoying the egg-and-spoon race, coconut shy, bouncy castle and a tug-of-war. Even the local MP, Labour's Helen Goodman, had come along to open the fair and give a speech to her constituents.

Goodman talked powerfully and eloquently about Ingleton – the beautiful waterfalls, the deep caves and the majestic peaks which offered hikers a glimpse of heaven. The only problem was that her voters had no idea what she was talking about. There were no waterfalls, caves or peaks in Ingleton. The one person who was supposed to represent their voice in Westminster – who also happened to have graduated from the University of Oxford with a degree in Philosophy, Politics and Economics (PPE) – had confused their village with another village that was seventy miles away and represented by a different MP.

What happened on that day is a curious instance of how, in Britain and across the West, the era of democratic pluralism has now been fully replaced by what Michael Lind calls the new era of 'technocratic liberalism' – a grim new reality for many people in which the new elite have taken full control of the political institutions, the think tanks, the civil service, the public bodies, the universities, the creative industries, the cultural institutions and much of the media, while many of the organizations which used to provide other groups with a voice and serious bargaining power, including the trade unions and political parties, have increasingly been hollowed out.[11] While the voice of the new elite has been put on steroids, blaring out to the rest of the country through a megaphone, the voice of the wider majority has been marginalized if not completely removed.

In turn, the entire national conversation has been reshaped around the values of the new elite, a synthesis of the New Right's free-market economic liberalism and the New Left's radical cultural liberalism. Increasingly, those who criticize or merely question this new consensus find themselves marginalized or stigmatized as morally inferior or illegitimate members of the community. In turn, at least until the revolts of the last decade, politics simply became far more apolitical, anti-majoritarian, elitist and removed from the lives and aspirations of the rest of the country. And, as we will see, this has had profound political effects.

The rise of this technocratic liberalism has been visible on both the left and right, but it has been most clearly displayed in the remarkable transformation of the Labour Party. Over the last two decades, Labour, like other left-wing parties, has morphed into a political home for what French economist Thomas Piketty has called 'the brahmins' – a highly educated caste of politicians and voters who have little interest in reforming the economy and the wider system to help the left behind.[12] Instead, as the trade unions have been weakened and intermediary organizations have collapsed, a new generation of Labour politicians has pushed aside the very groups their party was once founded to represent.

The story of how this happened is not complicated. When Neil Kinnock led Labour into battle against Margaret Thatcher in the 1980s, there had been sixty-four Labour MPs who had previously held working-class jobs. When Tony Blair won his second landslide, in 2001, the number had fallen to forty-nine. When Ed Miliband was defeated by David Cameron in 2015, it was down to twenty. When Jeremy Corbyn took over, promising to restore the voice of the working class, there were twelve. And when Keir Starmer replaced him, promising to repair the Labour Party's relationship with the Red Wall, there were only seven.[13]

Like one of those strange creatures on David Attenborough's *Planet Earth*, the working-class or non-graduate politician has become an endangered species. On both the left and right, ever since Margaret Thatcher came to power the percentage of politicians who have previously worked in a blue-collar job has crashed from 16 per cent to just 1 per cent. At the same time, Westminster has been taken over by the new elite. The share of MPs from the university-educated minority has soared to nearly 90 per cent. And nearly one in four of those university-educated MPs graduated from Oxbridge while one in three hold not just undergraduate but postgraduate degrees. In turn, the political class has steadily drifted away from much of the rest of the country.[14]

Whereas in the old days, Labour pulled a wide range of voices into politics, today, remarkably, its MPs are more likely than Conservative ones to have a degree and are twenty times more likely than the average voter to have graduated from Oxbridge. Labour's new status as a party for the brahmins was powerfully underlined at the last election, in 2019, when its candidates were the most likely of all to have postgraduate degrees and were just as likely as Tory candidates to have gone to Oxbridge.[15] By doubling down on the new elite, a political party which was founded to tackle economic inequality is now stoking political inequality, leaving millions of people without a voice in Westminster.

The new elite make much of the fact that politics is becoming more diverse, with record numbers of women and people from ethnic and sexual minorities elected at the last two general elections, in 2017 and 2019. But, when it comes to class, education and values, politics has become less diverse, organized ever more tightly around the values, interests and priorities of the new elite.[16] Only one in four British adults belong to the graduate class. But, today, that class, along with its very distinctive values, reigns supreme. The education and cultural divides that are pushing cosmopolitans and traditionalists apart are simply nowhere close to being represented in our politics.

These changes played a direct role in Labour's electoral collapse. As Labour was reshaped around the new elite, references to left-behind workers were purged from Labour speeches, manifestos and its electoral strategy. 'Political appeals to the working class', conclude professors Geoff Evans and James Tilley, in their insightful study of how Labour's electorate unravelled over the last ten years, 'have now effectively disappeared from the lexicon of party politics.'[17]

The political exclusion of these groups was also clearly visible on the campaign trail long before Nigel Farage, the Brexiteers, Theresa May and then Boris Johnson powered through the Labour heartlands. 'Here's my confession,' wrote pollster Deborah Mattinson, who advised Labour through the years of Blair and Brown, and now advises Sir Keir Starmer,

> other than the occasional by-election, at no point in the decades that I spent advising Labour did we ever consider running focus groups or polling in any of the Red Wall seats. Their reliability was seen as a given – quite frankly, they were taken for granted. These voters were neglected by the entire political class. Labour felt that they didn't need to worry about their 'heartland constituencies', populated by voters who would never let them down, who would always be on side. The Conservatives ignored them for a different reason: they were deemed totally unwinnable, so there was really no point.[18]

At the time, Labour strategists clearly thought they could win over the new middle-class graduate elite while Britain's workers and non-graduates, hidden behind massive majorities in the Labour heartlands, had nowhere else to go. But this was a miscalculation which underestimated the size of the latter and exaggerated the size of the former, further setting the stage for the rise of populism, Brexit and Boris Johnson which all appeal strongly to workers.

It is certainly true, as we saw in Chapter 1, that Britain's working class has, *objectively*, declined in size relative to other groups in society. But it remains a big and important part of the country, with working class jobs still making up around one-third of the entire workforce. Furthermore, *subjectively* most people in Britain today still identify as working class. Ever since the 1980s, consistently, about 60 per cent of people feel working class. And those who feel this way are also more likely than others to hold more working-class, traditionalist values: feeling sceptical of immigration, favouring a tough approach on crime, wanting their leaders to prioritize morality, order and stability, and wanting to slow the overall pace of demographic and social change in the country.[19]

Crucially, many people in the professional middle class also feel this way. In their study of people in the new elite who continue to identify as working class, academic Sam Friedman and his colleagues suggest that much of this is 'performative', intended to downplay and deflect from their privileged positions in society. Instead of acknowledging their economic, political and cultural power, the new elite reach back into their family histories to find stories of working-class struggle among their grandparents and great-grandparents which they use to misrepresent their lives and themselves as being more worthy and deserving than they are.[20]

Whether real or fake, the point remains that when much of the country looks out at Westminster today they see very few politicians who share their values and voice. And this has undermined Labour in particular. Throughout the 2000s and 2010s, while the party's more managerial, professional, economically centrist and culturally liberal image appealed to the new elite, entrenching the party's strength in the big cities and university towns, it has simultaneously alienated millions of Labour traditionalists whose left-wing views on the economy and right-wing views on culture were no longer visible in politics.

As Labour doubled down on the new elite, on people who look and sound like them, their relationship with the working class and people without degrees steadily deteriorated, giving these voters another reason to switch to populists.[21]

Consistently, between 1986 and 2019, Britain's workers and people without degrees have been significantly more likely than their middle-class and graduate counterparts to feel that 'people like me have no say in government'. As shown in Figure 9, throughout much of the last forty years, the very groups who increasingly found themselves excluded from the world of Westminster have been the most likely to feel they no longer have a voice. And ever since the Brexit referendum in 2016, the divide between the graduate minority and the non-graduate majority has become enormous.

This large reservoir of disillusionment has also been reflected in the

Figure 9: 'People Like Me Have No Say in Government'

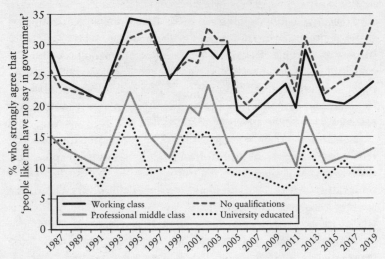

Source: British Social Attitudes 1986–2019.

extent to which these different groups of voters have been willing to even participate in elections. In the early postwar era, the difference in the rate of turnout between the country's working-class voters and professional middle-class voters was only 5 points; they both took part, believing they could make a difference. But by the time Blair and Brown left office, the gap between them had grown to 20 points. One group have felt their voice was recognized and respected while the other had come to feel the exact opposite.[22] This is not an irrational response; they have been excluded.

This damaged Labour's brand in other ways. As the party fell increasingly dependent on the new elite – prioritizing hyper-globalization, European integration, mass immigration and the hollowing-out of democracy – the share of people who thought Labour was still looking out for the working class collapsed. Between Neil Kinnock, in the 1980s, and the departure of Gordon Brown, in 2010, the share of all voters who thought Labour represented workers slumped by 25 points, to 64 per cent, while the share who felt that Labour prioritized big business surged from one-third to more than half, 54 per cent.[23]

At the same time, almost half the country felt 'Labour used to care about the concerns of people like me, but doesn't nowadays', compared to only 8 per cent who felt the same way about the Conservatives. And when voters were asked which two or three groups Labour want to help, the most popular answer was 'immigrants and non-white Britons', while the least popular were pensioners and white Britons.[24] Labour was now seen, especially by those who had been pushed aside, as a party for the new elite, immigrants, minorities and big business.

And this remained the case after Labour's heavy defeat to the Conservatives in 2019. Many of the older traditionalists who had abandoned Labour for the Conservatives wanted to prioritize workers, pensioners and the poor. But when they looked at Labour they often saw a party which, in their eyes, was out to prioritize immigrants, non-white Britons, sexual minorities and the rich.

'Many of those voters who switched to the Conservatives', noted one study, 'believe that Labour fails to share their concern for ordinary working people and pensioners . . . Instead, these voters think the party cares far more than they do for immigrants and non-white Britons as well as the LGBTQ+ community.'[25]

Focus groups with people who left Labour have also thrown light on how, in their eyes, the party's image changed for the worse. When they were asked what kind of person the Labour Party would be if it suddenly came to life, during the Ed Miliband era between 2010 and 2015 they described a man who was at a party, sitting awkwardly in the corner, shuffling CDs rather than talking to other guests. He wore an expensive suit, ate sausage en croute, was drinking craft ale from a micro-brewery and would rather be at a trendy pub in a trendy city. The conclusion was stark. The problem for Labour was not that it was no longer seen as authentically working class; the problem was that it was no longer seen as authentic at all.[26]

Then, during the Jeremy Corbyn era, things were not much better. Now, Labour was posh, living in a grand house in London and looking like the 'young, quinoa-eating, graduate, city-dwelling, socially liberal Remainers and Labour voters who . . . do not put Britain first and judge people like them harshly and unfairly for their views'. When voters were asked to describe the party in just a few words they said: old-fashioned, chaotic, disarray, lazy, the past, losers, broken, a mess, lost, antiquated, weak, liars, spenders. One described Labour as 'lawless, like an out-of-control car careering downhill knocking things over'. Another: 'They thought we'd always vote Labour – we'd always be their little puppets. They just took it for granted that everyone up north would vote Labour. Well, they were wrong.'[27]

Another warning sign that something was going terribly wrong for Labour had been the short-lived rise of the far-right British National Party, between 2001 and 2010. The BNP's leaflets told voters: 'We are the Labour Party your grandfather voted for.' Then, a much larger number of voters began to switch to Nigel Farage's national populist UK Independence Party, which, by the mid-2010s, had mobilized the most working-class electorate in the country. While the new elite blamed Farage's rise on social media, dark money and his confrontational billboards, which targeted mounting concerns over mass immigration, in reality his rise to power had been cleared by the new elite and their exclusion of people's voice in politics. It was, ultimately, the establishment that created anti-establishment populism.

None of this is unique to Britain. It is a similar story across the West, where workers and non-graduates are consistently the most likely to endorse statements such as 'the government does not care what people like me think', 'I have no influence in what my government does' and 'politicians are only in politics for personal profit'. Whereas the new elite are the most likely to express confidence and trust in politics, to feel included and respected, and to participate, workers and non-graduates are far more likely to feel powerless, to mistrust institutions, to feel less confident and more cynical about politics, to feel politicians are uninterested in what people like them have to say, and to think they are not being listened to.[28] The blunt reality, as we have seen, is that they have good reason to feel this way.

This is not just a story about the left, however. The exclusion of these voters has also been reinforced by the right, which remains, as it has always been, deeply unrepresentative of British society. Today, fewer than one in ten people in the country, 7 per cent, go to private schools, and only 1 per cent graduate from Oxbridge. Yet the Conservative Party has routinely drawn the bulk of its MPs from among these two groups. Between the eras of Margaret Thatcher and David Cameron, the share of Conservative MPs who went to fee-paying schools never fell below 50 per cent, while the share of Oxbridge graduates remained at least 40 per cent – if not much higher.[29]

In 2017 and 2019, Theresa May and Boris Johnson did begin tap into these feelings of disillusionment by, symbolically, promising to give more of a voice to 'ordinary workers' by 'levelling up' the country, delivering Brexit and reforming immigration. Theresa May's promise to prioritize ordinary working families, and Boris Johnson's pledge to level-up left-behind communities help to explain why they were able to make so much progress in the Labour heartlands, capturing some of the most working-class seats in Britain. While people's cultural values did much of the heavy lifting, their feelings of voicelessness and strong distrust of the established political class played an important supporting role.

Remarkably, this briefly left Boris Johnson – an Old Etonian who had studied Classics, ancient literature and philosophy at the University of Oxford – as the leader of Britain's non-graduate majority, and Jeremy Corbyn – who briefly attended a polytechnic before dropping out – as the leader of the university-educated minority.

But neither the Conservative Party nor the governments it has subsequently produced have ever truly connected – economically, socially, culturally – with the voters who found their values and voice purged from politics and the institutions. Theresa May's Cabinet certainly included more state-educated ministers than any previous Conservative government and had the lowest proportion of privately educated ministers since Clement Attlee's government of 1945. But, even so, of the twenty-seven ministers around her cabinet table, no less than 44 per cent were Oxbridge graduates.

Nearly two-thirds of the people who sat around Boris Johnson's cabinet were privately educated, while nearly half, 47 per cent, had gone to Oxbridge. More than two-thirds of Liz Truss's cabinet, in 2022, were privately educated, more than one-third had gone to Oxbridge and more than one-quarter had gone to *both* an independent school and then Oxbridge.[30] And when Rishi Sunak replaced her, in October 2022, more than 60 per cent of his cabinet ministers had gone to private schools, almost half had gone to Oxbridge and one-third had gone to both.

On both the left and right, therefore, Westminster is completely dominated by the new elite, who often have very few if any serious connections to the people who have found themselves on the wrong side of the revolution, feeling as though their values are no longer represented and their voice is no longer heard.

This narrowing of the range of voices has also been compounded by other trends. The once formidable trade unions who helped to bring alternative voices into Westminster and the debate have become much weaker. Their membership had collapsed from a peak of 13 million in 1979 to just 6.5 million by the time of the Brexit referendum.[31] Between the 1950s and the 1980s, one in ten Labour MPs had been a union official; by the 2010s it was only 1 per cent.[32]

Westminster, meanwhile, has been flooded with political careerists who have little work or life experience outside SW1. At least until the 1970s, as we noted in Chapter 1, it was not unusual to find politicians who had fought alongside their fellow citizens in the world wars, or had had serious careers outside politics. These experiences mattered; they helped to prevent groupthink from taking hold and forged qualities that are essential for leading a nation, such as empathy, a sense of obligation to others and familiarity with other classes.

But today things are very different. Between Margaret Thatcher and David Cameron, the share of MPs in the House of Commons whose previous job was 'politician' or 'political organizer' surged more than fivefold.[33] Remarkably, by the time of the Brexit rebellion, half of all Labour MPs and close to one-third of Conservative MPs were careerists who had only ever worked in politics.[34] For many, their entire 'experience' amounts to having served as a party councillor, party researcher, party official or party lobbyist, perhaps with a semester or two at an Ivy League university. And this has been just as visible on the left, where Labour once took pride in being connected to the people: while in the 1980s the party had only twenty careerists, today there are nearly 100.[35]

The professional politicians Clement Attlee had once warned about have now morphed into the largest single tribe in Westminster, ushering in a far more remote, self-serving and inexperienced class. 'The Political Class', noted Peter Oborne, before the revolts of the 2010s erupted, 'is distinguished from earlier governing elites by a lack of experience of and connection with other ways of life. Its members make government their exclusive study. This means they tend not to have significant knowledge of industry, commerce or civil society, meaning their outlook is often metropolitan and London-based. This converts them into a separate, privileged elite, isolated from the aspirations and the problems of provincial, rural and suburban Britain.'[36]

Political scientists have developed another term for this shift. Instead of the more rooted mass parties of the twentieth century, from the 1990s Western democracies have increasingly found themselves in the grip of 'cartel parties' – professional, technocratic and ideologically indistinguishable parties, filled with politicians who collude to keep questions that might challenge the dominant orthodoxy off the table, who do not dare challenge the consensus and who no longer appear interested in what other groups have to say.[37]

This, too, became a major tributary of the Brexit vote and the unfolding realignment, handing even more ammunition to populists, mavericks and renegades who have drawn their strongest support from the very people who have been pushed out of politics. 'Look at the three so-called "big parties" and look at their front benches,' boomed Nigel Farage. 'They are made up of people who go to the same handful of schools, they all go to Oxford, they all get a degree in PPE ... then they all get a job as a researcher in a political office ... this country is now run by a bunch of college kids who have never done a proper day's work in their lives.'[38] It is the same story across much of Europe, where populists such as Georgia Meloni in Italy and Marine Le Pen in France have railed against technocracy.

As studies since Brexit have shown, contrary to what many elites think most voters do not want their representatives to come from a narrow identikit of wealthy, Oxbridge-educated, homogeneous elites. Rather, they want to see a much wider range of voices in Westminster, including leaders from more humble origins.[39] Unfortunately, they have been given exact opposite – a highly educated, careerist and insular political class.

The people who belong to this class, furthermore, also think very differently not only about Brexit, immigration, diversity and British-ness but about representative democracy. In their study, published in 2021, Professors Oliver Heath and Rosie Campbell find that many of the people elected to Westminster are not only consistently more lib-eral than much of the rest of the country but are also more likely to want to prioritize the representation of ethnic and sexual minorities, women and the disabled, but less likely to want to prioritize the rep-resentation of working class and local white voters,[40] which is no doubt feeding these feelings of exclusion.

This loss of voice for Britain's workers, non-graduates, and oth-ers who share traditionalist values has not only been on display in the House of Commons. It is also clearly visible across Whitehall, where the new elite also dominate the Civil Service, the courts, the quangos and public bodies. Britain's permanent secretaries, diplo-mats, civil servants, chairs of public bodies, think-tankers and academic experts are all drawn disproportionately from this group,[41] and so entrench its dominance.

Britain's political institutions have always been dominated by a narrow elite, of course, but in a world where debates about culture, identity and belonging have surged up the agenda, and the graduate class has become far more liberal than it used to be, this large and widening gulf has become far more problematic, fuelling a sense among traditionalists that their voice is no longer included in the con-versation and the institutions.

One example is the Civil Service Fast Stream, which trains the leading civil servants of tomorrow. 'Much progress has been made in relation to some diversity indicators, including Black, Asian, and Minority Ethnic (BAME) and disability,' concludes the first major study into the people being fast-tracked. 'However, in relation to socio-economic diversity, the Fast Stream is unrepresentative of the population at large. To put this in context, the profile of the intake is less diverse than the student population of Oxford.'[42]

It is worth reiterating that while civil servants were always an elite group, there is evidence to suggest they have become even less representative of the wider country. One study, published in 2021, found that the most senior and influential civil servants were not only far more likely than the average voter to belong to the elite graduate class but were more elite than their predecessors were fifty years ago. Today, 72 per cent come from the most privileged educational backgrounds, compared to a lower figure of 67 per cent in 1967.[43]

Clearly, all societies need a highly educated professional class to help run the organs of the state and deliver solutions to complex problems. But when one class becomes so dominant, it risks undermining free thinking, creativity and viewpoint diversity and clearing the way for contrarian political goals to be either watered down or simply ignored.

EXCLUSION BIAS

None of this unique to Britain. Across the West, while the new elite only comprise a minority, they dominate almost all the political institutions, which magnifies their voice, influence and power over the rest of society and breeds resentment. 'Blue-collar workers and citizens with little formal education', summarizes one review of the international evidence, published in 2021, 'have all but disappeared from the ranks of parliamentarians.'[44] In fact, the new elite are now so dominant in the world of politics that some scholars warn we have left the era of mass democracy which characterized the twentieth century and instead entered a dark new era of 'diploma democracy', in which the system has been rewired to service the graduate class.[45]

'Most contemporary democracies', write Mark Bovens and Anchrit Wille, in their comprehensive study of how the new elite have taken over politics, 'are governed by a select group of well-educated citizens. They are diploma democracies – ruled by those with the highest formal qualifications. University graduates have come to dominate all relevant political institutions and arenas, from political parties, parliaments and cabinets to organized interests, deliberative venues and internet consultations.'[46]

Across Western Europe, it is no longer unusual for the minority graduate class to hold between 75 and 95 per cent of all seats in their respective legislatures. Aside from leaving people in the non-graduate majority with a palpable sense that they no longer have a voice, this stokes other problems which have carved out even more space for populists. Perhaps the most pressing has been the emergence of what academics call an 'exclusion bias' in the corridors of power, whereby the entire policy-making process has been reshaped around the values, interests and priorities of the new elite, while those who share neither their degrees nor values are marginalized.

In America, Professor Nicholas Carnes has shown how, long before the rise of Donald Trump, his path to power had at least been partly cleared by how the elite pushed the interests of working-class people and people without degrees out of Washington. 'Social safety net programs are stingier,' he writes, 'business regulations are flimsier, tax policies are more regressive, and protections for workers are weaker than they would be if more lawmakers came from lower-income and working-class backgrounds.'[47] The end result is what he calls 'white-collar government' – a politics that has been repurposed to serve the new elite.

Much the same is visible across Europe, where, contrary to the noble idea of representative democracy giving everybody an equal voice, the policy-making process has been completely taken over by the new elite. In their study, published in 2021, Dutch scholars Wouter Schakel and Daphne van der Pas find highly educated politicians devote far more time and energy to other 'high-status' graduates than they do to 'low-status' workers and non-graduates.[48] In fact, people who have low or medium levels of education, they find, have 'no independent influence on policy'. Unless things change, they warn, we will soon be living in entirely rigged political systems which 'could cement and deepen the divisions between educational groups, for example by causing increased resentment among those whose voice is silenced in the policy process'.[49]

In Germany, similarly, government policies have been shown to be 'systematically skewed' in favour of highly educated and wealthy citizens, findings which have been replicated in many other Western democracies.[50] One of the most comprehensive studies, of ten democracies including Britain, finds that when different groups want different things out of politics – with the less-well-educated wanting more done on crime, immigration and unemployment, and the highly educated wanting more done on climate change – the highly educated win.[51]

In Britain, this exclusion bias found its expression during the New Labour years when the party's more middle-class MPs behaved very differently from their dwindling number of working-class colleagues. They were more likely to stay loyal to the leader, were more interested in the swing voter than their local voters and were much more supportive of slashing welfare for the left behind.[52]

Nor is this bias just about the economy; it is also visible in many other areas of our national life. It is reflected in the historic failure of governments on both the left and right to invest just as seriously in people who belong to the non-graduate majority as they have invested in the graduate class. And it is reflected in the historic underinvestment in apprenticeships, adult skills and further education colleges, the failure to address the plight of white working-class children in Britain's schools, to rebalance the economy away from its heavy dependence on London's financial services, to lower immigration and to reform Westminster so as to ensure there is a wider range of values and voices present in the corridors of power.

It is also reflected in a very large and widening gulf between the views of the people who are running Britain and the views of the people they are representing. As the political system has been reshaped around the new elite, politicians – whether Labour or Conservative – are today much closer to the world view of liberal cosmopolitans than they are to the many traditionalists who either lean left on the economy and right on culture, or who combine their right-wing views on the economy with traditionalist views on culture. As a result, millions of people have reached the conclusion that neither their values nor their voice are now represented among Britain's political class.

The old elite, in the 1950s and the 1960s, largely shared the traditionalist views of voters. While the Conservatives have always stressed faith, flag and family, even Labour politicians embraced a 'nation first' mindset, sharing the 'small c' conservatism of voters. While they are ignored today, heavyweight Labour figures such as Clement Attlee, Hugh Gaitskell and, in later years, Peter Shore, talked passionately and eloquently about their love of the country while railing against efforts to integrate it with the European Community, with Gaitskell warning it would be 'the end of a thousand years of history'.

Another example was the contentious issue of immigration, symbolized, in 1968, when Labour home secretary James Callaghan introduced the Commonwealth Immigrants Act to prevent the entry of Kenyan Asians into Britain. 'Jim', wrote Labour's Richard Crossland at the time, providing an insight into what would have been a fairly common view on the left at the time, 'arrived [at the cabinet meeting] with the air of a man whose mind was made up. He wasn't going to tolerate any of this bloody liberalism.'[53]

In more recent decades, as the country has changed, Britain's MPs have become far more liberal. In the 1990s, surveys of party candidates found they were more supportive than voters of Britain's EU membership and immigration, and were less likely to think equal opportunities for minorities had 'gone too far'.[54] But in recent years this cultural gulf between the rulers and the ruled has become far more pronounced and is now unsustainable.

Consistently, the new elite who dominate Westminster are far more supportive of most of the things which alarm their traditionalist voters: hyper-globalization, immigration, EU membership and social liberalism. Brexit was the most obvious example of this gulf, though it is not the only one. Prior to the referendum, Britain's ruling class were far more likely than voters to think the country benefitted from being a member of the European Union; while 57 per cent felt this way, only 41 per cent of voters agreed. And, whether left or right, MPs were far more supportive of the free movement of EU nationals to work and live in Britain and of their right to claim benefits from the welfare state while they were living and working in Britain.[55]

At the Brexit referendum, in 2016, this underlying tension then burst out into the open for everybody to see. When all votes had been counted, 52 per cent of voters asked for something that only 3 per cent of Labour MPs and 43 per cent of Conservative MPs wanted.

This striking rift, however, was especially visible on the left, where only ten Labour MPs campaigned for something that won a majority of votes in nearly 150 Labour-held seats.[56] It was a remarkable and depressing illustration of the extent to which the political class had come adrift from the rest of Britain.

Beyond Brexit, the same void has been visible in many other areas of national life. As detailed surveys of MPs show, the blunt reality is that neither the left nor the right have been in tune with a large chunk of Britain. While Labour MPs are well aligned with voters on the economy, when it comes to culture, identity and belonging they are usually in a galaxy of their own, holding extremely liberal or progressive authoritarian views that are not shared by much of the rest of the country. Conservative MPs, meanwhile, are a little closer on culture but they too are a world apart when it comes to the economy. Neither of the main parties is connected to many of the voters who have been flocking to join the counter-revolution against the new elite, pushing politics into an unfolding realignment.[57]

It is worth exploring this divide in more depth, as it is now central to our politics. Whereas Labour MPs share the widespread public view that Britain's economy is rigged for the rich and the powerful, that there is one law for the rich and another for the poor and that the economy needs serious reform, when it comes to debates about identity, culture and belonging they are often completely adrift from the rest of the country.

While almost two-thirds of voters think young people no longer respect British values, not even one in ten Labour MPs agree; while 70 per cent of voters think people who break the law should be given stiffer sentences, only one in four Labour MPs feel the same; and while half of voters support the death penalty, *not a single Labour MP* agrees. 'For Labour', concluded one study, 'there is a serious disconnect between their voters and the party, and even more so between the party and the average voter.'[58]

Labour's cultural isolation from the rest of the country is also reinforced by the radical progressives who have joined the party at the grassroots and whose values, as we saw in the last chapter, are often a world away from the values that are held by the average voter. When

Jeremy Corbyn took over the Labour Party, he claimed he had restored the voice of the working class but in reality the party's membership both expanded and narrowed at the same time.

Instead of repairing its relationship with traditionalists, Labour doubled down on the new elite, with three-quarters of its new recruits coming from this group, with university degrees, above-average incomes, secure jobs in the public sector and homes in London. 'This finding may be disappointing to those who believe Labour should be the party *of*, not only *for*, the working class,' notes Professor Tim Bale, 'especially when one learns that it is not so very different to the 80 per cent figure for the Conservative Party.'[59]

This is making it even harder for the left to reconnect with traditionalists, who, as we saw in the last chapter, have been switching to the right. While almost nine in ten people who switched from Labour to the Conservatives at the last election, in 2019, think young people do not respect British values, only 9 per cent of Labour MPs and 17 per cent of Labour members agree; while over 80 per cent of Labour to Conservative switchers say schools should teach children to obey authority, only 41 per cent of Labour MPs and 29 per cent of Labour members agree; and while almost 90 per cent of these switchers back stronger sentences for criminals, only one-quarter of Labour MPs and members do.[60] Perhaps unsurprisingly, some New Labour figures who helped lead the party over the last twenty years, such as Jack Straw, now concede that their embrace of widely unpopular policies such as mass immigration was, in his words, a 'spectacular mistake'.[61]

Similar tensions can be seen on the right, where on economics Conservative MPs are disconnected from many of the people who have been turning to them. Conservative elites are far more likely than their voters to oppose redistribution, the idea that ordinary workers are being exploited, that ordinary people are not being given their fair share of the nation's wealth, and that there is one law for the rich and another for the poor.

And when it comes to questions about culture and identity, Conservative MPs are also more liberal than their own supporters – they are less likely to back things such as the death penalty, to believe that young people do not respect British values or to deliver the lower levels of migration that many of their new voters want to see – a point we will return to in the final chapter. In fact, Conservative MPs are often more closely aligned with the average Labour voter than with their own voters. The key point, in other words, is that the average voter, is more economically left-wing and more culturally conservative than the average MP in Westminster, which helps to explain why so many of these voters have been rebelling against the elite.

THE INSTITUTIONS

This loss of voice, however, is not just visible in politics. Beyond Westminster, many voters are also united by a sense that their voice is no longer heard in many of the other institutions which shape the national conversation about who we are.

The liberal cosmopolitan and progressive values of the new elite increasingly pervade not just politics but the country's prevailing culture. Traditionalists need only turn on the news, read the newspapers or leading columnists, scan the latest books released by publishers, visit cultural institutions such as galleries and museums or send their children to university to encounter a very one-sided view of Britain.

While the new elite routinely see their values and voice reflected back at them, from the BBC homepage through to the museums, bestseller lists, advertisements, television dramas, politics and more, traditionalists routinely struggle to recognize their world view at all. Furthermore, the only insight into traditionalists that the new elite are given is usually only provided by other members of the ruling class, who routinely portray their fellow citizens in profoundly negative ways, as morally inferior racists, gammons, Little Englanders, reactionaries or uneducated thickos.

As writer Jonathan Rutherford points out, the class power of the new middle-class graduate elite comes not only from their control over the political institutions in Westminster; it also comes from their control over 'institutions of culture, media and learning, and its function as the national arbiter and communicator of aesthetic taste and values'.[62]

Clearly, many of these institutions were always dominated by a narrow elite who were not exactly representative of British society. But, today, two things have changed. First, as we have seen, the axis of politics has moved away from an exclusive focus on debates about the economy to encompass new and more polarizing debates about identity and culture; second, graduates have themselves increasingly moved leftwards on these issues, in turn pushing many of the institutions which rely heavily on them further to the left. This explains why, today, many of the most important and influential institutions in Britain reflect the cosmopolitan or radically progressive world view of the new elite, implicitly sharing their belief that the country is 'institutionally racist', that whites should acknowledge and reflect on their 'white privilege' and that Britain's history, if not its identity, is a source of shame and embarrassment. Much like the people who work in them, more than a few of these institutions appear to be instinctively hostile towards traditionalist values and obsessed with diversity and inclusion.

Britain's film, television, radio, fashion, advertising, design, music, performance, visual arts, publishing and digital industries are all disproportionately dominated by the new graduate elite.[63] In 2021, to give only one example, the regulator Ofcom found that almost 60 per cent of workers in Britain's television industry, and 64 per cent in the radio industry, came from families in the professional and managerial class –nearly double the national average.[64]

None of these areas in our national life comes close to giving voice to both sides of the growing cultural rift between cosmopolitans and traditionalists. This not only explains why so many people in Britain today no longer believe their voice is heard but also why so many of the people who work in these institutions were so shocked by the political events of the last decade. Had they been in touch with the people gearing up to vote for populism, Brexit and Boris Johnson, ensuring their voice was reflected in the national conversation, then they would have seen these upheavals coming.

Britain's creative and cultural institutions are similarly dominated by the new graduate elite who use this power and influence to shape the national conversation about who we are around the values, the interests and the political priorities of their own group. 'Who gets on stage, page and screen is currently a major question for media and policy discussions,' concludes one of the most comprehensive studies to date, 'and our data suggests those from privileged backgrounds dominate key creative roles.'[65] At 64 per cent, the share of graduates in the creative industries is more than double the national average, as it is in film, television, radio and publishing, where the figure surges to 71 per cent.[66]

'The story', conclude Dr Orian Brook and her colleagues, in their study, 'is of a set of cultural and creative industries with attitudes that are the most liberal, most pro-welfare and most left wing of any industry.'[67]

Similarly, nearly half of Britain's authors come from families in the new elite, while only one in ten have any serious connection to the working class.[68] Unsurprisingly, therefore, when it comes to the books, the authors and the plays which shape how we think about British politics, culture, history and values, the conversation is once again one-sided.

This might explain why publishers recently attracted attention after their staff refused to work on books or with authors who challenged the dominant orthodoxy of the new elite, such as J. K. Rowling, former Republican vice president Mike Pence, academic Jordan Peterson and other former officials who worked in the Trump presidency.

Most of Britain's famous actors, including its Oscar and BAFTA winners, are also children of the new elite. While Sean Connery dropped out of school to work a milk round, three-quarters of Britain's most accomplished actors – Tom Hiddleston, Eddie Redmayne, Benedict Cumberbatch, Damian Lewis, Dominic West – come from the same elite.[69] It is not hard to find celebrities simultaneously proclaiming their love of diversity while berating voters who have sought to reassert their voice in the national debate through politics.

Instead of working to close the country's divides by ensuring that a wide range of views and voices are present in the debate, many institutions have instead chosen to double down on the new elite. Even on the rare occasion when other voices have been included, such as those from the working class, they are routinely portrayed in crude, simplistic and insulting ways, as criminals, teenage mums, feckless dads, chavs, alcoholics, drug addicts, racists or idiots. 'So, in fact', write Drs Sarah McNicol and Andrew McMillan, in their commentary,

> the myriad voices of the UK working classes in all their diversity are often getting lost because we simply don't recognise them – or simply refuse to listen to what they're actually saying ... the working class is still all too often seen from the outside as a monolith – uneducated, white, racist – where the reality is obviously much more diverse and complex.[70]

Much of Britain's media, like its politics, has also morphed into a highly educated caste, dominated by the new elite. In decades gone by, it was not unusual to find people in media who did not have a degree or had worked their way up through local and regional media. This was important as it ensured there were journalists who had different views and experiences with people from different parts of the country and perspectives. But, today, in a world where local media has collapsed and the media rely on unpaid internships which benefit the better-off, this is unlikely to happen. The end result is, once again, a narrowing of the range of views.

Journalists are now far more likely to go straight from an elite university into the media newsroom, taking their strongly cosmopolitan if not progressive values with them. Between the 1980s and the 2000s, the share of leading journalists who went to private schools *increased* from 49 per cent to 54 per cent, while the share with a degree *increased* from 78 to 81 per cent, more than half of whom graduated from Oxbridge.[71]

By the time of Brexit, which for many people in the country became an outlet for their utter exasperation with this stifling orthodoxy, the situation had not improved. More than half of Britain's 100 leading journalists were educated at private schools or graduated from Oxbridge.[72] And this is especially the case at the most senior and influential levels where almost 60 per cent of editors at the leading media outlets were privately educated, nearly 20 points *higher* than the figure in the 1980s.[73]

The growing remoteness of the media class from the rest of the country has also been underlined by the Reuters Institute for the

Study of Journalism, University of Oxford. By the mid-2010s, they find, and unlike decades past, British journalism had become 'fully academised', meaning 98 per cent of the journalists who began work at this time had at least a bachelor's degree while more than one third had a master's. 'Given the increasing costs of university education in the UK, especially when that education may include a master's degree, and given the competitiveness of university entry,' they write, 'questions need to be asked about the socio-economic diversity of future generations of UK journalists'.[74]

Even in 2019, after the vote for Brexit should have shaken up more than a few of these industries, leading them to make room for a wider range of voices, Oxbridge was still producing one-third of the most senior BBC executives, more than one-third of the country's female newspaper columnists, one-third of the most senior editors in the leading media outlets, 44 per cent of all columnists, and half of the most senior female editors.[75] On any given day, it is entirely normal to find that the vast majority of national commentators, if not all of them, had gone to one of two universities – including many of the women and minority ethnic writers who are held up as evidence of 'diversity'.

'The educational backgrounds of people in the top jobs in UK media', pointed out the Sutton Trust, 'look very different to the general population, with newspaper columnists the least like the audiences they write for.'[76] In 2022, the National Council for the Training of Journalists also drew attention to the fact that an overwhelming majority of journalists look and sound nothing like many of the people who are reading their content.[77]

Much the same is true of the largest and most influential organization of all: the BBC. While the BBC talks passionately about diversity, like other media it continues to rely heavily on the new elite. BBC staff are significantly less likely than the surrounding population to have relied on free school meals or to have come from a working-class background.[78]

Once again, the most senior levels are the least representative; 29 per cent of BBC executives were privately educated: almost one-third went to Oxbridge, 70 per cent went to a Russell Group university – up

8 points on 2014 – and 93 per cent were graduates.[79] Perhaps for this reason, when the BBC announced its '50:20:12' diversity target – 50 per cent for gender, 20 per cent for ethnicity, 12 per cent for disability – it said very little if anything about education, class and viewpoint diversity.[80]

Not everybody is ignoring the problem, however. One journalist who has reflected on the implications is Justin Webb, presenter of the flagship Radio 4 *Today* programme. 'The current presenters' roster', he wrote in 2021, 'boasts two Oxford graduates, two from Cambridge and me. It is unlikely that another non-graduate like John [Humphrys] will present it any time soon and we are reduced as a result. Our perspectives are less diverse.'[81]

Nor is he the only one to raise the issue. Other journalists have also expressed their frustration with the lack of genuine diversity in Britain's media. 'We journalists are the ones who day after day, are supposed to reflect Britain unto itself,' complained one, who noted how a furore over a gender pay gap in the BBC, while important, glossed a much deeper divide. 'We're supposed to be the ones who find and tell the stories that matter to our audiences, and for the BBC all of its licence fee payers. How are we supposed to do that if we are drawn from an increasingly narrow social caste?'[82]

'In the 1810s,' he continued, shortly before GB News and Talk TV would emerge to fill this gap, 'it was said that the Battle of Waterloo was fought and won on the playing fields of Eton so dominant was the school in the top brass of the Army. In 2017, it is the six o'clock news.' Shaped by their elite backgrounds, many journalists sit on one side of the unfolding divide, holding cosmopolitan values which are not shared by much of the country. When Oxford's Reuters Institute asked Britain's journalists to place themselves on the political landscape, more than half, 53 per cent, put themselves on the left, while only 23 per cent put themselves on the right (the rest were in the centre).[83] Among rank-and-file journalists 56 per cent identified on the left while only 18 per cent identified on the right (see Figure 10).

As American writer Batya Ungar-Sargon points out in her book *Bad News*, published in 2021, this problem is by no means unique to Britain. Across many Western democracies journalism has morphed into a profession of astonishing privilege, from a trade where people used to have little training or formal education and had often earned their stripes in local and regional media, to one that is now dominated by highly educated, often wealthy elites from privileged families, who have moved direct from an elite university into the newsroom and who are often united by their radically progressive views.[84]

The dominance of these voices, she argues, helps to explain the so-called 'Great Awokening' in American media, where references to liberal progressive ideas such as white privilege, cultural appropriation, intersectionality, whiteness, institutional racism and others have skyrocketed in recent years, particularly as young zoomer graduates from Generation Z have made their way into the newsrooms and embraced a more activist approach to media. One study, based on analysis of 27 million news articles in American media between 1970 and 2019, found a 500 per cent increase in the number of references to radically progressive terms such as white privilege, intersectionality,

Figure 10: Political Affiliation of UK Journalists

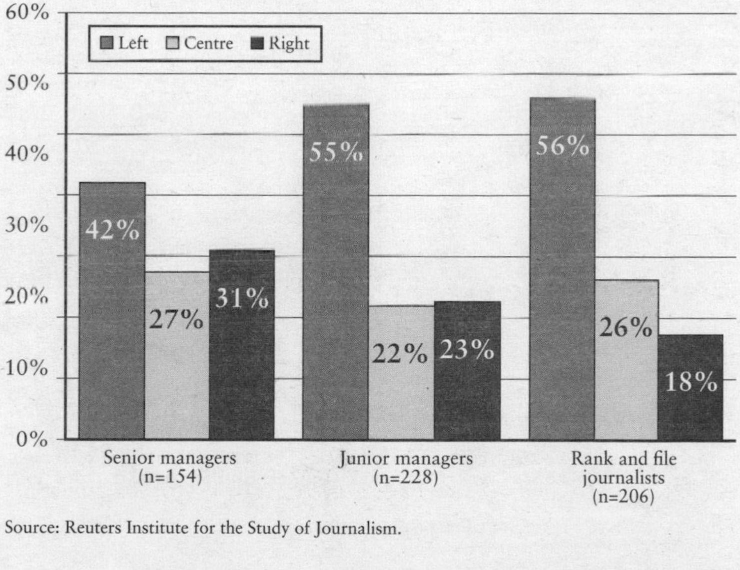

Source: Reuters Institute for the Study of Journalism.

Figure 11: UK News Media Coverage of Words Denoting Prejudice

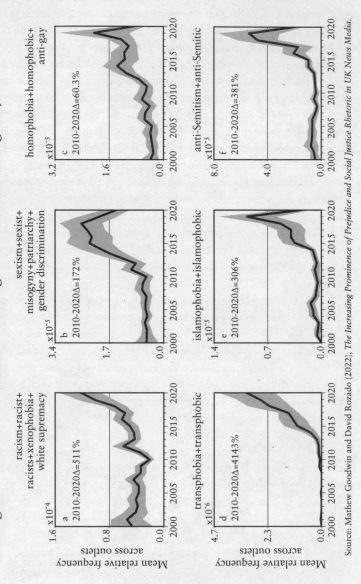

Source: Mathew Goodwin and David Rozado (2022), *The Increasing Prominence of Prejudice and Social Justice Rhetoric in UK News Media.*

cisgender, patriarchy, racism, transphobic and homophobic. Beginning around 2014, before the rise of President Donald Trump, the use of terms such as 'racist' increased by 638 per cent in the *New York Times* and 514 per cent in the *Washington Post*, and 'sexist' by 403 per cent in the *New York Times* and 141 per cent in the *Washington Post*. [85] Rather than being driven by an actual increase in prejudice, the authors of the study suggest this has more to do with a 'preoccupation with bias and discrimination among the literati', namely, a growing left-wing progressive slant in media which is increasingly shaped by the elite graduates from elite universities who work in media and, in turn, attract criticism from the right.[86]

My own research with David Rozado has found remarkably similar trends in Britain, where, despite levels of racism and prejudice declining sharply over the last fifty years, as we will see in the next chapter, the number of references in British media to terms such as racism, sexism, transphobia, homophobia, white privilege, whiteness, cultural appropriation and unconscious bias has surged over the last decade (see Figure 11).

Consistent with findings in America and Spain, between 2000 and 2020, terms such as racism increased by 769 per cent, white supremacy by 2,827 per cent, sexism by 169 per cent, patriarchy by 336 per cent, misogyny by 237 per cent, transphobia by 2,578 per cent, islamophobia by 289 per cent and anti-Semitism by 469 per cent. Other studies find British media have become more likely in recent years to characterize people on the other side of the political divide as extremists, though left-wing media is more likely to describe people on the right as 'far-right' than vice versa.[87]

Clearly, these trends might reflect new debates about the legacy of history and the need to tackle lingering discrimination in British society. But, arguably, they owe much to the changing profile of the media class, which is now dominated by elite graduates who are the most likely to hold radically progressive values and often show little interest in representing other voices.

Given these trends, it is perhaps unsurprising to find evidence of a sharp decline of public trust in media, including the BBC. While in 2003 81 per cent of British people said they 'trusted BBC News journalists to tell the truth', since then this figure has collapsed to 60 per cent in 2010 and a record low of 44 per cent in 2019, by which time only 8 per cent of people trusted BBC journalists 'a great deal'.[88] This is clearly problematic for the BBC. A national broadcaster that no longer talks to the nation, and which is no longer trusted by much of it, has no clear purpose.

There are also striking differences in the extent to which people on the left and right trust media. While four in ten Remainers and Labour voters no longer trust BBC journalists to tell the truth, this jumps to six in ten Leavers and Conservatives who feel this way. In 2022, similarly, Edelman found that the British are among the least trusting of media in the world, with only 35 per cent doing so.[89]

Amid this climate, many people clearly feel unable to voice their real views in society and instead feel they should 'self-censor' or hide their views. In 2021, remarkably, nearly six in ten people in Britain agreed with the statement 'I sometimes find myself stopping myself from expressing my views on political and/or social issues because of fear of judgement or negative responses from others.'[90] Researchers at the University of Cambridge have found the same share of people now believe 'political correctness is undermining free speech' while the British, remarkably, were more likely than the Americans, the French, the Germans, the Hungarians and the Poles to feel this way.[91]

Once again, it is the very people who have been left on the wrong side of the revolution – who are sceptical about immigration, who think minorities have things just about as good as white Britons, who disagree that 'a transgender woman is a woman' and who think there should be a law against wearing full body and face veils (i.e., burkas and niqabs) – who are the most likely of all to feel the need to hide their real voice, fearful of what might happen to them if they express their real views in society.[92]

Worryingly, this narrowing of the range of voices in British life is now also visible beyond politics and media, in the very institutions that are supposed to protect the marketplace of ideas and ensure that the next generation of citizens is being exposed to a diverse range of voices: Britain's universities.

Increasingly, over recent decades, they too have swung sharply leftwards, pushing the new elite and the next generation of degree-holders further away from the values and the voice of the non-graduate majority. The popular claim that Britain's universities have always leaned to the left is true but misleading. In the 1960s, fewer than half of Britain's academics identified on the left, while one in three placed themselves on the right.[93] This was not ideal, but it at least ensured that students and academics were exposed to alternative perspectives.

Today, however, this picture has changed dramatically. By the 1980s, the ratio of right to left academics had fallen to one in five and by the time of Brexit had fallen to one in eight. At the last election, in 2019, 70–80 per cent of Britain's academics voted for left-wing parties while only 10–15 per cent voted for right-wing ones.[94] Around the same time, the Center for the Study of Partisanship and Ideology found that while 52 per cent of British voters had supported Brexit, only 17 per cent of the people who are teaching in universities had done the same. And while more than one in two voters want to lower immigration, only one in eight academics feel the same way.[95]

Such findings point to the clear risk that Britain's universities, like many other institutions in society, are now morphing into 'ideological monocultures', where liberal cosmopolitan and progressive values are completely dominant, those who do not share them feel they cannot speak, and political minorities, such as conservatives and gender-critical scholars, are either marginalized or openly discriminated against. Recent studies suggest one in four of Britain's university students and one in three academics are self-censoring their voices in seminars and lectures, fearful of what might happen to their careers or friendships if they reveal their views.[96] Once again, it is those who do not share the outlook of the new elite who are especially likely to feel this way; while 75 per cent of academics on the right say they regularly hide their views when they are on campus, only 35 per cent of academics who place themselves on the left say the same thing.[97]

Britain's universities, like the new elite more generally, routinely preach the value of 'diversity', 'openness' and 'tolerance'. Yet, re-markably, one-third of Britain's academics say they would openly discriminate against somebody who supported Brexit, more than half would feel uncomfortable sitting next to a Brexiteer over lunch, and one in three would feel uncomfortable sitting next to somebody who held gender-critical feminist views, such as Kathleen Stock, who, in 2021, was forced to resign from her professorship at Sussex University after being harassed by student activists on university campus.[98]

Many other cases have similarly demonstrated the extent to which alternative voices are unwelcome in universities, including Cambridge's decision to rescind a fellowship for Jordan Peterson after student and staff protests; Cambridge's decision to dismiss a young researcher from his prestigious fellowship after students and staff branded him 'racist'; 150 Oxford lecturers refusing to teach unless a statue of Cecil Rhodes was removed; Edinburgh University's decision to rename the David Hume Tower; Nottingham's decision, in 2022, to withdraw the offer of an honorary degree to Dr Tony Sewell, whose government report challenged the progressive belief that Britain is 'institutionally racist'; the suspension of a professor at Durham University who invited columnist Rod Liddle to speak to students (who later threatened to withhold their rent payments until somebody apologized); and Cambridge's short-lived plan to encourage staff to anonymously inform on each other if they felt they had suffered 'micro-aggressions'.[99]

None of this is unique to Britain. In America, since 2015, there has been a sharp rise in the number of academics who have been investigated, penalized or sanctioned by students or staff because of something they said in class or wrote on social media, with most of these attempts to silence or discredit other voices coming from the left.[100] My own research finds that while nearly two-thirds of academics in Britain feel positively about people who vote for the left, only 10 per cent feel the same way about people who vote for the right.[101]

Some of this recalls older ideas that circulated on campuses in the 1960s and 1970s, when left-wing thinkers such as Herbert Marcuse, in an influential essay on 'repressive tolerance', argued that the objective of tolerance required that people show intolerance towards others. Marcuse called for 'intolerance against movements from the Right and toleration of movements from the Left', suggesting the need for 'new and rigid restrictions on teachings and practices in the educational institutions'.[102]

Britain's higher education system, therefore, looks increasingly like its counterpart in America, where universities have swung even more sharply to the left and it is no longer unusual to find left-wing academics outnumbering right-wing ones by ten or fifteen to one.[103] Jonathan Rauch points out in his book *The Constitution of Knowledge* that nearly 40 per cent of the top liberal arts colleges in America have zero Republicans or so few as to make no difference.[104] 'You need to go about with a lantern in broad daylight, Diogenes-style, to find a conservative in a humanities department,' writes Rauch. 'Many academics and students who do lean right are closeted. The university does not reliably feel like a safe space for them. On campus, conservative speakers are often shunned, shouted down, denounced in hysterical terms.'[105]

The risk facing universities in Britain can already be seen in the United States. Such a dramatic imbalance has found its expression in intensifying culture wars about the extent to which universities are drifting to the left, as well as a sharp decline in levels of public trust in these institutions, especially among Republicans, who feel their voice has been excluded from yet another influential institution. Over the last decade, as the Pew Research Center points out, while Democrats became more likely to think universities are having a positive impact on society, the share of Republicans who think this way collapsed from 58 to 33 per cent.[106]

One reason why the new elite have risen to dominate these institutions – political parties, think tanks, media, the creative industries, the universities – argues American academic Richard Hanania, is because, ultimately, they care more about political outcomes.[107] People who hold strongly liberal views are not only more likely to follow politics but are more likely to donate to campaigns, arrange protests and commit their lives to jobs which might not pay as much as others but are 'high status', allowing them to wield considerable influence.

In Britain and Europe, people who are the most active in politics and on social media are also more highly educated, wealthier and more liberal than the average voter.[108] Whereas traditionalists put more emphasis on practical rather than expressive roles, these jobs in politics, think tanks, media, internships and universities appeal to the new elite because they allow them to exert considerable influence over the rest of society. 'People who engage in protesting care more about politics than people who donate money, and people who donate money care more than people who simply vote,' writes Hanania. 'Imagine a pyramid with voters at the bottom and full-time activists on top, and as you move up the pyramid it gets much narrower and more left-wing.'[109]

This is part of the story, but it is only one part. Many of the trends we have discussed are connected to the growing cultural divide between the new graduate elite and everybody else. As graduates have increasingly embraced the cosmopolitan and progressive values of the revolution, the institutions which rely heavily on them are now also drifting leftwards, moving further away from the rest of the society. Alongside the rise of a more insular political class in Westminster, this has left many people with a powerful sense they are being cut adrift not only by the economic and political transformation of Britain, but a prevailing culture that no longer makes room for them and, even worse, is not particularly interested in what they believe or what they have to say.

5

Virtue

The populist revolts which have reshaped British politics and the country over the last decade have not only won support from voters who feel they have been cut adrift from the new values of the mainstream and left without a voice, they have also appealed strongly to people who feel that, relative to other groups in society, they are no longer seen by the new elite as having the same degree of social status, esteem and moral worth. Feeling derided and dismissed as an uneducated, racist and morally inferior underclass, many people have either given up on politics altogether or searched for more radical leaders who promise to treat them and their group with respect. This brings us to the third and final divide in the new politics.

The word 'virtue' refers to being morally good or righteous. Centuries ago, thinkers such as Aristotle saw politics as not just a way of organizing society but as a means through which people can lead a virtuous life, acquiring things such as character, a sense of honour, feelings of moral worth and respect from others.[1] But today, amid the rise of the new elite, many people feel the exact opposite – they have been not only silenced by the new elite but also stigmatized as belonging to a morally inferior underclass.

These feelings are not irrational; they reflect the rise of a new social order, a new way of distributing social status, esteem and moral worth around society. At the top, as we will see, are the highly educated new elite who have the right degrees from the right universities and the right set of elite beliefs to feel valuable and virtuous; at the bottom, by contrast, are people from the white working class, the non-graduate majority and older generations whose lack of university education and traditionalist beliefs, or whose very identities as straight, white men, leave them feeling as though they are no longer treated with as much respect as other groups in society.

It wasn't always this way. In a much earlier era, which still lingers on in the House of Lords and the monarchy, members of the old elite saw birth and ancestry as the most important markers of people's status and respect, with the upper-class aristocratic elite sitting at the top of the social ladder. In later years, in the second half of the twentieth century, people's occupation became a more important marker of their social status, with the rising number of professionals accumulating a greater sense of respect than manual workers. Today, instead, one of the main markers of somebody's status and position in society is whether they belong to the new elite.

THE NEW STATUS HIERARCHY

In his book *The Road to Character*, David Brooks usefully describes this shift as one that has pushed Western societies away from the 'eulogy virtues' which guided earlier generations towards today's obsession with what he calls 'resumé virtues'. Eulogy virtues are what gets talked about at somebody's funeral, such as whether they were a nice, courageous, faithful and generous person; résumé virtues are the individual achievements that people list on their résumé or CV, such as their university and degree.[2] Increasingly, over the last fifty years, as the revolution swept through society, the new elite rebuilt society around people who look and sound like them, doubling down on résumé virtues. The only route to leading a valuable and virtuous life, worthy of respect from others, has come to be seen as having the right degree from one of the right Oxbridge or Russell Group universities, and holding the right set of elite beliefs to accompany this education.

Whether on the right or left, this obsession with reshaping society around a university-based meritocracy has now become so entrenched that some thinkers argue we have fully evolved into 'schooled societies' – an entirely new era in which people's cognitive ability, certified by the universities, has become the main if not only way for people to win respect and recognition from others.[3]

In turn, this has given rise to a new 'status hierarchy' in Western societies, which Professor Tak Wing Chan, a leading expert on social status, defines as 'a perceived and often accepted hierarchy of social superiority, equality and inferiority'.[4] At the top of this new hierarchy are people who belong to the highly educated new elite who went to the right schools, the right universities, and who spend much of their day sitting on social media signalling their elite credentials and sense of moral superiority to other members of the elite; at the bottom are the much larger number of people who either went to a much less prestigious university or did not go to university at all.

This is why, ever since the rise of national populism, Brexit, Boris Johnson and similar revolts across the West, a growing number of thinkers have drawn a straight line from their strong support among the non-graduate majority to the problems that are baked into this university-based meritocracy, a system that appears hard-wired to stoke intense feelings of disillusionment among people who have not gone to the 'right' schools or the 'right' universities.

In his book *Head Hand Heart*, British thinker David Goodhart rightly points out that while the expansion of the universities improved many people's lives, it also had a profoundly negative impact on many others, not least by reshaping Western societies around a small cognitive elite who have become too powerful, too dismissive of others and too disconnected from the rest of society. Along the way, it has also changed how people are perceived by others, giving rise to a potent new divide in society. 'In the last two decades', he writes, 'it has sometimes felt as if an enormous social vacuum cleaner has sucked up status from manual occupations, even skilled ones, and reallocated it to the middling and higher cognitive professions and the prosperous metropolitan centres and university towns.'[5] While the winners of this new settlement are those he calls the Heads – the new graduate elite – whose innate cognitive ability and degrees from the right universities mean they feel recognized and respected; the losers have been the non-graduate Hands – Britain's plumbers, mechanics and factory workers – and the Hearts – people who choose to look after their families or fellow citizens in low-status jobs, such as nursing and social care. The Hands and Hearts now realize they are being pushed down the social ladder and have been turning to politics to express their intensifying disillusionment.

For many working-class men, in particular, this loss of status has been compounded by the loss of jobs which once gave them a greater sense of usefulness, dignity and meaning. As Britain's economy was opened to hyper-globalization, many jobs were either lost or replaced by low-skilled, insecure and much less prestigious ones. Between 2016 and 2021, the share of mainly male workers who are employed by online driving and delivery platforms, such as Uber and Deliveroo, increased more than fourfold, to 9 per cent of the workforce, equivalent to about 4.5 million people, many of whom cobble together several different jobs to try to stay afloat during long days, and with few rights.[6]

Their diminished sense of status and growing resentment of the new elite has also been amplified by an economic model that relies on a mass influx of cheap migrant workers into the same low-skill, low-wage, service industries. Squeezed between the new elite above and the unskilled and unemployed below, it is perhaps unsurprising to find that Britain's hard-working, traditionalist and skilled workers – whom pollsters call the 'C2s' – were the most likely of all to support populism, Brexit and Boris Johnson.[7]

One powerful symbol of their diminished status has been the historic failure of governments, on both the left or right, to invest anywhere near the same amount of attention, energy and interest in the non-graduate majority as they lavish on the graduate class. Britain's universities and their students, concludes one major review, have been 'both cared for and cared about'.[8] They receive the bulk of funding. They receive the bulk of attention from the institutions, which, as we have seen, are dominated by other graduates. And their interests are consistently advanced by dedicated 'mission groups', such as the Russell Group and Universities UK, which lobby, continuously, on their behalf. But it is a different story for the non-graduate majority.

While the new elite and their descendants have benefitted the most from meritocracy and moved on to better jobs, better salaries and the most powerful and influential positions in the institutions, many others have found themselves and their group devalued. In sharp contrast to the universities, Britain's further education colleges experienced the harshest spending cuts of all. Over the last decade, while government spending on university students soared, spending on everybody else collapsed. In 2022, the Institute for Fiscal Studies found that, over the last decade, total government spending on adult education and apprenticeships had fallen sharply, by 38 per cent, with a 50 per cent fall in spending on classroom-based adult education. Even by 2025, total spending on these alternative routes will be 25 per cent lower than it was in 2010.[9] 'Not surprisingly', concluded Dr Philip Augar and his team, at the end of their lengthy investigation into Britain's broken education system,

> the [further education] sector is demoralised, has little to spend on mission groups and is consequently under-reported in the media and under-represented in Westminster. No prior government of any persuasion has considered further education to be a priority. The consequence has been decades of neglect and a loss of status and prestige amongst leaders, employers, and the public at large.[10]

The general obsession with doubling down on the graduate class is even more remarkable given that the advantages of having a degree are nowhere near as obvious as they once were. Between 2015 and 2019, more than one in three of Britain's graduates were working in jobs that did not require a degree, while British graduates were more likely than their counterparts in other advanced countries to be over-qualified for their jobs.[11]

The 'pay premium' for graduates, that is, the financial advantage they enjoy over non-graduates, is also moving in the wrong direction. By the age of twenty-six, the pay premium for recent graduates born in 1990 was 8 points lower than for graduates who were born twenty years earlier. For people who graduate with a second-class degree, the premium is barely visible at all, while some studies estimate that, today, around one in eight students are studying for a degree or at a low-ranked university which will bring them negative or negligible earnings returns. Unsurprisingly, in 2022, more than half the country felt that university degrees were no longer offering people value for money.[12]

This is not just about money, however. The new elite's obsession with reproducing itself has also stoked other, profoundly negative effects. In his book, *The Tyranny of Merit*, Harvard philosopher Michael Sandel points out how the system has also fuelled what he calls the 'politics of humiliation' – a galling sense among many people that the highly educated new elite are looking down on those at the bottom with disdain if not contempt.[13] The core problem, he argues, building on older arguments by British thinker Michael Young, is that meritocracy, which contends that anybody can be successful so long as they work hard and apply their talent, is hard-wired to push society apart. It encourages the so-called 'winners' to see themselves as exactly that – winners who deserve their success.[14]

Yet, in reality, many people have only joined the new elite because they benefitted from in-built advantages that they didn't earn and that were not available to others, such as their innate cognitive ability, their privileged families, the social networks that come with these families, an education system that has long been rigged to favour the children of the new elite, or their sheer luck. 'It congratulates the winners but denigrates the losers, even in their own eyes,' writes Sandel, who rightly argues that these feelings have become central to the appeal of populism. 'For those who can't find work or make ends meet, it is hard to escape the demoralizing thought that their failure is their own doing, that they simply lack the talent and drive to succeed.'[15]

These negative thoughts are then reinforced by how the so-called losers are talked about in the institutions and much of the prevailing culture, which, as we have seen, are disproportionately dominated by the new elite. Routinely, the implicitly superior 'strivers', 'Winners of Globalization', the 'smart' and 'mobile' people who are 'getting ahead' are contrasted with the implicitly inferior 'takers', 'skivers', 'shirkers', 'scroungers', 'thickos', 'Losers of Globalization' and 'gammons'.[16]

How this resentment translates into politics has been shown by Arlie Hochschild, in America, who interviewed hundreds of people who went on to vote for Donald Trump, in 2016. She writes powerfully about how this way of talking about the world stoked a powerful sense among the mainly white working-class men without college degrees whom she met that not just their jobs, but their sense of social honour, was being steadily eroded.[17]

Seen through their eyes, an alliance of the new elite, immigrants, minorities, women and public-sector employees (who are also usually minorities and women) have not only 'cut in line' for an American Dream that is becoming harder to realize because of rising inequality, but are now also competing with them for cultural honour in wider society. These feelings of loss and resentment have not only been stoked by out-of-touch politicians but by a liberal cultural elite in Hollywood and the media who switched from portraying African Americans in simplistic, unflattering and racist ways, to, today, portraying the white (non-graduate) working class as moronic, raggedy, ignorant, fat, racist rednecks and white trash. Summarizing the world view she frequently encountered from one area to the next, Hochschild writes:

> You are a stranger in your own land. You do not recognize yourself in how others see you. It is a struggle to feel seen and honored. And to feel honored you have to feel – and feel seen as – moving forward. But through no fault of your own, and in ways that are hidden, you are slipping backward. You turn to your workplace for respect – but wages are flat and jobs insecure. So you look to other sources of honor. You get no extra points for your race. You look to gender, but if you're a man, you get no extra points for that either. If you are straight you are proud to be a married, heterosexual male, but that pride is now seen as a potential sign of homophobia – a source of dishonor. Regional honor? Not that either. You are often disparaged for the place you call home. As for the church, many look down on it . . . You are old, but in America, attention is trained on the young. People like you – white Christian, working and middle class – suffer this sense of fading honor demographically too, as this very group has declined in numbers.[18]

In Britain, much the same could have been said in the aftermath of the Brexit referendum, when the new elite lined up to stigmatize the mainly working-class and non-graduate traditionalists who had voted to leave the EU as uneducated thickos who did not know what they were voting for. 'Study reveals mainly stupid people will vote Brexit', read one headline, while the day after Brexit, in 2020, 'thick' trended on Twitter – a platform dominated by liberals.[19]

Such feelings of disillusionment and resentment have played an important role in unifying these voters. In 2021, Dutch scholar Jochem van Noord and his colleagues analysed more than 65,000 people across thirty-six countries, including Britain. They found that people who did not belong to the new elite were united not simply by their economic experiences but, rather, by their 'feelings of misrecognition, that is, the extent to which people have the feeling that they do not play a meaningful role in society, that they possess a (stigmatized) identity that is looked down upon and feel less valued than other groups'.[20]

Similarly, in their study of why millions of people across Europe have abandoned the old parties to vote for populists, Noah Gidron and Peter Hall found that, even after accounting for their income and class, many of these voters were pulled together by their shared sense that both they and their group are losing status, relative to other groups in society. 'What distinguishes them from voters for mainstream parties', they write, 'is the feeling that they have not been treated with respect – a sense that they are not fully valued by society. They care as much about recognition as about redistribution.'[21]

In Britain, it is no coincidence that the very same groups – workers, people without degrees, and pensioners who grew up before this obsession with the university class – have been rebelling against the new elite. When David Cameron finally brought the Blair and Brown years to a close, in 2010, the Conservative Party's lead over Labour among the skilled working class was just 8 points; when, in 2019, Boris Johnson won his majority, the Conservative Party's lead among this group had more than doubled, to nearly 20 points.[22] Many of these workers have been the most likely to drift into apathy, the most likely to feel politically disillusioned and the most likely to vote for populism, Brexit and Boris Johnson. For many, this was not just a quest to reassert their values and voice, it was also an attempt to restore their sense of virtue and moral worth against a new elite who appear neither to respect them, nor even like them.

Many of these voters are united by a belief that they are steadily being pushed down the social hierarchy, forced to watch the highly educated elite reshape Britain around their own values, interests and priorities and left to wonder if they are even respected at all. While they are aware that Britain's economic and geographical inequalities remain largely unresolved, many of these voters also sense a more fundamental separation in modern Britain – a divide in the perceived moral worth of 'people like them' and people who belong to the new elite.[23]

Nor are they necessarily wrong to think this way. While the new elite routinely talk about diversity, openness, tolerance and fairness, academic Toon Kuppens and his colleagues have found that the highly educated who belong to this new ruling class often look down on the less well-educated and feel more positively about other highly educated elites. Interestingly, the less well-educated did not exhibit the same bias towards the highly educated.[24]

This is why, in his book *The New Snobbery*, British writer David Skelton argues that the profoundly negative treatment of the working-class and non-graduate voters who rallied behind populism, Brexit and Boris Johnson has become one of the last acceptable forms of prejudice among the new elite – and one they would never countenance were it directed towards racial, sexual and gender minorities.[25]

'Large parts of the often liberal, professional elite', he writes, 'seem to believe that working-class views are not of the same worth as professional views; working-class jobs are not as valuable as middle-class jobs; and working-class places are less desirable to live in than middle-class places. This has created a new snobbery, through which it has become socially acceptable for the economically successful to look down on working people.'[26]

Skelton is right to point to this snobbery, but he is wrong to focus so heavily on class. Ever since Brexit, people's concerns about their lost status have been shown to be independent of their objective class position in society. People's support for Nigel Farage and Brexit was not merely driven by the old, class-based loyalties which shaped politics through the twentieth century; rather, it was rooted in a more diffuse sense that they and their group are rapidly losing social honour and moral worth relative to other groups in society.[27]

This is why Oxford academics Erzsébet Bukodi and John Goldthorpe suggest it makes more sense to see the populist revolts that are erupting across the West not so much as an expression of the old class politics but as an expression of status politics – as revolts that appeal strongly to people who come from different classes but who share a sense that they and their group are being pushed to the bottom of the new moral hierarchy.[28] This is a crucial point, not least because it points to the ongoing potential for these revolts in the years ahead. No matter how prosperous or well educated a society becomes, there will always be people who, relative to others, feel they are losing social status, esteem and honour. But treating these groups with more respect would be a good start.

THE LUXURY BELIEF CLASS

Today, however, these feelings are not only stoked by the dark side of meritocracy, they are also strengthened by how the new elite have also come to see their elite beliefs, not just their elite education, as a key marker of somebody's status, esteem and moral worth. In her book, *The Sum of Small Things*, Professor Elizabeth Currid-Halkett points out that as Western societies became more economically prosperous and better educated it became harder for people in the elite to find ways of signalling their status to other elites and distinguishing themselves from the masses.[29] In prosperous countries such as Britain, where nearly one in two young zoomers are now enrolling in university each year, having a degree from an elite university is necessary to join the ruling class but is no longer sufficient. This is why, increasingly, the new elite now also signal not just their elite education but their elite beliefs to project their heightened sense of moral superiority, righteousness and virtue to others, to try to win approval and recognition from other elites, and to distinguish themselves from the masses below.

Over the last decade, notes Cambridge academic Rob Henderson, this has increasingly given rise to what a he calls 'luxury belief class' in Western societies – highly educated members of the elite who no longer measure somebody's status or moral worth through money, estates, titles or education but through the new lens of ideas and beliefs. In the past, the old elite used to signal their status and sense of superiority through delicate and restrictive clothing, such as tuxedos and top hats, and by engaging in time-consuming leisure activities which manual workers did not have the time to do, such as playing golf, visiting galleries and museums and going on very long holidays. Today, in sharp contrast, the new elite have decoupled social status from goods and reattached it to beliefs. Being wealthy, highly educated and professionally successful are no longer enough; now, the new elite must be seen as more morally righteous and more virtuous – they must embrace these elite beliefs and signal them to others.[30]

While they are often driven by good intentions, this drive for status and recognition is what has been leading many members of the elite to embrace a more divisive and radical brand of progressive 'woke' politics, which is pushing apart rather than pulling together members of different racial, sexual and gender groups. Anchored in ideas that have been trickling out of the universities since the 1960s and the 1970s – though mainly 'critical theories' related to race, ethnicity and gender – radical progressive ideology contends that Britain and other Western states are inherently and irretrievably racist, that racial, sexual, gender and other minorities must be prioritized above the majority, that Western culture, identity, history and ways of life must be revised if not 'deconstructed', and that people who belong to the white majority or who hold traditionalist beliefs are morally inferior and suspicious, if not profoundly dangerous.

The rise of this radical belief system, concentrated among the new elite, has been a long time coming. Writing in 1940, George Orwell famously took aim at England's left-wing intellectuals, who, in his words, took their 'cookery from Paris' and their 'opinions from Moscow'. England, he wrote 'is perhaps the only great country whose intellectuals are ashamed of their own nationality. In left-wing circles, it is always felt that there is something slightly disgraceful in being an Englishman and that it is a duty to snigger at every English institution, from horse racing to suet puddings.'[31]

Throughout the 1960s and the 1970s, leading intellectuals in the West, such as Daniel Bell, then wrote about the rise of 'adversary culture' – a new class of highly educated, professional elites in the media, the arts, publishing and education who were increasingly trying to win prestige and recognition from other elites not just by signalling their wealth but by their rejection of Western identities, history, culture and ways of life.[32] Whereas the old elite had once stressed the importance of a shared national culture and identity, some members of the new elite have now begun to revolt against what they argue are backward, imperialist and racist societies in the West which are riddled with structures of power and privilege.

Many of these ideas were once encouraged by the likes of Michel Foucault, Jacques Derrida, Herbert Marcuse and other thinkers who essentially saw the traditions, languages, narratives and knowledge of the West as concealing or reflecting power structures that benefited the old elite. For this reason, it was argued, they had to be 'deconstructed' if not dismantled altogether.[33] Drawing on these ideas, today's radical progressives crudely reduce society to a zero-sum competition between different racial, sexual and gender groups, becoming intolerant of views which deviate from or challenge their new orthodoxy. They have become dismissive of free speech and increasingly use political correctness, speech codes or cancel culture to force their beliefs on the rest of society and silence or stigmatize those who question their world view.

Whereas Marxists saw societies through the lens of an economic struggle between powerful and oppressive capitalists on one side and powerless and oppressed workers on the other, radical progressives instead see societies through the lens of an identity struggle between supposedly powerful and privileged identity groups on one side and supposedly powerless and victimized minorities on the other. Whereas whites, heterosexuals, men and the able-bodied are seen as morally inferior oppressors who should be stripped not just of their power and privilege but their social status, sense of esteem and moral worth, a loose alliance of other groups --minorities, women, the disabled, and their highly educated white 'allies' – are seen as morally righteous, superior and virtuous.[34]

The rise of this moral hierarchy, as Greg Lukianoff and Jonathan Haidt point out in their book *The Coddling of the American Mind*, is increasingly dividing Western societies. 'Life is a battle between good people and evil people,' they write. 'Furthermore, there is no escaping the conclusion as to who the evil people are. The main axes of oppression usually point to one intersectional address: straight white males.'[35]

These views, as we noted in Chapter 1, are pushed by progressives who represent somewhere between 13 and 23 per cent of the country, have undergraduate if not postgraduate degrees, are financially secure if not very wealthy, come from privileged families, live in the big cities and university towns and often spend much of their time promoting their elite beliefs on social media platforms such as Twitter.[36]

Whereas almost half of Britain's middle-class professionals say they have heard the word 'woke' and know what it means, not even one-third of people from the working class say the same. Remainers, Labour voters, Londoners and young zoomers are all more likely than Brexit voters, non-Londoners, workers and older boomers to say they know what woke means, to describe themselves as woke, and think that being woke 'is a good thing'.[37] These ideas are also especially strongly concentrated in Britain's most elite schools and universities, as symbolized by the American School in London, which, in 2021, was downgraded by the Office for Standards in Education because of concerns about how radical progressive beliefs were impacting on the quality of teaching and left students feeling unable to speak in class. Parents pay £32,000 a year to send their children to this school.[38]

Only members of the new elite have the money and the connections to send their children to the right schools and universities, to embrace these beliefs and learn the vocabulary which is required to signal this knowledge to others – terms such as cultural appropriation, intersectionality, heteronormative, cisgender, pansexual, white privilege, white guilt, white fragility, allyship. When people use these terms, as Rob Henderson notes, what they are really doing is engaging in a display of status. They are saying, 'I was educated at a top university', 'I have the right values', 'I am morally righteous' and 'I am virtuous, at the top of the new moral hierarchy'.[39]

In fact, highly educated white liberals have become so committed to this new belief system that Professor John McWhorter has called it a 'new religion'.[40] Unlike political ideologies, he argues, radical progressive or 'woke' ideology exhibits all the hallmarks of a religion. It is led by those he calls 'the Elect', highly educated white liberals who portray themselves as the morally righteous bearers of unique wisdom who are fighting to save sacred minorities. The Elect, he continues, engage in superstition by drawing a simplistic straight line from every disparity between different groups to alleged racism while downplaying or ignoring the role of other factors, such as economic inequality or disproportionately high rates of family breakdown in some minority communities. People in the white majority, including children in schools, are urged to 'do the work' by acknowledging and seeking forgiveness for their white privilege, a modern-day original sin, and their complicity in perpetuating racism.

They also have their own anointed high priests, or clergy, who write pseudo-religious texts about white guilt, white fragility and anti-racism that are often free of evidence. Like Christians who put an ichthus (fish) symbol on their car to signal their faith to others, radical progressives use hashtags, Facebook profile pictures and vocabulary to signal their allegiance to these elite beliefs. Progressives routinely treat criticism of their pseudo-religious creed as blasphemous. 'The Elect consider it imperative', writes McWhorter, 'to not only critique those who disagree with their creed, but to seek their punishment and elimination to whatever degree real-life conditions can accommodate. There is an overriding sense that unbelievers must be not just spoken out against, but called out, isolated, and banned.'[41]

This is why others, such as economist Paul Collier, similarly argue how the newly successful people in Western societies today are neither capitalists nor workers,

> they are the well-educated with new skills. They have forged themselves into a new class, meeting at university and developing a new shared identity in which esteem comes from skill. They have even developed a distinctive morality, elevating characteristics such as minority ethnicity and sexual orientation into group identities as victims. On the basis of their distinctive concern for victim groups, they claim moral superiority over the less-well educated.[42]

As the new elite took over the Labour Party, these elite beliefs have also become far more visible in politics. Rather than offering voters broad and unifying narratives around things such as calls for greater equality or social patriotism, in more recent years Labour, like other left-wing parties around the globe, has embraced radical progressivism. By the early 2020s, as writer Ben Cobley charts in his book *The Tribe*, Labour had fully embraced what he calls 'the system of diversity', displaying many of these elite beliefs.[43] Labour and other institutions that are dominated by the new elite increasingly come to see British society in a way that directs favour, status and protection to non-white minorities, women, homosexuals, Muslims and immigrants, while considering whites, men, heterosexuals, Christians and, especially, the English in distinctly unfavourable terms. 'Favoured groups receive protection against criticism and other negativity,' writes Cobley, 'but unfavoured groups receive no such protection, leaving them open to disparagement and generalised disfavour in the public sphere.'[44]

Labour's embrace of radical progressivism is demonstrated by the party developing different manifestos for different groups in British society, and a rulebook which contained 139 mentions of women, 43 of ethnic, 41 of BAME, 26 of gender and 11 of race but only 2 of class, both of which were linked to women and minorities.[45] Unsurprisingly, many of the voters who have abandoned Labour for the Conservatives feel that the left has become more interested in prioritizing immigrants and minorities than the majority (see the next chapter).

None of this is unique to Britain. In the United States, frustrated liberals such as Mark Lilla have tracked how his fellow Democrats have become obsessed with what he calls identity liberalism. 'In recent years,' he wrote, after Trump's Republicans attracted considerable support from white working-class men without degrees, 'American liberalism has slipped into a kind of moral panic about racial, gender and sexual identity that has distorted liberalism's message and prevented it from becoming a unifying force capable of governing.'[46] These changes, as Lilla notes, have not only given rise to a new generation of young, urban, university-educated progressive activists who are narcissistically unaware of conditions outside their own group, and who often appear indifferent to reaching out to other parts of society; they have also entrenched this new moral hierarchy. Whites, workers, rural communities and the religious are increasingly encouraged by this elite belief system – which is now visible across the institutions – to think of themselves as morally inferior groups who often feel that not just their social status, but their very identity are under threat.

The spread of these elite beliefs is now also visible outside of politics and the universities, in business, where 'woke capitalism' is leading multinational corporations to co-opt radical progressivism to try to signal their own sense of moral righteousness and virtue to consumers, albeit while often failing to pay tax or provide rights to workers. In his book *Woke, Inc.*, Vivek Ramaswamy criticizes what he calls the Woke-Industrial Complex, arguing that corporations are now appropriating radical progressive beliefs in the service of profit.[47] It is easier, he argues, for the likes of Coca-Cola or Amazon to preach the virtue of anti-racism or hire diversity consultants to advise their workers how to be 'less white' than it is to address how corporations have hollowed out blue-collar communities and how Dickensian conditions in warehouses undermine the dignity of their workers.

In Britain, this was symbolized by Sainsbury's, in 2020, which, to celebrate Black History Month, tweeted: 'We are proud to celebrate Black History Month together with our Black colleagues. We proudly represent and serve our diverse society and anyone who does not want to shop with an inclusive retailer is welcome to shop elsewhere.'[48] This exercise in virtue-signalling came two years after the company had sought to cut paid breaks, bonuses and premium Sunday pay for workers while its CEO, paid 131 times the pay of an average worker, was revealed to belong to the controversial Invicta tax-avoidance scheme, whereby elites write investments down as losses to claim 40 per cent back through the British taxpayer.[49]

One of the key characteristics of luxury beliefs is that they not only confer social status on members of the elite at little cost to them, but they have profoundly negative effects on people from other groups in society who have to live with their consequences. While the new elite, as we have seen throughout this book, routinely call for things such as mass immigration, hyper-globalization, individual autonomy, looser sexual norms and the removal or weakening of traditional cultural guardrails, such as the family or a strong national identity, they have seldom had to deal with the negative effects of these changes.

Meanwhile, those who have been more likely to lose their jobs, wages, families, communities and sense of dignity and purpose have simultaneously been derided as racists and thickos for clinging to these cultural guardrails or for refusing to subscribe to these elite beliefs.[50] Whether promoted by elites, politicians or CEOs, radical progressives portray white working-class, non-graduate, and older traditionalists as a morally inferior underclass of racists and ignorant bigots. They also portray the nation, to which these groups feel more attached than others and consider an important source of social status, esteem and pride, as institutionally racist and a source of embarrassment and shame.

One way progressives do this is through 'concept creep', expanding the definition of 'racism' so that traditionalists who hold alternative beliefs and challenge the status-quo, such as by advocating a tighter immigration policy, can be stigmatized as 'racist', cancelled and removed from the public square. Ever since the Brexit referendum, researchers have found that the new elite and younger Britons are more likely than others to subscribe to a looser definition of racism than other groups. They are more likely to see a range of actions that are not racist as racist – such as imitating the accent of another group, assuming somebody is of a particular race based on their name or people feeling uncomfortable about somebody speaking another language in Britain. As researchers at YouGov have found, 18–24 year olds are far more likely than their older counterparts to think that disliking people who live in Britain and speak languages other than English in public, or imitating an accent that is associated with another racial group, are racist actions.[51] In this way, by expanding the concept of racism, progressives brand those who disagree with them as racist, which becomes another way for them to signal their virtue and distinguish themselves from the masses below.[52]

In Britain, this too became especially visible in the aftermath of the Brexit referendum when many people in the new elite lined up to try to reassert their sense of moral righteousness and superiority by stigmatizing much of the rest of the country as an uneducated, racist underclass. Brexit voters were 'bigots', 'clowns', 'pretty odd people' who 'led disappointing lives', the 'lumpen mass with . . . half formed thoughts and fully formed prejudices'. 'The English air is as foul as it has been at any point since my childhood,' wrote the Oxford PPE graduate Nick Cohen. 'It is as if the sewers have burst. The Leave campaign has captured the worst of England and channelled it into a know-nothing movement of loud mouths and closed minds.' 'It was a referendum on the modern world,' wrote privately educated Oxford graduate Laurie Penny, 'and yesterday the frightened, parochial lizard-brain of Britain voted out, out, out.' Matthew D'Ancona, another privately educated Oxford graduate, likewise traced the revolt to those 'who just don't much like people of foreign extraction'.[53] Terms such as 'Nazis' and 'gammon' trended on social media, while Labour MP David Lammy compared Britain's pro-Brexit politicians with Adolf Hitler's Nazi Party and proponents of South African apartheid before suggesting that the comparison was 'not strong enough'. The outpouring of hostility was so great that even *The Economist* was repulsed: 'Enlightened liberals, even less tolerant than cultural conservatives, behaved like middle-class passengers forced to sit next to a working-class party on an overcrowded Ryanair flight.'[54]

Meanwhile, across media, education, creative and cultural institutions – which, as we have seen, are disproportionately dominated by the new elite – important symbols of national identity, culture, history and nationhood are routinely branded racist. Examples of things that have been branded racist include but are not limited to: England, the justice system, the prime minister, the home secretary, the police, Oxbridge, the countryside, the Conservative Party, physical education (PE) lessons, science, schools, the Church of England, English cricket, sport, the Barbican, *Top Gear*, *Strictly Come Dancing*, the Royal family and British architecture.[55] In politics, many things that are clearly not racist are branded as such, including Labour's pledge to introduce immigration controls, displaying the Union Jack, voting for the UK Independence Party, voting for Brexit, voting for Boris Johnson and Labour MP Lisa Nandy suggesting her party should 'stand up for British people, stand up for British interests and [will] always put that first'.[56]

'In all of these cases, and more,' write Professors Robert Ford and Maria Sobolewska, who show how highly educated liberals subscribe to looser definitions of racism, 'the strategy employed by identity liberal campaigners has been to expand the definition of racism to include these actions directly or to achieve the same goal indirectly by ascribing racist motives to ambiguous behaviours.'[57]

Unfortunately, radical progressives offer a distorted view of British society which downplays if not ignores the evidence. Contrary to many of their gloomy narratives about the country, much evidence that has emerged in recent years points in the opposite direction. Britain, overall, has become not only a more inclusive country but a much less racist and prejudiced one.

One way social scientists measure prejudice is by asking people whether they feel comfortable with the idea of one of their relatives marrying somebody from a different group – which is a so-called 'social distance' measure. Using this measure, serious, rigorous, peer-reviewed academic studies have now tracked a sharp decline in levels of racial prejudice since the 1980s, finding that large majorities of British people feel entirely comfortable with these intergroup relationships. 'Taken together,' summarizes academic Ingrid Storm and her colleagues, who analysed British Social Attitudes survey data, 'the results suggest that racial boundaries between whites, blacks and Asians have blurred in recent decades, and continue to do so. Far fewer people express opposition to intermarriage with other ethnic groups.'[58] Similarly, in 2020, amid the George Floyd protests, the reliable pollster Ipsos-MORI found that 90 per cent of British people have no problem with their child marrying somebody from a different ethnic or religious group, up from 75 per cent in 2009.[59]

Interestingly, while radical progressives routinely frame the white majority as racist and intolerant, it is often minorities who express the strongest levels of opposition to the idea of one of their relatives marrying across group lines – such as the six in ten British Indians who would oppose one of their relatives marrying a British Muslim, the four in ten British Indians who would oppose a relative marrying somebody who is black British, the four in ten British black Africans who would oppose a relative marrying a British Muslim, or the significant numbers of British Pakistanis and Bangladeshis who would oppose a relative marrying somebody who is white British or black British.[60]

And while the white British majority have become increasingly liberal in their views on women's rights and same-sex couples, British Muslims are significantly more likely than others to think that 'wives should always obey their husbands', that homosexuality should be illegal and that it is unacceptable for homosexuals to teach children.[61] Minorities, in other words, are just as likely, if not more so, to voice prejudiced views as white Britons, revealing how these crude narratives which contrast a racist and morally inferior white majority with virtuous minorities are usually wide of the mark.

Many of the narratives that circulate widely among the new elite also downplay or ignore the remarkable softening of British public attitudes towards issues such as minority rights, or what academics call the 'populist paradox' in the new politics. At the same time as many voters rallied behind populism, Brexit and Boris Johnson, the country overall has become more relaxed about immigration, minority rights and Britishness.[62] The populist paradox is reflected not only in falling levels of racial prejudice but in widespread public support for welcoming refugees who are fleeing war and persecution – such as the two-thirds of British people who felt the country should welcome Hong Kongers fleeing China, the more than seven in ten who felt the same way about Afghan interpreters and the almost eight in ten who felt the same way about refugees from Ukraine.[63]

Many of these findings are curiously absent in progressive narratives that portray Britain as institutionally racist, defined as a system in which racism is deeply embedded in laws, regulations and institutions. There is certainly no doubt that some people from some minority groups experience discrimination in some areas of British life. They are more likely than white Britons to say they experience discrimination and, in recent years, a series of gold standard studies, known as 'meta-analyses', have found that British black Caribbeans, British black Africans and British Pakistanis face discrimination in Britain's labour and rental markets (though, regarding the latter, they find a sharp decline in recent years).[64]

But, at the same time, the picture is far more complicated than many people imply. British black African, British Chinese, British Indian and British Asian children routinely outperform their white

British peers in the education system, as we noted in Chapter 1. They are usually more likely than their white counterparts to get good GCSE grades and strong A-levels and to progress to university, where they often outperform white Britons.[65] Between 2007 and 2021, consistently, white British children were the least likely of all to progress into the higher education system. In 2021, only one-third did compared to almost half of black British children, 55 per cent of British Asians and 72 per cent of British Chinese.[66]

While historically university applicants from minority groups were less likely than their white counterparts to be offered places at elite universities, and less likely to leave with a first-class or upper-second-class degree, this picture has now changed significantly. In 2010, white British students entered Britain's elite universities at 2.4 times the rate of black British students but, by 2020, this had declined to a ratio of just 1.1 to 1.[67] In 2021, a record number of British black, British Asian and other minority ethnic applicants were accepted into Oxford and comprised 24 per cent of the UK intake.[68]

In health, similarly, the picture is complex. White British people have a lower life expectancy at birth than every other ethnic group, while British black Africans enjoy some of the longest life expectancy. In 2021, as the Office for National Statistics pointed out, white Britons had a statistically significant higher (age-standardized) mortality rate from all causes of death than any other ethnic group and had higher mortality rates than most other groups for the leading causes of death – dementia, Alzheimer's, most common cancers and also suicide. While British Bangladeshis, British Pakistanis and British Indians have higher mortality rates from things such as heart disease, the overall story is far more nuanced than many imply.[69]

In the economy, too, throughout the last decade British black, British Bangladeshi and British Pakistani citizens were more likely to experience unemployment, but while the median hourly pay of white Britons was marginally higher than it was for British black Caribbeans and British black Africans, it was lower than pay for British mixed ethnic groups, British Indians and British Chinese. British Indians usually enjoy higher median pay than other groups in society.[70]

And when it comes to longer-term social mobility, namely, the extent to which people move within or between social classes, the picture is once again nuanced. Over the last fifty years, respected Professor Yaojun Li points out, minority ethnic children from families of unskilled workers were more likely to achieve upward mobility than their white counterparts. 'Overall', he writes, 'there were more signs of social progress than social regress. We have witnessed a dynamic society in the last 50 years, with some ethnic minority groups like British Indian and British Chinese now doing very well and even better than the White ethnic group, and with other groups catching up.'[71]

In the institutions, meanwhile, minorities are either well represented or rapidly catching up with their white counterparts. In 2020, British Asians and blacks were over-represented in the NHS, where half of NHS doctors came from minority backgrounds – including 44 per cent of the most senior doctors. In Westminster, contrary to claims of systemic discrimination, there is huge variation across government departments, with minorities representing 28 per cent of staff in the Treasury and 25 per cent in the Department for Health and Social Care but less than 5 per cent in the Ministry of Defence, though almost every department has recorded sharp increases in recent years.

In the House of Commons, the 2019 election delivered the most diverse parliament in history, while Boris Johnson's cabinet and then Liz Truss's cabinet were among the most ethnically diverse in history. While minorities remain less visible at the most senior levels of business, by 2022 more than 90 per cent of leading companies had at least one person from a minority group on their board, up from 47 per cent in 2016, while the share of directors from a minority background is also rising sharply.[72] None of this is to deny that racism and discrimination exist in British society, much as they do in every society around the globe. But it is to say that the available evidence does not support the dreary narratives about modern Britain that are pushed by radical progressives, used to stigmatize much of the country.

Many of these radically progressive beliefs are now clearly having a profound impact on our politics, fuelling the polarization and populism that went mainstream over the last decade. Many of the people who have abandoned Labour and the Conservatives in recent years for populism have told researchers they felt they had been relegated to second-class status in British society, no longer considered as morally worthy as graduates, minorities and immigrants, who they often felt were routinely prioritized by Labour and the elite.[73] Seen through their eyes, the country's new ruling class appear more interested in helping immigrants than the British majority and use 'anti-racism' campaigns to try to silence and stigmatize those who hold different views.

'In many ways', writes academic Justin Gest, who conducted one of the most comprehensive studies of the people who abandoned the mainstream for populism over the last ten years, 'UKIP harvested enormous political capital among alienated unionists and leftists who felt like the Labour Party abandoned their interests after aligning with London's cosmopolitan financial class and ethnic minorities.'[74] In focus groups, too, after Boris Johnson's victory in 2019, many people conveyed their view that, far from feeling respected, they felt that the new elite and the young zoomer graduates from Generation Z who often had limited life experience did not see them as equal members of the community; they were 'looking down' on the 'little people' who shared neither their elite education nor their elite beliefs.[75]

Many of these voters feel intensely angry about how, in their eyes, they are now routinely portrayed by the new elite as 'misguided', 'ignorant' or 'stupid', which has stoked even more resentment of the institutions which exclude their values and voice. In their own words, they see the Labour Party as being dominated by metropolitan, graduate elites who are obsessed with political correctness and who are 'more concerned with telling the people they were supposed to represent that they were "wrong" than with trying to understand the conditions under which they were living and their responses to these conditions'.[76]

These views are especially strongly held among older voters who have switched from left to right in recent years. When one study asked them to list their main criticisms of Labour, they certainly said they did not trust the party to run the economy and that Jeremy Corbyn had been 'useless'. But they also expressed a broader exasperation – that Labour had 'changed for the worse in the past two or three years', that 'whenever it's in government, it messes things up', and 'it allowed too many immigrants to come to Britain'.[77] Many also did not believe Labour really is interested in people like them.

While 60 per cent of the older voters who abandoned Labour want Britain to prioritize pensioners, only 17 per cent think Labour is prioritizing these voters. 'The point here', concluded a report, commissioned by none other than Tony Blair to try and make sense of who had abandoned his party, 'is that Labour's reputation among millions of older voters has been shot to pieces ... Pensioners rank second in their own list of priorities but only seventh out of nine in their perception of Labour's priorities, behind immigrants and LGBTQ+ voters, and only ahead of white Britons and the rich.'[78]

While Labour was once seen in the mid-twentieth century as a party for the working class, during the 1990s and the 2000s the party's image steadily deteriorated, even as the number of working-class identifiers remained stable. By the 2010s, while only 63 per cent of white people felt Labour looked after working-class people's interests, a noticeably higher 80 per cent felt the party was looking after the interests of blacks and Asians.[79] Nor was this helped by how Labour removed many working-class and non-graduate voices from the party.

There are also good reasons to expect this tension to grow in the years ahead, as more radical progressive Labour elites double down on their liberal cosmopolitan and progressive values. In America, amid the so-called 'Great Awokening', whereby highly educated liberals have become even more strongly committed to their radical views, the academic Zach Goldberg finds that some members of the new elite have become so strongly committed to radical progressive values that they now feel more positively towards minorities than they do towards members of their own group. He finds many highly educated white liberals exhibit what is known as 'pro-outgroup bias'; they are the only group in America who feel more positively towards racial and ethnic minorities than their own majority group. It is not hard to see how this could trigger an even stronger political backlash in the years ahead.[80]

Though few Labour politicians have been willing to speak out, it is clear that the emergence of a far more radical 'woke' politics and more aggressive identity politics is playing a key role in this, fuelling a sense among many voters they are now at the bottom of the new moral hierarchy in British society. As Professor Geoffrey Evans and Zack Grant have shown in a working paper, in recent years white working-class voters came to believe that Labour more closely looks after non-white interests than working-class interests, particularly in comparison to the new elite and minorities. Furthermore, the belief that Labour now represents minorities more closely than it does the working class has been a significant reason why voters from the white working class have shunned Labour. This, they argue, has not just weakened Labour's support at recent elections but introduced a new and more profound electoral dilemma for Labour and the centre-left. Whereas the old dilemma for the centre-left was how to unify the new middle-class graduate elite and the working class around shared economic interests, the new dilemma for the centre-left is how to reconcile its rapidly diversifying electorate with a growing sense among the white working class that the new elite's heavy focus on diversity is now coming at their expense. Many workers feel deeply alienated by many of the narratives about Britain that are promoted by radical progressives who now dominate the Labour Party and many of the institutions, such as the media and universities. The many voters who Labour lost over the last decade simply do not share the belief that their British identity is a source of embarrassment, that British history is overwhelmingly negative and that Britain is deeply racist. There are no easy answers for Labour; the more its progressive activists double down on this more radical ideology, the more they will alienate the white working class.

Some Labour sympathizers suggest the party can essentially ignore the steadily declining white working class in favour of doubling down on the new elite and minorities. But this is simply not a viable strategy if the party wants to return to power. The white working class remains a large block of voters, representing 24 per cent of all voters in Britain and 18 per cent of Labour voters. Crucially, as we will see in the next chapter, they are also more evenly distributed around the country than the graduates and minorities, who are usually based in the cities. And if, as Evans and Grant point out, woke identity politics cannot work for the Democrats in a country like America, where non-white voters represent 40 per cent of the entire electorate, then it is highly unlikely to work in Britain, where non-white voters represent just 13 per cent of the electorate.

The populist revolts that have erupted in British politics and elsewhere, then, have not only given voters an opportunity to reassert their values and their voice; they have also offered an opportunity to reassert their sense of virtue and moral worth against an increasingly radical new elite. Unless these feelings are addressed, seriously, they will almost certainly continue to provide ongoing potential support for populists who, by their very nature, claim to speak on behalf of a plain, common and virtuous people against what they argue has become a politically correct, technocratic, highly educated and out-of-touch 'woke' elite who neither respect nor particularly like the people around them.

Conclusion: Counter-Revolution

Today, there are two competing views of British politics. There are those who argue that because Brexit has been delivered and Britain has left the European Union, all the political turmoil and turbulence of the last decade now belongs firmly in the past. Amid high inflation, a cost-of-living crisis and low rates of economic growth, politics will return to debates about the economy, the state and redistribution.

Then there are those who, instead, argue that all the revolts of the last decade represent the beginning, not the end, of a more profound realignment of politics, which is visible not just in Brexit Britain but across the West. Seen through this lens, irrespective of who wins the next general election, or even the one after that, because of the deeper divides that we have explored in this book, there will remain considerable potential for movements and leaders which mobilize opposition to the new elite.

In this book, we have encountered more evidence to support the latter than the former. When we look at the new politics through a wide lens, we see that the rise of national populism, Brexit and Boris Johnson's very different brand of post-Brexit conservatism were not just powered by the latest news cycle, policies, leaders or campaigns. Instead, they all tapped into a much deeper, longer-running and intensifying counter-revolution against the new elite, which has been building for decades and may still have a long way to run.

Politics, it is often said, moves in cycles. There are times when one political party or set of ideas dominates for a long period of time before being swept aside and replaced by a new zeitgeist. Historians would point to the long period of Tory rule in the early 1800s, the liberal ascendancy in the middle of the nineteenth century, the return of the Conservatives in the late nineteenth century, the return of the liberals in the early 1900s, their replacement by the Labour Party, and then, after the Second World War, the postwar consensus which lasted until the 1970s. More recently, between 1979 and the 2010s, as we have seen, politics entered a new cycle in which Margaret Thatcher and Tony Blair presided over a new revolution which was defined by its strong commitment to a radical economic and cultural liberalism.

But, ever since then, Britain has been in the grip of a growing public backlash against this political project and the new elite who have overseen it. This counter-revolution, as we will see in this final chapter, has not just drawn strength from the economically left behind. It has connected, strongly, with a very broad and cross-class coalition of voters who have been pushed together by the three beliefs we have explored throughout this book – they no longer feel their values are respected by the new graduate elite; they no longer feel their voice is represented in the institutions; and they no longer feel that, relative to others, their group is recognized as having the same amount of social status, prestige, dignity and moral worth.

All three of these drivers – values, voice, and virtue – will continue to have an enormous impact in the years ahead. This is not only because they reflect the failings of our current politics but because they are anchored in an intensifying education divide between the country's minority graduate class and the non-graduate majority. This growing rift between a more strongly liberal if not radically progressive graduate elite and much of the rest of the country will continue to shape people's values, the extent to which they feel their voice is heard in the institutions and whether they are being treated with respect.

It will also shape how these groups react to new debates that will increasingly influence politics in the years ahead – debates about rising sexual and gender diversity, how we interpret British history, the role of Islam in British society and identity 'woke' politics.

Looking forwards, and keeping the evidence we encountered in Chapter 3 in mind, it is hard if not impossible to see how these debates will not further prise apart the younger, middle-class, professional and urban liberal graduates in the big cities and the university towns, who are united by their cosmopolitan values, from older, blue-collar and non-graduate voters in the smaller towns, coastal areas and country-side who are instead united by their traditionalist values and oppose the Londonization of the rest of the country.

Contrary to the misleading narratives we encountered in Chapter 1, the emergence of this blowback is intimately wrapped up with the choices that were made by the new elite over the last fifty years – the decision to rebuild Britain around a highly unstable, London-centric, and damaging model of hyper-globalization, the rapid onset and acceleration of a new era of mass immigration, the hollowing-out of the country's national democracy and the rise of a homogeneous and largely indistinguishable political class in Westminster.

While all these changes reflected the values of the new elite, they simultaneously alienated much of the rest of the country. In response, many voters have been trying to swing the pendulum back towards a more traditionalist vision of the country: a country where politics makes more room for the values of the missing majority, where voices that have been purged from the institutions are brought back into the national conversation and where Britain's leaders bestow as much respect on the majority as they currently lavish on the elite graduate class and minorities.

A CROSS-CLASS COALITION

For these reasons, the counter-revolution has, so far, appealed to three specific groups of voters in British society who will likely remain receptive to similar revolts in the years ahead, especially if the Conservative Party under Rishi Sunak remain disconnected from this unfolding realignment.

The first is the non-graduate majority. Like their counterparts across the West, people who do not belong to the graduate class have increasingly been drifting from left to right. Disillusioned with the new elite, twenty years ago they began their journey by drifting into apathy and giving up on politics before switching to Nigel Farage's national populist crusade and then Brexit. In the aftermath, when it became apparent that much of the political class had little interest in respecting Brexit, they switched to the post-Brexit Conservatives Theresa May and Boris Johnson, who at least appeared interested in offering them a break from the revolution, by promising to see Brexit through.

Between the eras of Margaret Thatcher and David Cameron, there had never been much of a difference in the Conservative Party's levels of support between graduates and non-graduates. But, from 2015, this changed as the party began hoovering up votes from people who share neither the backgrounds nor values of the new elite. By 2017, the Conservatives were mobilizing a larger share of their support from people who did not have degrees than from people who had them. This shift then continued in 2019, when, remarkably, the Old Etonian and Oxford graduate Boris Johnson became the leader of the country's non-graduate majority, tapping into many of their values which had long been neglected by the new elite.

In this way, Britain, like America, is becoming more deeply polarized around the education fault line, and this too now looks set to remain as a permanent feature of the new politics. At the last election, in 2019, while almost seven in ten of the country's university graduates voted for the liberal left, more than six in ten non-graduates voted for the Conservative or Brexit parties. The sheer scale of this divide becomes even more dramatic when it is looked at by generation; while more than six in ten older Britons who have not gone to university voted Conservative, only one in five 18–34-year-olds who have a degree did the same.[1]

Across Europe and America, not just in Brexit Britain, graduates are routinely voting for parties which reflect their very distinctive liberal cosmopolitan if not radically progressive values. Having a degree and cosmopolitan values has now emerged as one of the strongest predictors of whether people support green and liberal parties, much like it is a reliable predictor of whether or not people are supporting the Liberal Democrats and the Greens in Britain. At the same time, people who do not have degrees and who hold traditionalist values are far more likely to vote for national populists and ultra-conservatives, which appeal to their values and promise to reassert the voice of the majority against minorities, especially on cultural issues.

The second key group in the counter-revolution are older voters, though especially the older baby boomers who are either in or approaching retirement and usually do not have a degree. These older voters came of age before the revolution swept through British society, before the rapid expansion of the universities, before Westminster doubled down on the graduate class, before hyper-globalization, mass immigration and EU integration, and before left and right converged around the same liberal consensus. Shaped by their memories of a very different Britain and by their traditionalist values, these older voters feel like strangers in their own country. They neither recognize nor like the values which dominate politics and the prevailing culture and resent the new elite for showing insufficient regard for people like them who hold different views.

Ever since Brexit, many people in the new elite have become fond of dismissing these older voters as a rapidly diminishing part of Britain. This was symbolized by the 'Deatherendum' website, which provided live forecasts of the likely result at a second Brexit referendum based on how many older and mainly pro-Brexit voters were passing away.[2] But these simplistic and insulting accounts ignore the fact that in Britain and across the West older voters are quickly becoming one of the most electorally powerful and fastest-growing groups in politics. Globally, 2020 was the first year on record when there were more pensioners than under-five-year-olds on the planet, while in Britain, because of lower fertility rates among the young and rising life expectancy among the old, the number of pensioners in the country will now surge – from 12 million at the Brexit referendum to 20 million by the 2060s.[3] The grey vote, in other words, will only become far more important in politics, not less.

And these voters, too, have been moving rightwards in politics, sitting in the driving seat of populism, Brexit and Boris Johnson's majority. The Conservative Party was always more popular among the over-45s than with the under-45s. But over the last decade, the age gap in the party's support expanded to the largest on record. Remarkably, when the Conservatives came to power in 2019, they held a

21-point lead over Labour among people in their fifties, a 35-point lead among people in their sixties, and a 53-point among people in their seventies. Since the days of Thatcher, the Conservative Party's lead over Labour among the over-55s has rocketed, from about 15 points to closer to 40 points.[4] This handed the counter-revolution another advantage.

It also weakened Labour and the left. At the last election, Labour won fewer votes from older Britons than at any time since Neil Kinnock's defeat to John Major in 1992. And this is not just about Brexit. Over the last decade, between 2010 and 2019, despite the rising number of older voters in the country, the Labour Party lost around 1 million of them, while the Conservatives gained around 3 million.[5] While many of these older voters are financially secure if not wealthy, it's their cultural values – on immigration, Europe, diversity, identity and Britishness – which have led them to join the counter-revolution. Like non-graduates, they too have been trying to push back against the cosmopolitan and progressive mindset which dominates not just the Labour Party but much of the political class in Westminster and many other institutions which rely heavily on graduates – from the media to the universities, from the creative industries to the cultural institutions.

Ever since Labour's historic defeat in 2019, research on the older voters who abandoned the party has found that, unlike those who stayed loyal, they were not just far more supportive of leaving the EU but also far more sceptical of immigration and its effects on the country, more likely to think 'immigrants today are a burden on our country because they take our jobs, housing and healthcare', more likely to describe themselves as nationalists, more opposed to Labour's decision to campaign for a second Brexit referendum, more likely to think Labour is incompetent, and still very distrustful of the party when it comes to immigration.[6]

And many of these concerns remain visible today. Ask the British whether immigration over the last ten years was too high, too low or about right, and while 54 per cent of all voters think it was too high, 75 per cent of older voters think this way. Ask them which party they trust to handle immigration, and only 12 per cent say Labour.

Though it is often overlooked, these older voters are also far more likely to vote than their younger millennial and zoomer counterparts. At all three of the most recent elections – in 2015, 2017 and 2019 – Britain's baby boomers were around 30 points more likely to vote than young zoomers from Generation-Z.[7] This 'generation gap' in turnout has also been widening over time, reinforced by the fact that Britain's boomers are a larger generation than both the Millennials and Zoomers. They are not only more likely to vote, but there are more of them. Younger voters care a great deal about issues such as climate change, gender diversity, Black Lives Matter and anti-racism but they are also much less likely than older voters to cast a ballot.

Whereas in 1964, the turnout gap between the young and old was only 3 points, by the mid-2010s it had increased to 25 points.[8] This is why, at key moments like the Brexit referendum, the counter-revolution also benefited from lower-than-average turnout in the young, trendy, hipster districts, such as London's Hackney and Shoreditch, while turnout was noticeably higher in older and more working-class areas, where people, clearly, felt more motivated.[9] Alienating these politically committed older voters by telling them they do not matter, they represent the past, or by insulting their decisions at the ballot box appears a rather curious strategy.

The third key group to join the counter-revolution have been the many working-class voters who share this sense that their values have been cast aside, that they no longer have a voice in the institutions and are now looked down on by radical progressives in the Labour Party and the new elite because of who they are. Their distrust of the new elite has also been stoked by the fact that while they had long suspected hyper-globalization was damaging their communities, and mass immigration was only having small or barely noticeable economic benefits, they were derided as the closed-minded ones who could not possibly understand the intricacies of globalization. But, in the end, as we noted in Chapter 2, they were right all along. Hyper-globalization has had many negative effects on people like them.

While many people in the new elite are fond of talking about these working-class voters as though they represent a small and rapidly diminishing share of Labour's electorate, this too is misleading. For much of the last twenty years, the working-class Labour voters who lean left on the economy and right on culture consistently outnumbered the university-educated Labour cosmopolitans who lean left on the economy and hold strongly liberal views on culture – often by a margin of at least two to one.[10] Working-class traditionalists are also distributed far more evenly across the country than liberal cosmopolitans. Alienating these voters by ignoring their values, excluding their voice, and telling them they belong at the bottom of a moral hierarchy because they happen to be white, male or straight, has poured petrol over this growing counter-revolution against the elite and, as we saw in Chapter 5, is making it harder not easier for the Labour Party and the left to win them back.

The decision taken by these workers to abandon the Labour Party has also had a deeper effect on our politics, by steadily reducing the power of social class. Throughout much of the twentieth century, one unwritten law was that people in the working class vote for the left, while people in the middle class vote for the right. There were always exceptions, of course, including the one-third of workers who broke with convention by voting Conservative.

'What do you say to the elections in the factory districts?' Friedrich Engels asked Karl Marx in the 1860s, after Britain's urban workers shattered their dreams by voting for the Tories. 'Once again', he continued, 'the proletariat has discredited itself terribly ... It cannot be denied that the increase of working-class voters has brought the Tories more than their simple percentage increase; it has improved their relative position.'[11]

Yet, for much of the next 140 years, class was the main driver of how the British voted, so much so in fact that Professor Peter Pulzer, in 1967, famously declared that class was the basis of British politics.[12] But nobody would say that today.

As the revolution swept through the country, as the new debates about immigration, Europe and national identity cut across the old fault lines, and as Labour purged itself of blue-collar and non-graduate voices, the party suffered a more profound breakdown in its relationship with the working class. In 1970, when Ted Heath defeated Harold Wilson, two-thirds of all voters had belonged to the working class and nearly six in ten had voted for Labour. By 2019, when Boris Johnson defeated Jeremy Corbyn, just over four in ten voters belonged to the working class, but only one-third of them voted for Labour. Over the same period, the share of Labour's vote that was composed of the working class and their families collapsed from 80 per cent to just 40 per cent.[13]

This too is the direct result of the choices Labour made when it was in office – the decision to double down on mass immigration, to prioritize the new elite, to embrace the EU and to install a far more technocratic and managerial politics. By the end of the Blair and Brown years, the party's relationship with the working class had come to resemble a bad marriage that was running out of steam and heading for a costly divorce. And, like at the end of most long-term relationships, the resentment between the two sides had not emerged suddenly but had been building up slowly over many years. Contrary to Blair's fateful miscalculation that Britain's workers had nowhere else to go, between the late 1990s and the mid-2010s growing numbers of them did find a place to go. They either abandoned politics or switched to populists, Brexit and then the Conservatives.

Between 2005 and 2015 – long before anybody had heard of Brexit – New Labour was already losing considerable ground in areas that were filled with these blue-collar, non-graduate and older white voters. Then, between 2015 and 2019, Labour's support continued to decline most sharply in the same areas – where people no longer related to the EU, felt under threat from mass immigration and loathed the new graduate elite in the institutions.[14] Those who switched to Farage's national populism were mainly driven by their cultural values and distrust of the new ruling class; they strongly opposed Britain's EU membership, they strongly opposed mass immigration and they strongly opposed the liberal consensus in Westminster.[15]

Contrary to misleading tropes, however, they were not all disgruntled Thatcherites; many had voted for Labour in the past. They often leaned left on the economy, believing that Britain's economy is rigged to favour the rich, and right on culture, believing that the political class prioritizes immigrants and minorities over the majority. By tapping into their cultural values, Farage mobilized the most working-class electorate in British politics and further eroded Labour's bond with them.

By the time Jeremy Corbyn was then crushed by Boris Johnson in 2019, this relationship had become even weaker. Labour's average share of the vote across England and Wales crashed by 9 points; but it collapsed by a remarkable 14 points in the most solidly working-class seats that Labour was defending and which had often been buckling for a while.[16]About four in ten people who voted for Boris Johnson in 2019 had voted for Labour in the past.[17]

These areas did not just vote differently from their Labour MPs at the Brexit referendum, they had been cut adrift by the new elite for the best part of half a century. Once they saw an opportunity to reassert their values and their voice they grabbed it with both hands. And this was also true in the northern Red Wall, where the erosion of Labour's support had been visible for a long time, not just since the Brexit referendum. In 1987, the Labour Party had averaged 50 per cent of the vote in Red Wall seats and 30 per cent of the vote across England, giving the party a Red Wall dividend of 20 points. But over the next thirty-two years this dividend steadily declined – to 18 points in 2001, 13 points in 2010, 11 points in 2015, 9 points in 2017 and then just 3 points in 2019.[18] Brexit and the unpopularity of Jeremy Corbyn certainly contributed to this trend, but the trend was already under way.

All these profound changes help to explain why the class foundations of British politics have been giving way. Back in the 1970s, the Conservatives had enjoyed a commanding 45-point lead among the middle class, while Labour enjoyed a 20-point lead among workers. This left a striking 'class gap' of 65 points. But over the next forty years – as hyper-globalization, mass immigration and EU membership cut across these old loyalties, and as Labour became obsessed with the graduate class – this gap collapsed to 28 points in 1997, 14 points in 2015 and then, in 2019, it disappeared altogether.[19] As the power of class collapsed, Boris Johnson was able to mobilize a much larger share of blue-collar Britain than Thatcher had ever managed.

While some on the left have since argued that Labour's losses among the working class at the 2019 election have been exaggerated, the independent British Election Study tells a different story: 18 per cent of Labour voters in routine, semi-routine or supervisory blue-collar jobs defected to the Conservatives, compared to 11 per cent of Labour voters overall. Even after the tumultuous decade of the 2010s, in other words, even after the legacy of the Global Financial Crash and nearly a decade of Tory rule, so strong were their cultural concerns and their utter exasperation with Westminster that workers handed the Conservatives a 21-point lead.[20]

It was all three of these groups – the country's non-graduates, pensioners and a large chunk of the working class – who have been leading the counter-revolution against the new elite, pushing through national populism, Brexit and then Boris Johnson to try and reassert their values, voice and sense of virtue against this ruling class.

THE EMERGING LIBERAL BACKLASH

The easiest way forward for the new elite today is to reply, seriously, to the grievances that have been expressed through these revolts. Unfortunately, however, rather than address them, many people prefer to fall back on misleading narratives, including the fashionable idea that demography is destiny. Instead of thinking about how they might better recognize the values of traditionalists, restore their voice in the institutions and award the majority as much respect as they award to themselves and minorities, the new elite point to trends which, they argue, mean they do not need to win these voters back at all.

They point to the fact that while the country's workers, non-graduates and pensioners have been moving from left to right, many other groups have been moving from right to left. All the groups which are central to emerging cosmopolitan alliance – the new middle-class graduate elite, the slightly larger graduate class, the rapidly rising number of minority ethnic voters, the young millennials and the even younger zoomers – are beginning to mobilize a counter-revolution to the counter-revolution – a completely new cycle which, some argue, will get the revolution back on track.

Much like the rise of Barack Obama in 2008, commentators talk excitedly about a completely new electoral realignment, the rise of a new electoral coalition that will push back against populism, Brexit and more than a decade of Conservative Party dominance.

There is no doubt that these trends are taking place. Almost all these groups are united in believing that Brexit was the wrong decision, in wanting their leaders to rejoin or forge a closer relationship with the European Union, in thinking more positively about immigration, minorities and diversity and supporting a more assertive 'anti-racism'. While traditionalists spent the last decade trying to reassert their values and voice in a system they feel no longer represents them, many of these other voters are now actively searching for ways to reassert *their* values and voice in a system they feel has been taken away from them. They feel much like traditionalists felt before Brexit.

Much like their counterparts across the West, three groups in particular have been reshuffling themselves politically, lining up in larger numbers behind Labour and the liberal left to try and stage this backlash to the populist revolts of the last decade.

The first are the new elite and the slightly larger graduate class who are moving rapidly to the left in politics, doubling down on their liberal cosmopolitan and progressive values. This shift had already been visible in the early 2000s, when Britain's liberal graduates in urban university seats began turning in larger numbers to Nick Clegg and the Liberal Democrats, to express their cultural liberalism. Since then, particularly after Nick Clegg joined with David Cameron in a coalition government, the country's graduate class have been switching to Labour in much larger numbers.

Whereas Labour used to poll more strongly among people who did not have a degree, it has continued to morph into a party for the graduate class. Jeremy Corbyn was heavily defeated by Boris Johnson in 2019 but left the election with a strong lead among graduates and, remarkably, a 35-point lead among the youngest 18–34-year-old graduates.[21] Had only the country's most highly educated people been able to vote at the last election, then Jeremy Corbyn, not Boris Johnson, would have overseen the Covid-19 pandemic, the war against Russia in Ukraine, high inflation and a cost-of-living crisis.

These trends have helped the Labour Party almost completely

capture Britain's university towns, where, as we have seen, the young zoomer students and their liberal professors lean heavily to the left. Of the country's seventy-seven seats with the largest number of university students, all but ten were won at the last election by the liberal left.[22] Support for the Conservatives increased across the country but fell back in these university seats.

The political implications of this shift can also be seen across England's southern shires – in seats such as Guildford, Esher and Walton, Beaconsfield and Hitchin and Harpenden – where highly educated professionals from the new elite are spilling out of London into the commuter suburbs. It is in these areas where, over the last decade, the Conservatives suffered their sharpest losses and where, looking ahead, many southern Conservative MPs will almost certainly pay the price of this unfolding realignment, losing their seats to their Labour or Liberal Democrat rivals.[23] Elsewhere, meanwhile, in the young, diverse and densely populated seats such as London's Hackney, Streatham, Tottenham, Tooting, Bristol West and Brighton, Labour and liberal left parties will likely cement their already formidable electoral majorities.

The second key group, reinforcing this trend, are Britain's millennials and zoomers, who have also been drifting leftwards. Unlike the older baby boomers, who came of age in a country before the revolution, the young zoomers, who were born after 1996, have known nothing other than the revolution. Many were not even born when Tony Blair came to power and will have no memory of his time in office. Most were in primary school when mass immigration and the Global Financial Crash began, and they were too young to vote in the Brexit referendum if not also the 2017 and 2019 general elections.

Having spent their entire lives online, they have come of age in a country and a world where not just the new elite but the celebrity class, social media influencers, schools and universities are passionately supportive of liberal cosmopolitan and progressive values, making clear their support for EU membership, immigration, diversity, gender identity theory, anti-racism, pulling down historical statues, 'decolonizing' reading lists, expressing their allegiance to social movements such as Black Lives Matter and embracing the elite beliefs we explored in Chapter 5. In 2022, one report by think tank Don't Divide Us also found that nearly one in four local councils in England and Wales who replied to their request for information are encouraging schools in their area to promote 'critical race theory' beliefs, teaching children about more radically progressive concepts such as white privilege, cultural appropriation and a divisive brand of identity politics.

Consistently, Britain's millennials and zoomers are far more supportive of the European Union, immigration, diversity, expanding rights for women and racial, sexual and gender minorities and BLM. Support for BLM is roughly twice as high among the young zoomers as among the older boomers, while zoomers are twice as likely as boomers to say they feel 'ashamed' of Britain's imperial past.[24] These are not the only differences. Young zoomers are also far more likely to share the new elite's much thinner or civic sense of Britishness, which around 40 per cent of them do. 'Younger generations', concludes the independent National Centre for Social Research,

> are less likely than their elders to think that ascribed factors such as being born in Britain, being Christian or having British ancestry matter in determining whether or not someone is 'really' British. Consequently, as older generations die out, we would expect to see a gradual increase in the proportion of people who think that only civic, and not ethnic, factors matter.[25]

Young Britons today also feel much less attached to the traditions, symbols and institutions of British nationhood, such as the monarchy. In 2020, for the first time on record, a plurality of young Britons favoured replacing the monarchy with an elected head of state.[26] Like the new elite, they are also less likely than their older counterparts to voice their pride in Britain's national identity and to see this identity as an important part of who they are; whereas half of the older boomers feel 'very proud' to be British, not even one in five zoomers feel the same way. Rigorous academic studies have also tracked a long-running decline in feelings of national pride in Britain, as each generation has replaced the last.[27] This suggests that debates about British identity and who we are will likely intensify in the years ahead as traditionalists worry that their distinctive and thicker sense of British identity is slipping away while young zoomers promote a much thinner and more civic vision of who we are, which will most likely be wrapped around the universal liberal themes of multiculturalism and diversity.

Like the graduate class, these younger Britons are also pushing back against the rise of national populism, Brexit and the Conservatives, which they see as violating their liberal cosmopolitan and progressive values. At the last election, remarkably, nearly eight in ten 18–24-year-old zoomers voted for the liberal left, while two-thirds of the older boomers voted for the right.[28] Some might shrug their shoulders and say the young have always voted for the left while the old have always voted for the right. 'A man who has not been a socialist before twenty-five', so the saying goes, 'has no heart; but if he remains one after twenty-five, he has no head'.[29] But this is misleading.

We have never seen an age divide like this before. Rewind the clock to the era of Ted Heath, Margaret Thatcher and Michael Foot, in the 1970s and the 1980s, and young Britons were not more likely than the old to support the left. It was between Tony Blair's final majority in 2005 and Boris Johnson's majority in 2019 when a far more dramatic age divide in British politics opened, when Labour's 6-point advantage among the young spiralled into the nearly 40-point advantage that the party has today.[30] This has led many to argue that it is only a matter of time until the pendulum swings back in the other direction, back towards the cosmopolitan and progressive values of a new generation.

Young women have also been central to this trend and are now pulling away from other groups in terms of both their rate of participation in the higher education system and their much stronger commitment to social liberalism. In 2022, 51 per cent of young women progressed to university by the age of nineteen, compared to only 38 per cent of boys. And this gap has been widening over time, from around 8 points a decade ago to 13 points today. So too has the rate at which women are being accepted into the most elite institutions and graduating with 2:1 or first-class degrees.

This partly helps to explain their changing politics. In the post-war years, women tended to be more conservative than men. But, during the 2010s, this changed. Ed Miliband and Labour lost the general election in 2015 but they still left with a noticeable lead among young women. Four years later, in 2019, about 85 per cent of 18–24-year-old women were voting for the liberal left with most of them, two-thirds, voting for the Labour Party.[31] Over time, therefore, it is not hard to see how working-class boys in particular could find themselves not only falling behind others, lacking the 'right' qualifications, but appearing unattractive to an increasingly liberal cohort of university-educated women. Britain may yet find itself confronted with a large number of left-behind, non-graduate, conservative, if not populist men who not only feel they have been cut adrift by the new graduate (and often female) elite but resentful of being asked to reflect on their 'white privilege', 'white guilt', 'unconscious bias' and alleged role in perpetuating 'systemic racism' and 'the patriarchy'. This will raise profound questions about democracy, not least given the fact that men are generally more likely than women to vote for populists and to rebel against the system.

Furthermore, as we have seen, while many people in the new elite and more recent generations feel far more passionately attached to a more radical progressive ideology, many of their views are simply not held by much of the rest of the country and might even entrench the counter-revolution going forward, as traditionalists seek to push back against what they see as an anti-British, if not anti-Western, ideology.

These trends may be exacerbated by the third key group of voters who have been moving leftwards in recent years: Britain's rising number of minority ethnic voters. While they do not always share the liberal values of the new elite – especially when it comes to issues such as same-sex marriage, women's rights, religion and sexual relations between different groups[32] – when it comes to politics Britain's minority voters do lean strongly towards the Labour Party, which they see as the true defender of minority rights and a bulwark against racism and discrimination.[33]

While Labour lost some of their support during the disastrous war in Iraq, by the mid-2010s the party had once again become the main home for minority voters and is now advancing strongly across the most ethnically and religiously diverse parts of Britain.[34] Consistently, more than three-quarters of minority voters now vote Labour, while even notable exceptions, such as British Hindu Indians, still lean heavily in the same direction.[35] At the last election, in 2019, while white voters handed the Conservative Party a nearly 20-point lead over Labour, Britain's black and minority ethnic voters gave Labour a 44-point lead over the Conservatives. Overall, more than three in four minority voters support parties on the liberal left.[36] Labour is also especially popular among Britain's rapidly growing Muslim communities, where the party often relies on *biraderi* networks to rally support.[37] At the last election, nine in ten British Muslims voted for the left. Labour won all thirty seats with the largest share of Muslims and usually with massive majorities. Of the fifty seats in the country with the largest share of Muslim voters the Conservatives only won three.

Yet, as we saw in Chapter 5, Labour's growing dependency on these voters is raising a serious dilemma for a party that is now often seen by the white working class in particular as wanting to prioritize minority voters over the majority. Labour's heavy focus on minority voters, alongside its embrace of a more aggressive and divisive identity politics, is one reason why blue-collar workers have been shunning the party in recent years. This dilemma over how to carve out more unifying appeals which reject this obsession with fixed identity groups, is also especially acute given another major problem for Labour and the left: geography.

All three of the groups that have been trending leftwards in recent years – graduates, zoomers and minorities – tend to live in the same parts of the country, which is weakening their electoral punch. At the last election, in 2019, graduates represented a majority of the working-age population in only 82 of 650 seats. Of the thirty seats with the largest number of degree-holders all but three are in London, while the rest are in university towns such as Oxford, Cambridge and Manchester. This is why, despite imposing its values, voice and sense of moral righteousness on everybody else, the university-educated minority struggled to fend off the revolts among traditionalists who are larger in number and spread across the country more evenly. In 2022, the British Social Attitudes survey estimated that Britain's most strongly committed group of liberals only represent 20 per cent of the population and are still outnumbered by their traditionalist counterparts.[38]

While the Conservative Party's embrace of the realignment allowed it to break into new territory, widening rather than narrowing their reach, ever since Brexit, Labour has doubled down on the cosmopolitan alliance, becoming even more dependent on Britain's big cities and university towns, where these voters are heavily but narrowly concentrated.[39] In England and Wales, over the last decade, Labour has advanced on average by an impressive 15 points in the most densely populated parts of Britain but by only 5 points in the least populated. The Conservatives, in sharp contrast, have fallen back by 5 points in the former but surged by 12 points in the latter. Labour's support, in other words, has been growing most sharply in highly educated, hyper-diverse and strongly liberal parts of the country – in the likes of Birmingham, Bristol, Cambridge, Cardiff, Canterbury, Bradford, Manchester, Sheffield, Hove, and London districts such as Bethnal Green and Bow. But the party's support has fallen off a cliff across blue-collar, white and older communities in the Midlands and Yorkshire, in seats such as Bassetlaw, Bolsover, Brigg and Goole, Amber Valley, Wentworth and Dearne, Cleethorpes, Barnsley, and Normanton, Pontefract and Castleford. Because of these longer-term trends, such areas will remain far more competitive in the years ahead, irrespective of what happens at the next election.

In the shadow of the revolution, then, Labour has been transformed into a party for the new graduate elite and their allies, who are often too small in number and too geographically concentrated to fend off the counter-revolution. Labour has often been stacking up votes in urban areas where the party does not need them while losing votes in more traditionalist areas where it desperately needs them if it is ever to return to a serious and sustainable position of power. In places like London, Liverpool and Birmingham, Labour MPs now hold the safest seats in Britain with massive majorities; of the twenty seats with the largest majorities no less than sixteen are held by Labour, while of the thirty largest majorities no less than twenty are held by Labour. Progressives might cheer these victories on, celebrating Labour's dominance in London and other cities, but unless they find a way of winning over non-London, non-metropolitan England they will struggle to return to Downing Street with a commanding lead.

Much like Britain's institutions, as the Labour Party has become even more dependent on these groups it is also being pushed in a more pro-EU, pro-immigration, pro-diversity, and more radically progressive direction. And while this has clearly weakened the party's relationship with the white working class, it might also yet undermine its relationship with other large groups in its new coalition. One warning sign comes not from Britain but America, where the more radically progressive Democrats have lost considerable support not just among white working-class and non-graduate voters but minority Latino and Hispanic voters who have been turned off by the new elite's beliefs. In areas such as San Francisco, Seattle and Virginia, radical progressive politicians have lost office and been replaced with more ideologically moderate or even Republican candidates. While the new elite have rushed to endorse radical progressive calls to 'defund the police' and denounce America as being institutionally racist, in the aftermath of the George Floyd protests and the rise of Black Lives Matter the independent Pew Research Center found only 16 per cent of American Hispanic and Latino voters and only 23 per cent of African Americans want to decrease spending on police. Many of these voters were in the front line of a wave of crime that followed these protests, providing another example of how the luxury elite beliefs that are promoted by the new elite often entail very negative consequences for other groups in society.[40]

Other research, by the pro-Democrat Equis group, finds that in key swing states, such as Florida, around 60 per cent of fourth-generation migrants feel concerned about how the Democrats, in their eyes, have embraced the radical left. 'Concern over socialism', they conclude, 'does appear to increase the likelihood of voting for Trump, all else being equal. The effect is the highest in Florida but is not contained to Florida.'[41] At the 2022 midterm elections the Republicans won nearly 40 per cent of Hispanic and Latino voters – their highest since George W. Bush in 2004.

Such findings contain a clear message for Britain's Labour Party: while it might currently be dominating the big cities and the minority vote, there is no guarantee these trends will continue, particularly if British Indians and Muslims who hold traditionalist values on sex, gender, same-sex marriage and what children should be taught in school begin to feel alienated by the radical progressive left and move rightwards in politics. Labour, in other words, needs to find ways of toning down this divisive identity politics and returning to more unifying themes. The more it reshapes itself around the values, interests and priorities of only a small number of radical progressives in the cities and university towns, the more it will alienate a much larger number of voters.

These trends have not only raised a dilemma for the left, however, they have also raised one for the incumbent Conservative Party. One of the great puzzles in British politics, observed Professor Andrew Gamble after the Conservative Party's fourth straight victory, in 2019, is why the party has been so successful for so long.[42] In the more than 100 years since the British people began to be given voting rights, the Conservative Party has governed alone or in coalition for 72 per cent of the time, which, by the next election, will have risen to 75 per cent. No less than ten Conservative leaders since the Second World War have become prime minister, while not even half of the Labour Party's twelve leaders can say the same. How can we explain this?

The answer is reinvention. Throughout its long history, the Conservative Party has consistently demonstrated a willingness to reinvent itself to tap into the public mood. And in the aftermath of Brexit, the party reinvented itself once again to tap into the unfolding realignment, hoovering up support from traditionalists.

Much of this was made possible not only by the divides over values, voice, and virtue but also by how the Conservative Party itself appeared to change its message to tap into them. Post-Brexit conservatism, under Boris Johnson, downplayed the neoliberal conservatism of the 1980s and the 2010s and became openly committed to dismantling key pillars of the revolution. The party swung behind leaving the EU, reforming immigration, 'levelling-up' the left-behind regions and investing far more seriously in the non-graduate majority, through a new skills agenda and apprenticeships.

A new generation of conservatives, led by Nick Timothy, senior advisor to Theresa May, openly criticized their neoliberal predecessors, railing against the destabilizing and damaging effects of the revolution, the deregulation of financial markets, a rampant and narcissistic individualism, mass immigration, the erosion of workers' rights and the general obsession with the new graduate elite.[43]

Though Timothy and prime minister May failed in their quest, in 2017, to win a majority in their own right, their diagnosis of the new electoral coalition that was available was accurate. Their repositioning of the party, including the most economically left-wing manifesto since 1964, coupled with a strong commitment to reforming immigration and seeing Brexit through, attracted the highest share of the national vote for the Conservatives since Margaret Thatcher's second landslide in 1983. They also advanced most strongly across a large swathe of Labour's territory, clearing the way for Boris Johnson's far more impressive majority in 2019.[44] Johnson then tapped even more successfully into the emerging counter-revolution, not only by capitalizing on his strong personal appeal among workers, non-graduates and pensioners, but by offering the country something the revolution ruled out. He promised to 'Get Brexit Done', replace uncontrolled immigration with a controlled Australian-based points system, strengthen workers' rights and invest in non-graduates. There is no doubt the party still remains adrift from many of the people who are yearning for change. Today's Conservative voters, as we saw in Chapter 4, often sit further to the left on the economy and further to the right on culture than many of the party's more economically and socially liberal MPs in Westminster. Nor is the voice of these working-class and non-graduate voters adequately represented within the Conservative Party, which remains far too dependent on the privately and Oxbridge-educated. But these changes did help bring the party an electorate that was very different from the one that had voted for David Cameron only three years earlier.

These new post-Brexit Conservatives were far more strongly committed to Brexit, more sceptical about immigration, more determined to prioritize the majority over minorities, more convinced that opportunities for minorities have gone too far, more traditionalist in their views on crime and morality, more supportive of a thicker conception of what it means to be British and more populist in their attitudes – they are more likely to think politicians no longer care about people like them, the system is rigged against them and the country's rulers have been ignoring people like them for decades.[45]

Their strong support for Johnson's Conservatives not only reflected his success at tapping into the counter-revolution, and the groups that are central to it, but how the centre-right almost fully absorbed the populist tradition in British politics. Boris Johnson won over more than eight in ten people who had voted for Nigel Farage.[46]

While Labour's reach shrunk, the Conservative's reach increased. The party unlocked a large swathe of the country where, historically, Conservatives had struggled to break through. By offering a more compelling message to traditionalists, the party advanced most strongly across the small, coastal and post-industrial towns. Whereas historically the party had once polled its strongest support in more prosperous, leafy and graduate-heavy southern shires, from 2017 it began to score its strongest gains across the post-industrial, working-class Midlands, Yorkshire, and Northern regions. Remarkably, Labour's sharpest *losses* came in areas which had struggled the most with unemployment, while the Conservative's most impressive gains came in areas which had been consistently cut adrift by the revolution – whether defined by their average earnings, education or class.[47]

Throughout the 2010s, remarkably, the Conservatives advanced on average by more than 20 points in the most strongly committed parts of Leaveland – in seats such as Boston and Skegness, Walsall, Castle Point, Stoke-on-Trent, Mansfield, Dudley and Cleethorpes. Two-thirds of all seats Boris Johnson took from Labour were among the most working class in the country. Many had not elected a Conservative for generations – including Great Grimsby (Labour since 1945), Bishop Auckland (1935), Bassetlaw (1935), Wakefield (1932), Leigh (1922), Don Valley (1922) and Bolsover (a seat Labour had never lost).

Today, there are many more Labour seats that look like these Red Wall constituencies. There are about three dozen seats in the Red Wall 2.0 which have small Labour majorities but are filled with many of the same working-class, non-graduate and older voters who have been drifting from left to right in recent years. They include Yvette

Cooper's seat of Normanton, Pontefract and Castleford in Yorkshire and Humberside, Ed Miliband's seat of Doncaster North and seats such as Wolverhampton Southeast, Huddersfield, Kingston-upon-Hull East, Wentworth and Dearne, Sunderland Central, Wansbeck, Oldham East and Saddleworth, Warrington North, and Hemsworth. While the Conservatives look set to lose a large chunk of territory in the southern shires, making further gains in these areas might have helped to offset those losses among graduates, professionals and younger voters.

Though it is often forgotten today, the Conservatives then continued to win these types of areas even after the country had officially exited the European Union, in 2020. The next year, at a by-election, Boris Johnson and the Conservatives captured yet another historic Labour fiefdom, this time the northern working-class seat of Hartlepool. The last time a Conservative won this seat, England had not yet won the World Cup, Cliff Richard topped the charts with 'Living Doll', *Ben-Hur* was in the cinema, Winston Churchill was still alive, Tony Blair was six years old, and Sir Keir Starmer had not yet been born. The party then made further gains in local elections, in 2021, when they forced Labour to lose historic strongholds such as Durham County Council, held since 1925. By leaning into the realignment, in other words, the party was able to continue to make gains in areas of the country in which it had previously been weak.

It was only after Boris Johnson presided over a string of major scandals in Number 10 Downing Street, including 'Partygate', the holding of numerous parties during nationwide Covid-19 restrictions, that the counter-revolution he had successfully tapped into began to lose steam. The Conservative Party collapsed in the polls, and during the summer of 2022, Boris Johnson was forced to resign.

In the aftermath, the party reinvented itself once again, only this time choosing to pursue a path that was far more disconnected from the counter-revolution and the groups that have flocked to it. After Boris Johnson was replaced by Liz Truss, the party returned to the radical economic liberalism of the 1980s, prioritizing tax cuts, a small state and economic reforms that would mainly benefit London and the south-east of England far more than other regions of the country. This injected a fundamental and irreconcilable tension between the minority 'liberal Leaver' vision of what the counter-revolution is all about and the majority traditionalist vision that unites many new Conservative voters.

While Conservative elites, donors and a relatively small share of the Conservative electorate are united by this vision of a low-regulation, high migration and economically liberal Davos-on-Thames, a much larger share of the new Conservative electorate dream of a very different Britain – one where the government is more willing to intervene to fix a rigged economy and broken institutions, where immigration is not just controlled but much lower, where the needs of the nation are prioritized above the needs of global markets and where the values, priorities and interests of the majority are respected just as much as those of minorities.

And this divide is especially visible when it comes to one issue which has lain at the very heart of the realignment over the last decade and could yet deliver more shocks in the years to come: immigration. While all British people have become more positive about immigration, the Conservative Party has continued to preside over a model of mass immigration that is much closer to the goals of the revolution than the goals of their new voters.

In 2022, despite promises to lower the number of immigrants, the party was still presiding over a rate of net migration at 239,000 – one of the largest on record, while Liz Truss and a new generation of Conservative libertarians made clear their intention to increase immigration to even higher levels to try to reboot economic growth.[48] Much of this reflects the fact that while the free movement of EU nationals has come to an end, Conservative elites have replaced this with a relatively liberal points-based system that will continue to drive record levels of ethnic, cultural and religious diversity in the years ahead. Work permits have been relaxed. The definition of what constitutes a 'skilled worker' has been diluted. British employers are no longer required to prioritize British workers before recruiting from overseas. The salary threshold – originally designed to encourage very high-skilled workers – is only £25,600 and, for some jobs, only £20,480. And international students have been given the right to stay and work in Britain at the end of their degrees.

These changes explain why, in the aftermath of the Covid-19 lock-downs, the number of work visas, family visas and student visas soared to more than one million – changes that have not yet been noticed by many people who have switched to the Conservatives. The nature of migration into Britain will now also change in fundamental ways. Unlike the last twenty years, when much migration came from within Europe, most of the workers who are now arriving in Britain come from even more culturally and religiously distinctive areas of the world – India, Nigeria, the Philippines, Pakistan, Zimbabwe, South Africa.[49] By 2061, it is now forecast that the share of the UK population that is white British will fall from 83% in 2011 to 62%. These very different migration flows will soon become a visible reminder to many traditionalists of why their vision of the counter-revolution is not one that is shared by the people who sit at the top of the Conservative Party. Contrary to claims of 'Taking Back Control', many voters may soon conclude once again that they have no control at all.

The potential for this disillusionment to drive a more sweeping realignment of the Conservative Party or a resurgent national populism can already be seen. In 2022, three years after Boris Johnson's election victory, immigration was still the second most important issue for Conservatives, most of whom still felt just as disgruntled with this issue as they had before the Brexit referendum. Amid a spiralling cost-of-living crisis, no less than 72 per cent of Leavers and 67 per cent of Conservatives felt the government was managing immigration 'badly'. And when Ipsos-MORI asked people why they felt so unhappy with immigration in Britain, the four most popular responses were 'not enough is being done to stop the Channel migrant crossings', the government 'is allowing too many people to claim asylum in Britain', 'immigration numbers are too high' and 'the government is being too generous to migrants and asylum seekers'.[50]

In the aftermath of the 2019 general election, a window of opportunity briefly opened for the new elite to finally bring the turbulence of the last decade to an end and address the country's deepening divides by bringing forward a new social settlement – one that is defined by moderate not mass immigration, evolutionary not revolutionary change and a national conversation that better reflects the wide range of voices in British society. Given the current direction of both the Conservative Party and the Labour Party, that window of opportunity is swiftly closing.

More broadly, now that the counter-revolution is underway, much will also depend on the willingness of the new elite to address the widening divides over values, voice and virtue. Now that the shock of Brexit has passed, will the new elite do more to recognize and represent people's traditionalist values? Will they slow, not stop, the pace of social and cultural change? Will they spend as much time celebrating the distinctive identity, history and culture of Britain and England as they spend celebrating universal liberal themes, such as multiculturalism and diversity? Will they make room for a wider range of voices in the country's political, creative, cultural, media and university institutions and ensure that they are just as present at the most senior and influential levels? Will they move away from a more radical progressive ideology which views Britain and the West narrowly and crudely through the lens of identity and race, and which only appeals to a small subset of the country? And will they instead return to carving out more unifying narratives for the country that appeal beyond these narrow and divisive categories?

The future of the realignment, British politics and the country more generally will be shaped by how the new elite answer these questions. The alternative is both obvious and profound. As we have seen throughout this book, neither the established left nor established right is fully in tune with a large swathe of the country. Many voters hold values and a voice that are no longer represented in Westminster and the institutions. One clear and present danger is that the revolts of the last decade will spiral into a full-blown rebellion against the new elite and the wider system. As we have seen with the rise of the Yellow Vests in France, the radicalization of the Republicans in America and increased support for Marine Le Pen in France, the tremors that are now regularly shaking politics could yet be followed by a more devastating earthquake.

The stunning collapse of the established centre-left and centre-right at France's presidential election in 2022, the implosion of the centre-right in Germany in 2021, the temporary collapse of the Conservatives and Labour during the spring of 2019, when they plummeted to a combined 22 per cent share of the vote, and the record number of British voters who are today switching their support from one party to another all point clearly towards this more volatile, polarized, febrile and divisive politics.

Nor does the new elite's initial reaction to the counter-revolution bode well for the future. Rather than listen and respond to the grievances of the majority, as we saw in Chapter 5, over the last five years they have routinely derided much of the rest of the country as ignorant bigots, racists, fascists, Nazis and gammons, or, in the words of Richard Dawkins, 'an ignorant and misled public'.[51] Rather than viewing the last decade as a moment in which many people registered their opposition to a project that was not working for the wider country, the new elite refused to engage with it at all.

Some have turned in on themselves and away from society. In the universities, scholars demand the return of 'epistocracy', an elitist conception of democracy in which the votes of people who are more knowledgeable count for more than the votes of those who know less.[52] And in the media, journalists from the new elite, such as Janan Ganesh of the *Financial Times*, have wondered aloud whether '[d]emocracy works better when there is less of it'.[53]

Whether the new elite can push these arguments aside and find their way to representing the values of the wider majority, recognizing the voice of many people who feel excluded and respecting all groups in society will ultimately determine whether the counter-revolution against them will now gradually fade away or, alternatively, soon escalate to all new heights.

Afterword

Less than three years after Boris Johnson's emphatic victory, in 2019, the Conservative Party had lost touch with the realignment of British politics. A unique opportunity to completely reshape Britain and its politics around a very different consensus from the one that has dominated the country for the last half century was lost.

In the shadow of the Partygate scandal, the mass resignation of Conservative MPs which triggered Boris Johnson's downfall and then the party's disastrous experiment with Liz Truss, who sought to return to the Thatcherite policies of the revolution, the Conservative Party suffered a catastrophic collapse of support in the polls.

Confronted with a party that no longer appeared all that interested in representing the values and the voice of its new voters, a party that had delivered Brexit but in many other respects remained firmly committed to the social and economic liberalism of the revolution, including the continuation of mass immigration, many people up and down the country abandoned the party in droves.

Between Boris Johnson coming to power in 2019 and the hapless Liz Truss being replaced by former chancellor Rishi Sunak in late 2022, the share of Brexit voters supporting the Conservatives crashed from 76 to 37 per cent, the share of working-class voters who supported the party fell from 51 to 24 per cent, and the share of pensioners who did so collapsed from nearly 70 to just 40 per cent.[1]

The very distinctive cross-class coalition of voters which found its expression through the rise of populism, Brexit and Boris Johnson, which represented a revolt against the new elite, fell apart. A realignment that was supposed to extend the Conservative's period of dominance deep into the late 2020s was brought to a premature end.

On the surface, this owed much to two specific events. The first, beginning in late 2021, was the Partygate scandal, which violated the British people's sacrosanct sense of fair play and severely damaged the Conservative Party's image in the eyes of many voters. Prior to Partygate, even after the worst of the Covid-19 pandemic, Boris Johnson and the Conservatives had still led Labour in the polls and could realistically set their sights on achieving what no other party has ever achieved in British history: a fifth consecutive term in office. After Partygate, however, the party lost an average of six points in the polls, Labour pulled ahead and would remain there throughout 2022.

The second event, made possible by the first, was the replacement of Boris Johnson by Liz Truss and the party's disastrous experiment with 'Trussonomics', a return to the supply-side politics of Thatcherism. Calls to remove a cap on bankers' bonuses, slash taxes for high earners, put financial services, London, and the south-east on steroids and retain a strong commitment to global free trade and mass immigration signalled not a bold new offer that was in tune with the post-Brexit realignment but rather a return to the broken politics of the revolution which much of the country had already rejected.

Trussonomics was completely adrift from the economic and social outlook of voters who had been drifting around the political landscape for years, looking for an alternative to the broken status quo. As the British Social Attitudes survey made clear, in late 2022, only one in twenty voters, including just 7 per cent of Conservative voters, shared Liz Truss's instinctive desire to slash taxes and cut spending on public services. The vast majority of people in the country, including most Conservatives, either wanted to keep taxes and spending as they are or increase them further.[2] Nor did they support her continued commitment to large-scale migration.

Rather than lean into the new, unfolding realignment, then, the Conservative Party openly rejected it by seeking to return to the old, broken consensus. Against the backdrop of Partygate, Trussonomics cost the party another twelve points in the polls and sent it crashing to some of its lowest support in British polling history. By the time Truss was replaced by Rishi Sunak, after only forty-four days in the job, the party's reputation for economic competence had been shredded while the number of voters who saw the Conservative Party as out of touch with ordinary people, incompetent, on the side of a small elite and as having no clear purpose rocketed. Together, Partygate and Trussonomics was a brutal and self-inflicted two-punch combination.

But at a deeper level, the inability of the Conservative Party to remain connected with the realignment is about more than this. While the party briefly tapped into the underlying fissures over values, voice, and virtue to rally an impressive coalition in 2019, it then became clear that neither the party nor its MPs, who lean further to the cultural left and further to the economic right than their new voters, ever really knew what to do with this new coalition of supporters.

On an array of issues which reflect the importance of the new cultural axis in politics, such as legal and illegal immigration, diversity, gender politics, free speech, preserving and promoting a distinctive national identity, and pushing back against a minority of radical progressives in the institutions, the Conservative Party struggled to appear in tune with its more traditionalist voters and find new cross-cutting issues which, like Brexit, might have otherwise allowed the party to hold its unique coalition together at the next election.

In the end, all realignments are about demand and supply. And while public demand for a very different politics remains on full display in modern Britain, reflected in the large number of people who say none of the main parties represent their values, who feel excluded by the institutions and believe they are being looked down upon by a progressive elite, the Conservative elites in Westminster consistently struggled to supply this demand with an appealing, resonant message.

Rather than address the divides that have powered the turmoil and turbulence of the last decade, therefore, the failure of all the main parties to respond to them has left more than enough space for yet another revolt against the new elite. It is revealing, for example, that in the final days of 2022 only one in ten of the people who had voted for Boris Johnson three years earlier had defected to Labour while a much larger number had either drifted into apathy, no longer sure who to vote for, or to the national populist Reform party, which is aligned to Nigel Farage. In late 2022, one poll suggested that 28 per cent of British people, including 43 per cent of Brexit voters, would be interested in supporting a new populist party, while other polls have suggested that one-third of the country would potentially be open to a party that specifically campaigned to lower immigration.[3]

All three of the revolts that reshaped British politics over the last decade – the rise of populism, Brexit and the post-Brexit realignment of the Conservative Party – were supposed to bring the rulers and the ruled closer together. But, in the end, they have done no such thing. Much like a decade ago, a large swathe of the electorate appear disgruntled and disillusioned with a new elite that does not reflect their values, represent their voice, or treat them with the same degree of respect and dignity as other groups in society.

And so now, once again, more than six years after the vote for Brexit, many people in the country are searching around for a radical alternative that will allow them to launch a revolt against the growing power of the new elite. The only question that remains is what form this radical alternative will take and when it will arrive.

Notes

PREFACE

1. Robert Ford and Matthew Goodwin (2014), *Revolt on the Right: Explaining Support for the Radical Right in Britain*, Routledge; see also Matthew Goodwin and Caitlin Milazzo (2015), *UKIP: Inside the Campaign to Redraw the Map of British Politics*, Oxford University Press.
2. Roger Eatwell and Matthew Goodwin (2018), *National Populism: The Revolt Against Liberal Democracy*, Penguin.
3. This observation was made by Emmanuel Le Roy, cited in David Cannadine (2000), *Class in Britain*, Penguin, p. 163.

INTRODUCTION

1. https://yougov.co.uk/topics/politics/trackers/do-the-main-political-parties-really-represent-brits-priorities-and-values.
2. 'Populist and nativist sentiment in 2019: a 27 country survey', Ipsos Global Advisor, https://www.ipsos.com/sites/default/files/ct/news/documents/2019-09/populist_and_nativist_sentiment_in_2019_-_global_advisor_report_-_gb.pdf.
3. Roger Eatwell and Matthew Goodwin (2018), *National Populism: The Revolt Against Liberal Democracy*, Penguin.
4. Andrew Gamble (2019), 'The Realignment of British Politics in the Wake of Brexit', *Political Quarterly* 90(S2), pp. 177–86.
5. Walter Dean Burnham (1975), 'Party systems and the political process', in W. N. Chambers and W. D. Burnham (eds.), *The American Party Systems*, Oxford University Press. Originally cited in John B. Judis and Ruy Texeira (2002), *The Emerging Democratic Majority*, Lisa Drew/Scribner, p. 12.

CHAPTER I: RISE OF THE NEW ELITE

1. Roger Eatwell and Matthew Goodwin (2018), *National Populism: The Revolt Against Liberal Democracy*, Penguin.

2. Helen Lewis, 'How the Brexit campaign lied to is – and got away with it', *New Statesman*, 30 June 2016.

3. Peter Geoghegan on dark money online advertising and electoral reform, *Common Wealth*, 19 October 2020, https://www.common-wealth.co.uk/reports/interview-peter-geoghegan-on-dark-money-online-political-advertising-and-electoral-reform.

4. 'People who use social media for politics skew Labour and Remain, but Leave is winning the Twitter war', *Hansard Society*, 17 May 2019; Jonathan Melon and Christopher Prosser, 'Twitter and Facebook are not representative of the general population: political attitudes and demographics of British social media users', *Research and Politics*, 13 July 2017; for similar findings in America see Pew Research Center, 'Sizing up Twitter users', 24 April 2019, https://www.pewresearch.org/internet/2019/04/24/sizing-up-twitter-users/.

5. Kaleigh Rogers, 'Why it's so hard to gauge support for QAnon', *FiveThirtyEight*, 11 June 2021, https://fivethirtyeight.com/features/why-its-so-hard-to-gauge-support-for-qanon/.

6. Eatwell and Goodwin, *National Populism*.

7. Levi Boxell, Matthew Gentzkow and Jesse M. Shapiro, *Cross-country Trends in Affective Polarization*, no. w26669, National Bureau of Economic Research, 2020.

8. We will discuss these trends throughout this book, but on earlier evidence see, for example, B. Särlvik, I. Crewe and R. MacDermid (1983), *Decade of Dealignment: The Conservative Victory of 1979 and Electoral Trends in the 1970s*, Cambridge University Press.

9. YouGov, 'Britons least likely of 22 nations to trust information on social media', 7 May 2019, https://yougov.co.uk/topics/technology/articles-reports/2019/05/07/britons-least-likely-22-nations-trust-information-.

10. Reuters Institute, 'People most likely to vote Conservative are the least likely to get news online', 13 December 2019, https://reutersinstitute.politics.ox.ac.uk/news/people-most-likely-vote-conservative-are-least-likely-get-news-online; Eran Amsalem and Alon Zoizner (2022), 'Do people learn about politics on social media? A meta-analysis of 76 studies', *Journal of Communication*. https://academic.oup.com/joc/advance-article/doi/10.1093/joc/jqac034/6726545?login=true.

11. Alan Gerber, James Gimpel, Donald P. Green and Daron R. Shaw (2011), 'How large and long-lasting are the persuasive effects of televised campaign ads? Results from a randomized field experiment', *American Political Science Review* 105(1); also David Nickerson and Todd Rogers (2020), 'Campaigns influence election outcomes less than you think', *Science* 369(6508), pp. 1181–2; Alexander Coppock, Seth Hill and Lynn Vavreck (2020), 'The small effects of political advertising are small regardless of context, message, sender, or receiver: Evidence from 59 real-time randomized experiments', *Science Advances* 6(36).

12. British Election Study, 'Most volatile British electorate in modern times', 8 October 2019, https://www.britishelectionstudy.com/wp-content/uploads/2019/10/PR-Explaining-Voter-Volatility.pdf.

13. Ipsos MORI, 'Jeremy Corbyn has lowest leadership satisfaction rating for any opposition leader since 1977', 20 September 2019, https://www.ipsos.com/ipsos-mori/en-uk/jeremy-corbyn-has-lowest-leadership-satisfaction-rating-any-opposition-leader-1977.

14. In October 2019, YouGov put Prince Andrew's rating at -48 (22 per cent positive, 58 per cent negative), https://d25d2506sfb94s.cloudfront.net/cumulus_uploads/document/j5w7s0m4z0/TheSun_RoyalFamily191003.pdf. In the same month Jeremy Corbyn held an approval rating of -61. See: https://yougov.co.uk/topics/politics/trackers/jeremy-corbyn-approval-rating.

15. For these figures and those in figure 1 see Achim Hildebrandt and Sebastian Jäckle (2021), 'The shifting class-base of social democratic parties in Western Europe', *European Politics and Society* 5, pp. 1–18.

16. Linn Rennwald (2020), *Social Democratic Parties and the Working Class: New Voting Patterns*, Springer Nature.

17. Sally Tomlinson and Danny Dorling (2019), '(Mis)Rule Britannia: Brexit is the last gasp of empire', LSE, https://blogs.lse.ac.uk/brexit/2019/02/20/misrule-britannia-brexit-is-the-last-gasp-of-empire/; Danny Dorling and Sally Tomlinson (2019), *Rule Britannia: Brexit and the End of Empire*, Biteback.

18. Fintan O'Toole (2018), *Heroic Failure: Brexit and the Politics of Pain*, Head of Zeus. See also Afua Hirsch, 'People are nostalgic for the British Empire, but how did we get that power?', *Metro*, 11 February 2020; Pankaj Mishra, 'The malign incompetence of the British ruling class', *New York Times*, 17 January 2019.

19. Sathnam Sanghera (2021), *Empireland: How Imperialism Has Shaped Modern Britain*, Penguin, pp. 115–19.

20. 50 per cent of Dutch voters said their former empire was 'more something to be proud of than to be ashamed of' compared to only 32 per cent of the British. See YouGov, 'How unique are British attitudes to empire?' 11 March 2020, https://yougov.co.uk/topics/international/articles-reports/2020/03/11/how-unique-are-british-attitudes-empire.

21. Arthur Marwick (2011), *The Sixties: Cultural Revolution in Britain, France, Italy and the United States, 1958–1974*, A&C Black; Bernard Porter (2004), *The Absent-Minded Imperialists: Empire, Society and Culture in Britain*, Oxford University Press.

22. Ipsos MORI, 'Attitudes to racism in Britain', research for *The Economist*, September 2020, https://www.ipsos.com/sites/default/files/ct/news/documents/2020-10/economist-survey-on-racism-2020-slides.pdf; YouGov, 'How unique are British attitudes to empire?', 11 March 2020, https://yougov.co.uk/topics/international/articles-reports/2020/03/11/how-unique-are-british-attitudes-empire.

23. Anyusha Rose, 'The Brexit debate has made Britain more racist', *Washington Post*, 22 June 2016.

24. Cassilde Schwartz, Miranda Simon, David Hudson and Jennifer van-Heerde-Hudson (2021), 'A populist paradox? How Brexit softened anti-immigrant attitudes', *British Journal of Political Science* 51(3), pp. 1160–80.

25. Robert Ford and Matthew Goodwin (2014), *Revolt on the Right: Explaining Support for the Radical Right in Britain*, Routledge.

26. 'Long-term trends in UK employment, 1861 to 2018', Office for National Statistics, 29 April 2019.

27. Ibid.; also 'Women and the UK economy', House of Commons Library, March 2022.

28. Geoffrey Evans and James Tilley (2017), *The New Politics of Class: The Political Exclusion of the British Working Class*, Oxford University Press; Daniel Oesch (2008), 'The changing shape of class voting', *European Societies* 10(3), pp. 329–55.

29. R. Florida (2019), *The Rise of the Creative Class*, updated edn, Hachette UK.

30. Rune Stubager (2013), 'The changing basis of party competition: education, authoritarian-libertarian values and voting', *Government and Opposition* 48(3), pp. 372–97.

31. K. Kiernan, S. Crossman and A. Phimister (2022), 'Families and Inequalities', *IFS Deaton Review of Inequalities*, https://ifs.org.uk/inequality/wp-content/uploads/2022/06/IFS-Deaton-Review-Families-and-inequality-.pdf.

32. R. Stubager (2008), 'Education effects on authoritarian–libertarian values: a question of socialization'. *The British Journal of Sociology* 59(2), pp. 327–50.

33. R. Scott (2022), 'Does university make you more liberal? Estimating the within-individual effects of higher education on political values', *Electoral Studies* 77, 102471.

34. E. Kaufmann (2021), *Academic Freedom in Crisis: Punishment, Political Discrimination, and Self-censorship*, Center for the Study of Partisanship and Ideology.

35. Ronald Inglehart (1971), 'The silent revolution in Europe: Intergenerational change in post-industrial societies', *American Political Science Review* 65(4), pp. 991–1017.

36. Evans and Tilley, *The New Politics of Class*.

37. David Brooks (2010), *Bobos in Paradise: The New Upper Class and How They Got There*, Simon and Schuster.

38. On the growing education divide and the different values of Britain's graduates and non-graduates see Ford and Goodwin, *Revolt on the Right*; Evans and Tilley, *The New Politics of Class*; Maria Sobolewska and Robert Ford (2020), *Brexitland: Identity, Diversity, and the Reshaping of British Politics*, Cambridge University Press; R. Stubager (2008), 'Education effects on authoritarian-libertarian values: a question of socialization', *British Journal of Sociology* 59, pp. 327–35; P. Surridge (2016), 'Education and liberalism: pursuing the link', *Oxford Review of Education* 42, pp. 146–64; B. Lancee and O. Sarrasin (2015), 'Educated preferences or selection effects? A longitudinal analysis of the impact of education on attitudes toward immigrants', *European Sociological Review* 31(4), pp. 490–501.

39. David Goodhart (2017), *The Road to Somewhere: The Populist Revolt and the Future of Politics*, Oxford University Press.

40. Stubager, 'Education effects on authoritarian-libertarian values'; Surridge, 'Education and liberalism'; Lancee and Sarrasin, 'Educated preferences or selection effects?'; Sobolewska and Ford, *Brexitland*.

41. https://www.ipsos.com/sites/default/files/ct/news/documents/2020–10/economist-survey-on-racism–2020-tables.pdf. Cite Alison Park government study effect of higher education on attitudes.

42. More in Common, 'Britain's choice', https://www.britainschoice.uk/.

43. Matthew Yglesias, 'The Great Awakening', 1 April 2019, https://www.vox.com/2019/3/22/18259865/great-awakening-white-liberals-race-polling-trump-2020; on British data cited see https://www.ipsos.com/

sites/default/files/ct/news/documents/2022-03/attitudes-towards-immigration-british-future-ipsos-march–2022.pdf.

44. Ibid.

45. Arthur Marwick (2011), *The Sixties: Cultural Revolution in Britain, France, Italy, and the United States, c. 1958–c. 1974*, A&C Black.

46. More in Common, 'Britain's choice', https://www.britainschoice.uk/; Rebecca Benson and Bobby Duffy (2021), 'The four sides in the UK's "culture wars"', Ipsos-MORI, Policy Institute and Kings College London, https://www.kcl.ac.uk/policy-institute/assets/the-four-sides-in-the-uks-culture-wars.

47. John Gray, 'The problem of hyper-liberalism', *Times Literary Supplement*, 30 March 2018; More in Common, 'Britain's choice'; https://www.kcl.ac.uk/news/uk-culture-war-debate-public-divide-into-four-groups-not-two-warring-tribes.

48. More in Common, 'Britain's choice'.

49. 'Education: historical statistics' (2012), House of Commons Library, SN/SG/4252; https://www.universitiesuk.ac.uk/latest/insights-and-analysis/higher-education-numbers.

50. *British Social Attitudes* and British Election Study data; see also P. Devereux and W. Fan (2011), 'Earnings returns to the British education expansion', *Economics of Education Review* 30(6), pp. 1153–66.

51. V. Boliver (2011), 'Expansion, differentiation, and the persistence of social class inequalities in British higher education', *Higher Education* 61(3), pp. 229–42.

52. Remarkably, applicants from state schools had to be better qualified than their elite counterparts by as much as two A-level grades before they were as likely to apply to elite universities. When they did apply, they needed to be better qualified than their elite counterparts, on average, by as much as one grade at A-level before they were as likely to receive the same offer of admission. V. Boliver (2013), 'How fair is access to more prestigious UK universities?', *The British Journal of Sociology* 64(2), pp. 344–64.

53. Office for Students, 'Continuation and transfer rates', 2019, https://www.officeforstudents.org.uk/data-and-analysis/continuation-and-transfer-rates/#:~:text=Transfer%20rates%20are%20lowest%20for,significantly%20higher%20than%20the%20benchmark.; Office for Students (2019), 'Differences in student outcomes', https://www.officeforstudents.org.uk/publications/differences-in-student-outcomes-further-characteristics/; see also Augar Review, *Independent*

Panel Report to the Review of Post-18 Education and Funding, 30 May 2019.

54. M. Triventi (2013), 'Stratification in higher education and its relationship with social inequality: a comparative study of 11 European countries', *European Sociological Review* 29(3), pp. 489–502.

55. Education Committee (2021), *The Forgotten: How White Working-class Pupils Have Been Let Down and How to Change It*, https://publications.parliament.uk/pa/cm5802/cmselect/cmeduc/85/8502.htm; see also Ethnicity Facts and Figures (2020), 'Students getting 3 A grades or better at A level', https://www.ethnicity-facts-figures.service.gov.uk/education-skills-and-training/a-levels/draft-percentage-of-students-achieving-3-a-grades-or-better-at-a-level/latest#:~:text=3%20A%20grades%20or%20better%20at%20A%20level,of%20Asian%20students%20and%205%25%20of%20Black%20students.

56. 'The "taboo" about who doesn't go to university', *BBC News*, 27 September 2020, https://www.bbc.co.uk/news/education-54278727; see also Sean Coughlan, 'Poorer white pupils let down and neglected – MPs', *BBC News*, 22 June 2021, https://www.bbc.co.uk/news/education-57558746.

57. 'Widening participation in higher education', 28 July 2022, https://explore-education-statistics.service.gov.uk/find-statistics/widening-participation-in-higher-education/2020-21.

58. Sam Baars, Ellie Mulcahy and Eleanor Bernardes (2016), *The Underrepresentation of White Working-class Boys in Higher Education*, Kings College London; also P. Bolton (2014), 'Oxbridge "elitism"', House of Commons Library.

59. Data from Office for Students, 2019, cited in Alex Blower, 'White working-class students have been let down', *Wonk HE*, 23 June 2021, https://wonkhe.com/blogs/white-working-class-students-have-been-let-down-just-not-by-a-debate-over-white-privilege/#:~:text=White%20working%2Dclass%20students%20have%20been%20let%20down%20%E2%80%93%20just%20not,be%20focussed%20on%20its%20concerns.

60. Paul Swinney and Maire Williams (2016), 'The Great British Brain Drain', Centre for Cities, https://www.centreforcities.org/wp-content/uploads/2016/11/16-11-18-The-Great-British-Brain-Drain.pdf.

61. Office for National Statistics, 'Regional gross value added by local authority in the UK', https://www.ons.gov.uk/economy/grossvalueaddedgva/

datasets/regionalgrossvalueaddedbalancedbylocalauthority
intheuk.

62. Michael Savage (years), *Social Class in Britain*, Pelican.

63. On Britain see Kings College London News Centre, 'UK "culture war" debate: public divide into four groups, not two warring tribes', 18 June 2021, https://www.kcl.ac.uk/news/uk-culture-war-debate-public-divide-into-four-groups-not-two-warring-tribes. On America see recent research by Pew Research Center at https://www.pewresearch.org/politics/2022/06/16/politics-on-twitter-one-third-of-tweets-from-u-s-adults-are-political/.

64. Christophe Guilluy (2019), *Twilight of the Elites: Prosperity, the Periphery, and the Future of France*, Yale University Press.

65. W. Jennings and G. Stoker (2017), 'Tilting towards the cosmopolitan axis? Political change in England and the 2017 general election', *Political Quarterly* 88(3), pp. 359–69; see also F. Mitsch, N. Lee and E. R. Morrow (2021), 'Faith no more? The divergence of political trust between urban and rural Europe', *Political Geography* 89, 102426.

66. S. Butt, E. Clery and J. Curtice (eds.) (2022), *British Social Attitudes: The 39th Report*, National Centre for Social Research.

67. Data from 2013 *British Social Attitudes* survey.

68. D. Luca, J. Terrero-Davila, J. Stein and N. Lee (2022), 'Progressive cities: urban-rural polarisation of social values and economic development around the world', International Inequalities Institute Working Papers (74), International Inequalities Institute, LSE.

69. David Brooks, 'How the Bobos Broke America', *The Atlantic*, September 2021.

70. 'Who doesn't want to hear the other side's view?', Noah Carl Substack, 28 April 2017, https://noahcarl.medium.com/who-doesnt-want-to-hear-the-other-s-view-9a7cdf3ad702.

71. YouGov, 'Does marrying someone with different politics matter to parents?', 27 August 2019, https://yougov.co.uk/topics/relationships/articles-reports/2019/08/27/labour-voters-more-wary-about-politics-childs-spou?utm_source=twitter&utm_medium=website_article&utm_campaign=labour_conservative_children. In America, similarly, while 61 per cent of Hillary Clinton's supporters felt it would be 'hard' to be friends with people who had voted for Trump, only 34 per cent of Trump voters felt the same way about people who had voted for Clinton. Single people who support the Democrats were about 20 points more likely than single people who support the Republicans to say they would not consider being in a committed relationship

with somebody from the other side of the political divide. 'Most Democrats who are looking for a relationship would not consider dating a Trump voter', Pew Research Center, 24 April 2020, https://www.pewresearch.org/fact-tank/2020/04/24/most-democrats-who-are-looking-for-a-relationship-would-not-consider-dating-a-trump-voter/.

72. Benson and Duffy, 'The four sides in the UK's "culture wars"'.

CHAPTER 2: REVOLUTION

1. Anthony King (1975), 'Overload: problems of governing in the 1970s', *Political Studies*, 23(2–3), pp. 284–96; also Anthony King (ed.) (1976), *Why Is Britain Becoming Harder to Govern?*, British Broadcasting Corporation.

2. Originally cited in Robert Saunders (2018), *Yes to Europe! The 1975 Referendum and Seventies Britain*, Cambridge University Press, pp. 27–62.

3. Margaret Thatcher (1993), *The Downing Street Years*, HarperCollins, p. 8.

4. Dani Rodrik (2019), 'Globalization's wrong turn and how it hurt America', *Foreign Affairs* 98(4).

5. David Edgerton (2018), *The Rise and Fall of the British Nation: A Twenty-First Century History*, Penguin, p. 469.

6. Harold Macmillan, speech to the Tory Reform Group, 8 November 1985.

7. Historical strike data, https://www.ons.gov.uk/employmentandlabourmarket/peopleinwork/workplacedisputesandworkingconditions/articles/labourdisputes/2018#historical-context; John Van Reenen, 'The economic legacy of Margaret Thatcher is a mixed bag', LSE, 13 April 2013, https://blogs.lse.ac.uk/europpblog/2013/04/13/the-economic-legacy-of-margaret-thatcher-is-a-mixed-bag-john-van-reenen/.

8. Anthony Heath, Elizabeth Garrett, Ridhi Kashyap, Yaojun Li and Lindsay Richards (2018), *Social Progress in Britain*, Oxford University Press; see also Richard Blundell and Ben Etheridge (2010), 'Consumption, income and earnings inequality in Britain', *Review of Economic Dynamics* 13(1), pp. 76–102.

9. 'Household income inequality, UK: financial year ending 2020', Office for National Statistics, 22 July 2020, https://www.ons.gov.uk/peoplepopulationandcommunity/personalandhouseholdfinances/income

andwealth/bulletins/householdincomeinequalityfinancial/financial
yearending2020provisional.

10. Rawi Abdelal (2006), 'Writing the rules of global finance: France,
Europe and capital liberalization', *Review of International Political
Economy* 13(1), pp. 1–27.

11. Peter Mandelson speech to executives in Silicon Valley, California,
October 1999. Cited in Andrew Rawnsley (2000), *Servants of the
People*, Hamish Hamilton.

12. Colin Hay (1999), *The Political Economy of New Labour: Labouring
under False Pretences?*, Manchester University Press, p. 42.

13. Henry Kissinger (2022), *Leadership: Six Studies in World Strategy*,
Allen Lane. Quote originally cited in Niall Ferguson, 'Henry Kissinger
at 99: how to avoid another world war', *Sunday Times Magazine*, 11
June 2002.

14. The evidence suggests the income of low-income working-age adults
without children rose very little, and their relative poverty rate
increased. Robert Joyce and Luke Sibieta (2013), 'An Assessment of
Labour's record on income inequality and poverty', *Oxford Review of
Economic Policy* 29(1), pp. 178–202.

15. 'Tony Blair's conference speech 2015', *Guardian*, 27 September 2005,
https://www.theguardian.com/uk/2005/sep/27/labourconference.
speeches.

16. Oliver Bullough (2022), *Butler to the World*, Profile.

17. 'Firms on Caribbean island chain own 23,000 UK properties', *BBC
News*, 13 February 2018; 'Foreign ownership of homes in England and
Wales triples', *Financial Times*, 21 November 2021.

18. Lawrence Summers, 'America needs to make a new case for trade',
Financial Times, 27 April 2008.

19. 'Manufacturing: Statistics and Policy', briefing paper 01942, House of
Commons Library, January 2020.

20. Philip McCann and Raquel Ortega-Argilés (2021), 'The UK "geography of discontent": narratives, Brexit and inter-regional "levelling
up"', *Cambridge Journal of Regions, Economy and Society* 14.3,
pp. 545–64.

21. Ibid.

22. Philip McCann (2016), *The UK Regional-National Economic Prob-
lem: Geography, Globalisation and Governance*, Routledge; W. Tanner,
J. O'Shaughnessy, F. Krasniqi and J. Blagden (2020), *The State of our
Social Fabric: Measuring the Changing Nature of Community over*

Time and Geography, Onward, https://www.ukonward.com/wp-content/uploads/2020/09/The-State-of-our-Social-Fabric.pdf; GBD 2016 Healthcare Access and Quality Collaborators, 'Measuring performance on the Healthcare Access and Quality Index for 195 countries and territories and selected subnational locations', *Lancet*, 23 May 2018, pp. 2236–71, https://www.thelancet.com/journals/lancet/article/PIIS0140-6736(18)30994-2/fulltext; UK2070 (2020), *Make No Little Plans: Acting at Scale for a Fairer and Stronger Future*, Final Report of the UK2070 Commission; P. Veneri and F. Murtin (2019), 'Where are the highest living standards? Measuring well-being and inclusiveness in OECD regions', *Regional Studies* 53, pp. 657–66.

23. P. Carneiro, S. Cattan, L. Dearden, L. van der Erve, S. Krutikova and L. Macmillan (2020), 'The long shadow of deprivation: differences in opportunities across England', Institute for Fiscal Studies, 15 September 2020, https://ifs.org.uk/publications/long-shadow-deprivation-differences-opportunities-across-england.

24. D. Dorn and P. Levell, 'Trade and inequality in Europe and the US', *IFS Deaton Review of Inequalities*, 16 November 2021, https://ifs.org.uk/inequality/trade-and-inequality-in-europe-and-the-us/; D. Autor, D. Dorn and G. Hanson (2013), 'The China Syndrome: local labor market effects of import competition in the United States', *American Economic Review* 103(6), pp. 2121–68; S. Hakobyan and J. McLaren (2016), 'Looking for local labor market effects of NAFTA', *Review of Economics and Statistics*, 98, pp. 728–41.

25. D. Rodrik (2021), 'A primer on trade and inequality', *IFS Deaton Review of Inequalities*, 16 November 2021, https://ifs.org.uk/inequality/a-primer-on-trade-and-inequality/.

26. David Autor, David Dorn and Gordon Hanson (2016), 'The China Shock: learning from labor-market adjustment to large changes in trade', *Annual Review of Economics* 8, pp. 205–40.

27. Mia Gray and Anna Barford (2018), 'The depths of the cuts: the uneven geography of local government austerity', *Cambridge Journal of Regions, Economy and Society* 11(3), pp. 541–63.

28. Ipsos-MORI, 'Broken-system sentiment in 2021: populism, anti-elitism and nativism', Ipsos Global Advisor 25, Country Survey, July 2021, https://www.ipsos.com/sites/default/files/ct/news/documents/2021-07/GA%20-%20Broken%20System%20Sentiment%20-%20Populist%20Anti-Elitism%20and%20Nativism%20in%202021%20-%20Graphic%20Report.pdf.

29. Christina Beatty and Steve Fothergill (2018), *The Contemporary Labour Market in Britain's Older Industrial Towns*, Centre for Regional Economic and Social Research/Joseph Rowntree Foundation.

30. Anne Case and Angus Deaton (2020), *Deaths of Despair and the Future of Capitalism*, Princeton University Press, 2020.

31. Veena Raleigh, *What Is Happening to Life Expectancy in England?* Kings Fund, 6 December 2021.

32. Public Health England, *A Review of Recent Trends in Mortality in England*; see also 'Drug deaths: England and Wales see highest number since records began', *British Medical Journal*, 15 October 2020.

33. 'Drug-related deaths hit record high in England and Wales after rising for eighth year in a row', *Sky News*, 2 September 2021.

34. D. Dorn and G. Hanson (2019), 'When work disappears: manufacturing decline and the falling marriage market value of young men', *American Economic Review: Insights* 1(2), pp. 161–78.

35. OECD, 'Further information on the living arrangements of children', https://www.oecd.org/els/soc/SF_1_3_Living-arrangements-children. pdf; G. R. Weitoft, A. Hjern, B. Haglund and M. Rosén (2003), 'Mortality, severe morbidity, and injury in children living with single parents in Sweden: a population-based study', *Lancet*, 361(9354), pp. 289–95; G. R. Weitoft, A. Hjern and M. Rosén (2004), 'School's out! Why earlier among children of lone parents?' *International Journal of Social Welfare* 13(2), pp. 134–44, https://www.ons.gov.uk/peoplepopulation andcommunity/birthsdeathsandmarriages/families/bulletins/ familiesandhouseholds/2019.

36. While nearly 30 per cent of births to low-educated women are to women not living with their partner, only 6 per cent of births to highly educated graduate women are. Kiernan et al., 'Families and inequality'.

37. R. Blundell, R. Joyce, A. Norris Keiller and J. P. Ziliak (2018), 'Income inequality and the Labour market in Britain and the US', *Journal of Public Economics* 162, pp. 48–62; Kiernan et al., 'Families and inequality'; W. Adema, C. Clarke and O. Thevenon (2020), 'Family policies and family outcomes in OECD countries', in *The Palgrave Handbook of Family Policy*, Palgrave Macmillan, pp. 193–217.

38. While nearly 30 per cent of births to low-educated women are to women not living with their partner. only 6 per cent of births to highly educated graduate women are. Kiernan et al., 'Families and inequality'.

39. On trade shocks see Italo Colantone and Piero Stanig (2018), 'Global competition and Brexit', *American Political Science Review*, 112(2), pp. 201–18; Francesco Nicoli, Dominik Geulen Walters and Ann-Kathrin Reinl (2021), 'Not so far east? the impact of Central-Eastern European imports on the Brexit referendum', *Journal of European Public Policy* 29(9), pp. 1–20. On immigration see M. J. Goodwin and O. Heath (2016), 'The 2016 referendum, Brexit and the left behind: an aggregate-level analysis of the result', *Political Quarterly* 87(3), pp. 323–32. On housing markets see B. Ansell and D. Adler (2019), 'Brexit and the politics of housing in Britain', *Political Quarterly* 90(S2); Miguel Carreras, Yasemin Irepoglu Carreras and Shaun Bowler (2019), 'Long-term economic distress, cultural backlash, and support for Brexit', *Comparative Political Studies* 52.9, pp. 1396–424.

40. Paul Collier (2019), *The Future of Capitalism: Facing the New Anxieties*, Penguin.

41. Hendrik Zorn, Armin Schäfer and Philip Manow (2004), *European Social Policy and Europe's Party-political Center of Gravity, 1957–2003*, MPIfG Discussion Paper, no. 04/6.

42. I draw here on British Election Study data.

43. Colin Crouch (2004), *Post-Democracy*, Polity.

44. Anthony King (2015), *Who Governs Britain?* Penguin.

45. Michal Moran (2018), 'Whatever happened to overloaded government?' *Political Quarterly*, 89(1).

46. R. A. Rhodes (2007), 'Understanding governance: ten years on', *Organization studies* 28(8), pp. 1243–64; B. Guerin, J. McCrae and M. Shepheard (2018), 'Accountability in modern government: what are the issues?', *Institute for Government* 23; C. J. Bickerton (2012), *European Integration: From Nation-states to Member States*, Oxford University Press; S. Strange (1995), 'The defective state', *Daedalus* 124(2), pp. 55–74. Peter Mair, 'Political opposition and the European Union', https://www.cambridge.org/core/journals/government-and-opposition/article/political-opposition-and-the-european-union1/7C9AEB444CBFE3FF85AE655C9CD4DD93.

47. Cited in Adam Tooze (2018), *Crashed: How a Decade of Financial Crises Changed the World*, Penguin.

48. Originally cited in Roger Eatwell and Matthew Goodwin (2018), *National Populism: The Revolt Against Liberal Democracy*, Penguin, p. 100.

49. Quoted in Philip Stephens (2003), 'The Blair Government and Europe', in Andrew Chadwick and Richard Heffernan (eds.), *The New Labour Reader*, Polity Press, p. 253.

50. As Blair told the London Business School in July 1999: 'Britain should join a successful single currency, provided the economic conditions are met . . . It is a position of genuine conviction. I happen to believe in it', Tony Blair, 'Making the case for Britain in Europe. The prime minister's full speech to the London Business School', 27 July 1999, https://www. theguardian.com/business/1999/jul/27/emu.theeuro2.

51. Simon Bulmer (2008), 'New Labour, new European policy? Blair, Brown and utilitarian supranationalism', *Parliamentary Affairs* 61(4), pp. 597–620.

52. 'EU vote: Where the cabinet and other MPs stand', *BBC News*, 22 June 2016.

53. Kyriaki Nanou and Han Dorussen (2013), 'European integration and electoral democracy: how the European Union constrains party competition in the member states', *European Journal of Political Research* 52(1), pp. 71–93; see also Vivien Schmidt (2006). *Democracy in Europe: The EU and National Polities*, Oxford University Press

54. Helen Thompson, 'How the EU bungled Brexit', *UnHerd*, 25 June 2021, https://unherd.com/2021/06/how-the-eu-bungled-brexit/.

55. Peter Mair (2007), 'Political opposition and the European Union', *Government and Opposition* 42(1), pp. 1–17.

56. Andreas Follesdal and Simon Hix (2006), 'Why there is a democratic deficit in the EU: A response to Majone and Moravcsik', *Journal of Common Market Studies* 44(3), pp. 533–62.

57. Bickerton. *European Integration*.

58. Originally cited in Matthew Finders (2012), *Defending Politics: Why Democracy Matters in the Twenty-First Century*, Oxford University Press, p. 90.

59. L. Rennwald (2020), *Social Democratic Parties and the Working Class: New Voting Patterns*, Springer Nature, p. 111.

60. Consistently, immigration has exceeded emigration by more than 100,000 in every year since 1998. For these and other statistics see 'Migration statistics briefing paper', House of Commons Library, no. CBP06077 (2021).

61. Steve Vertovec (2007), 'Super-diversity and its implications', *Ethnic and Racial Studies* 30(6), pp. 1024–54.

62. Office for National Statistics, 'Births by parents' country of birth, England and Wales: 2019', https://www.ons.gov.uk/peoplepopulation andcommunity/birthsdeathsandmarriages/livebirths/bulletins/ parentscountryofbirthenglandandwales/2019.

63. National Population Projections: 2021-based interim. Office for National Statistics, January 2022, https://www.ons.gov.uk/peoplepop ulationandcommunity/populationandmigration/populationestimates/ articles/overviewoftheukpopulation/january2021.

64. Andrew Neather, 'Don't listen to the whingers – London needs immigrants', *Evening Standard*, 23 October 2009.

65. Ibid.

66. M. Goodwin and C. Milazzo (2017), 'Taking back control? Investigating the role of immigration in the 2016 vote for Brexit', *The British Journal of Politics and International Relations* 19(3), pp. 450–64.

67. Toby Perkins (2021), 'Skilled approach: education and training for the opportunities of the future', in John Healey (ed.), *Hearts and Minds: Winning the Working-Class Vote*, Fabian Society, https://fabians.org. uk/wp-content/uploads/2021/04/FABJ8753-Fabian-Ideas-pamphlet- WEB-210406VI.pdf.

68. Carlos Vargas-Silva, Madeleine Sumption and Peter Walsh (2022), *The Fiscal Impact of Immigration in the UK: Migration Observatory*, University of Oxford.

69. Lauren McLaren and Mark Johnson (2007), 'Resources, group conflict and symbols: explaining anti-immigration hostility in Britain', *Political Studies* 55, pp. 709–32.

70. 'The Casey Review: a review into opportunity and integration', p. 5, https://assets.publishing.service.gov.uk/government/uploads/system/ uploads/attachment_data/file/575973/The_Casey_Review_Report.pdf; see also Ted Cantle (2001), *Community Cohesion: A Report of the Independent Review Team,* Home Office; 'Britain "sleepwalking to segregation"', *Guardian*, 19 September 2005.

71. Ed Husain (2021), *Among the Mosques: A Journey Across Muslim Britain*, Bloomsbury.

72. Ibid.

73. Ibid.

74. ICM polling 2015. Overall, 49 per cent said, 'I would like to fully integrate with non-Muslims in all aspects of life'; 29 per cent said, 'I would like to integrate on most things, but there should be separation in some

areas, such as Islamic schooling and laws'; 17 per cent said, 'I would like to integrate on some things, but I would prefer to lead a separate Islamic life as far as possible'; while 1 per cent said, 'I would like to live in a fully separate Islamic area in Britain, subject to Sharia Law and government'. https://www.icmunlimited.com/wp-content/uploads/2016/04/Mulims-full-suite-data-plus-topline.pdf.

75. *British Social Attitudes*, 2016. Only 12 per cent felt they could do a lot or a little to improve the situation.

76. 'Migration statistics briefing paper', House of Commons Library no. CBP06077, 2021.

77. Office for National Statistics (2012), 'Methods used to revise the national population estimates for mid-2002 to mid-2010', Office for National Statistics, http://ons.gov.uk/ons/guide-method/method-quality/specific/population-and-migration/population-statistics-research-unit-psru-/methods-used-to-revise-the-national-population-estimates-for-mid-2002-to-mid-2010.pdf.

78. For a useful breakdown of this see: https://researchbriefings.files.parliament.uk/documents/SN06077/SN06077.pdf.

79. James Dennison and Matthew Goodwin (2015), 'Immigration, issue ownership and the rise of UKIP', *Parliamentary Affairs* 68, pp. 168–87.

80. Edward Fieldhouse, Jane Green, Geoffrey Evans, Jon Mellon, Chris Prosser, Hermann Schmitt and Cees van der Eijk (2021), *Electoral Shocks: The Volatile Voter in a Turbulent World*, Oxford University Press, pp. 75–6.

81. Cameron returned with insignificant changes to in-work benefits for EU migrant workers, had to shelve more ambitious plans for a brake on migration and was unable to prevent EU nationals from sending benefits they received in Britain back to their countries of origin.

82. 'UKIP demands apology from Cameron', *BBC News*, 4 April 2006. http://news.bbc.co.uk/1/hi/4875026.stm.

CHAPTER 3: VALUES

1. Stanley Greenberg (2015), *America Ascendant*, Thomas Dunne Books. For very similar arguments in the UK see Robert Ford and Maria Sobolewska (2020), *Brexitland: Identity, Diversity, and the Reshaping of British Politics*, Cambridge University Press.

2. Polly Toynbee, 'On Saturday the UK turns remain. Parliament must force a second referendum', *Guardian*, 17 January 2019.

3. Pew Research Center, 'Attitudes on same-sex marriage', 14 May 2019, https://www.pewresearch.org/religion/fact-sheet/changing-attitudes-on-gay-marriage/; Equis Research (2021), '2020 post-mortem. The American dream voter', https://static1.squarespace.com/static/5d30982 b599bde00016db472/t/61b7e8e75c74f5558036268b/1639442667 560/Post-Mortem+Part+Two+FINAL+Dec+13.pdf. Published December 14 2021; Ruy Texeira, 'The Democrats' Hispanic voter problem', *The Liberal Patriot*, 9 December 2021.

4. John Curtice and Victoria Ratti (2022), 'Culture wars', in S. Butt, E. Clery and J. Curtice (eds.) (2022), *British Social Attitudes: The 39th Report*, National Centre for Social Research.

5. For further discussion of this point see John Curtice (2014), 'A revolt on the right? The social and political attitudes of UKIP supporters', *British Social Attitudes* 32, https://www.bsa.natcen.ac.uk/media/38974/ bsa32_ukip.pdf; also Robert Ford and Matthew Goodwin (2014), *Revolt on the Right: Explaining Support for the Radical Right in Britain*, Routledge.

6. Isabelle Kirk, 'Britons don't tend to support the death penalty . . . until you name the worst crimes', YouGov, 30 March 2022, https://yougov. co.uk/topics/politics/articles-reports/2022/03/30/britons-dont-tend-support-death-penalty-until-you-; Isabelle Kirk, 'Criminal sentencing is too soft, say two-thirds of Britons', YouGov, 30 March 2022, https:// yougov.co.uk/topics/politics/articles-reports/2022/03/30/criminal-sentencing-too-soft-say-two-thirds-briton.

7. Marc Hetherington and Jonathan Weiler (2018), *Prius or Pickup? How the Answers to Four Simple Questions Explain America's Great Divide*, Houghton Mifflin.

8. According to the British Election Study, traditionalists were more than twice as likely as the graduate class to think 'government takes better care of ethnic minorities than the white majority'. On Black Lives Matter see More in Common, 'Britons and gender identity', 2022, https:// www.moreincommon.org.uk/our-work/research/britons-and-gender-identity/.

9. More in Common, 'Britain's choice', https://www.britainschoice.uk/.

10. Kirby Swales (2016), *Understanding the Leave Vote*, National Centre for Social Research.

11. M. J. Goodwin and C. Milazzo (2015), *Britain, the European Union and the Referendum: What Drives Euroscepticism?* Chatham House.

12. Kirby Swales, 'Understanding the Leave vote', NatCen, natcen_brex-planations-report-final-web2.pdf.

13. Bobby Duffy et al., 'The "fault lines" in the UK's culture wars', https://www.ipsos.com/sites/default/files/ct/news/documents/2021-06/fault-lines-in-the-uks-culture-wars-kings-ipsos-mori-jun-2021.pdf.

14. Sara B. Hobolt, Thomas J. Leeper and James Tilley (2020), 'Divided by the vote: affective polarization in the wake of the Brexit Referendum', *British Journal of Political Science* 51(4), pp. 1–18.

15. Chris Hanretty (2017), 'Areal interpolation and the UK's referendum on EU membership', *Journal of Elections, Public Opinion and Parties* 27(4), http://dx.doi.org/10.1080/17457289.2017.1287081.

16. YouGov (2016), 'On the day poll', YouGov, https://d25d2506sfb94s.cloudfront.net/cumulus_uploads/document/640yx5morx/On_the_Day_FINAL_poll_forwebsite.pdf. Lord Ashcroft, 'How the United Kingdom voted on Thursday … and why', *Lord Ashcroft Polls*, 24 June2016,https://lordashcroftpolls.com/2016/06/how-the-united-kingdom-voted-and-why/.

17. https://www.britishelectionstudy.com/bes-findings/what-mattered-most-to-you-when-deciding-how-to-vote-in-the-eu-referendum/#.Ybn6R73P39M.

18. Centre for Social Investigation, Nuffield College, 'People's stated reasons for voting Leave or Remain', https://ukandeu.ac.uk/wp-content/uploads/2018/07/CSI-Brexit-4-People's-Stated-Reasons-for-Voting-Leave.pdf.

19. I draw here on British Election Study data.

20. I am drawing here on the latest *British Social Attitudes* survey data.

21. M. Goodwin and C. Milazzo (2017), 'Taking back control? Investigating the role of immigration in the 2016 vote for Brexit', *The British Journal of Politics and International Relations* 19(3), pp. 450–64. Regarding the point on 2019 I draw on British Election Study data.

22. *Things Not to Say to Someone Who Voted Brexit*, BBC Three, https://www.bbc.co.uk/bbcthree/clip/349b32a3-1fd6-4b73-8d0b-7fb6afbfccab.

23. Simon Hix, Eric Kaufmann and Thomas Leeper (2021), 'Pricing immigration', *Journal of Experimental Political Science* 8(1), pp. 63–74.

24. Matt Grossmann and Daniel Thaler (2018), 'Mass–elite divides in aversion to social change and support for Donald Trump', *American Politics Research* 46(5), pp. 753–78.

25. Ford and Sobolewska, *Brexitland*.

26. I draw here on *British Social Attitudes* data.

27. Pew Research Center, 'Europe's growing Muslim population', 29 November 2017, https://www.pewresearch.org/religion/2017/11/29/europes-growing-muslim-population/.

28. *British Social Attitudes* survey data 2013; YouGov survey results, 12–13 February 2019, https://docs.cdn.yougov.com/t9ukrh70x4/YGC%20Tracker%20GB%20Feb%2019.pdf.

29. Ipsos MORI, 'Attitudes to race and inequality in Great Britain', https://www.ipsos.com/en-uk/attitudes-race-and-inequality-great-britain.

30. 'National identity: exploring Britishness', *British Social Attitudes* 31, https://www.bsa.natcen.ac.uk/media/38984/bsa31_national_identity.pdf.

31. https://www.ipsos.com/sites/default/files/ct/news/documents/2021-07/ipsos-pridetabs-postmatch.pdf.

32. I am drawing here on *British Social Attitudes* survey data.

33. David Voas and Steve Bruce (2019), 'Religion: identity, behaviour and and belief over two decades', *British Social Attitudes* 36, pp. 17–44, https://www.bsa.natcen.ac.uk/media/39293/1_bsa36_religion.pdf.

34. *British Social Attitudes* survey data.

35. Sobolewska and Ford, *Brexitland*.

36. 'National identity: exploring Britishness'.

37. Francis Fukuyama (2018), *Identity: Contemporary Identity Politics and the Struggle for Recognition*, Profile Books, 2018.

38. Eric Kaufmann (2020), 'Liberal fundamentalism: a sociology of wokeness', *American Affairs* 4(4), p. 193.

39. John Curtice (2017), 'Why Leave won the UK EU Referendum', *Journal of Common Market Studies* 55, https://onlinelibrary.wiley.com/doi/abs/10.1111/jcms.12613.

40. Kirby Swales (2016), *Understanding the Leave Vote*, National Centre for Social Research.

41. L. Rennwald (2020), 'The class basis of Social Democracy at the beginning of the twenty-first century', in *Social Democratic Parties and the Working Class*, Palgrave Macmillan, pp. 51–69.

42. Paula Surridge (2018), 'The fragmentation of the electoral left since 2010', *Renewal: A Journal of Social Democracy* 26(4), pp. 69–78.

43. Ibid.; Labour Together (2020), *Election Review 2019*; Deborah Mattinson (2020), *Beyond the Red Wall: Why Labour Lost, how the Conservatives Won and What will Happen Next?* Biteback.

44. Peter Kellner (2021), *From Red Walls to Red Bridges: Rebuilding Labour's Voter Coalition.* Tony Blair Institute.

45. While only 36 per cent of Labour cosmopolitans felt that 'politicians don't care what people like me think', this rocketed to 71 per cent among Labour traditionalists. While only 44 per cent of Labour cosmopolitans felt 'people like me have no say in what government does', 75 per cent of Labour traditionalists felt this way. And while only 38 per cent of Labour cosmopolitans felt politicians were only looking out for their own interests rather than those of the people who had elected them, this surged to almost 70 per cent among Labour traditionalists. Surridge, 'The fragmentation of the electoral left since 2010'.

46. More in Common, 'Britain's choice'.

47. Rebecca Benson and Bobby Duffy (2021), 'The four sides in the UK's "culture wars"', Ipsos-MORI, Policy Institute and Kings College London, https://www.kcl.ac.uk/policy-institute/assets/the-four-sides-in-the-uks-culture-wars.pdf.

48. Kings College London News Centre, 'UK "culture war" debate: public divide into four groups, not two', 18 June 2021, https://www.kcl.ac.uk/news/uk-culture-war-debate-public-divide-into-four-groups-not-two-warring-tribes.

49. YouGov, 'How prevalent Brits think racism is', https://yougov.co.uk/topics/politics/trackers/how-prevalent-brits-think-racism-is?cross Break=ivotedtoleave.

50. More in Common, 'Britain's choice'.

51. Ibid.

52. More in Common, 'Britons and gender identity', 2022, https://www.moreincommon.org.uk/our-work/research/britons-and-gender-identity/.

53. Ibid.

54. Kings College London News Centre, 'UK "culture war" debate'.

55. Ibid.

56. L. Legault, J. N. Gutsell and M. Inzlicht (2011), 'Ironic effects of antiprejudice messages: How motivational interventions can reduce (but also increase) prejudice', *Psychological Science* 22(12), pp. 1472–7.

57. Patricia G. Devine and Tory L. Ash (2022), 'Diversity training goals, limitations, and promise: a review of the multidisciplinary literature', *Annual Review of Psychology* 73, pp. 403–29; see also F. Dobbin and A. Kalev (2016), 'Why diversity programs fail', *Harvard Business Review* 94(7), p. 14.

58. Devine and Ash, 'Diversity training goals, limitations, and promise'.

59. Lucian Gideon Conway, Meredith A. Repke and Shannon C. Houck (2017), 'Donald Trump as a cultural revolt against perceived communication restriction: priming political correctness norms causes more Trump support', *Journal of Social and Political Psychology* 5(1).

60. E. Cooley, J. L. Brown-Iannuzzi, R. F. Lei and W. Cipolli III (2019), 'Complex intersections of race and class: among social liberals, learning about White privilege reduces sympathy, increases blame, and decreases external attributions for White people struggling with poverty', *Journal of Experimental Psychology: General* 148(12), p. 2218.

CHAPTER 4: VOICE

1. 'Face it. PLU blew it for everyone but themselves', *Financial Times*, 15 December 2016.

2. Michael Lind (2020). *The New Class War: Saving Democracy from the Metropolitan Elite*, Atlantic Books, p. 45.

3. Ross McKibbon (1975), *The Evolution of the Labour Party, 1910–1924*, Oxford University Press.

4. 'Membership of UK political parties', House of Commons Library, briefing paper no. SN05125, August 2019.

5. Jane Wills and Melanie Simms (2004), 'Building reciprocal community unionism in the UK', *Capital and Class* 28(1), pp. 59–84.

6. R. Cherrington (2012), *Not Just Beer and Bingo! A Social History of Working Men's Clubs*, AuthorHouse; Z. Layton-Henry (1973), 'The Young Conservatives 1945–70', *Journal of Contemporary History* 8(2), pp. 143–56.

7. D. Butler and D. Stokes (1969), *Political Change in Britain*, St Martin's Press.

8. YouGov, 'Political disaffection is rising, and driving UKIP support', 29 October 2014, https://yougov.co.uk/topics/politics/articles-reports/2014/10/29/political-disaffection-not-new-it-rising-and-drivi.

9. Guttsman estimates that the percentage of Labour MPs from private school backgrounds jumped from 6.5 per cent in 1918–35 to 21 per cent in 1951, so still a minority. W. L. Guttsman (1965), *The British Political Elite*, Macgibbon and Kee. R. W. Johnson notes that that in 1951 the working-class proportion of the Labour Parliamentary Party was 45 per cent, while the proportion of middle-class professionals was 45 per cent. R.W. Johnson (1973), 'The British Political Elite,

1955–1972', *European Journal of Sociology/Archives Européennes de Sociologie* 14(1), pp. 35–77.

10. John Bew (2016), *Citizen Clem: A Biography of Attlee*, Hachette.

11. Lind, *New Class War*, pp. 47–8.

12. T. Piketty (2018), 'Brahmin left vs merchant right: rising inequality and the changing structure of political conflict', *WID World Working Paper*, p. 7.

13. Data collected by author. For recent years I updated a dataset kindly provided to me by Tom O'Grady, which is available upon request from the author.

14. 'Social background of Members of Parliament 1979–2010', House of Commons Library, February 2022, https://commonslibrary.parliament. uk/research-briefings/cbp–7483/; Chris Butler, Rosie Campbell and Jennifer Hudson (2021), 'Political recruitment under pressure, again: MPs and candidates in the 2019 General Election', in Robert Ford, Tim Bale and Will Jennings (2021), *The British General Election of 2019*, Palgrave Macmillan, pp. 387–420.

15. Butler, Campbell and Hudson, 'Political recruitment under pressure, again'.

16. Over the past decade, the proportion of non-white politicians has increased from one in forty to one in ten, while the proportion who are women is up from one in five to one in three. There are no official data on sexual orientation, but I follow the House of Commons briefing paper which notes that forty-six openly gay MPs were elected in 2019, one fewer than the record set in 2017: https://researchbriefings.files. parliament.uk/documents/CBP–7483/CBP–7483.pdf.

17. Michael Lind, *The New Class War*.

18. D. Mattinson (2020), *Beyond the Red Wall: Why Labour Lost, How the Conservatives Won and What Will Happen Next?* Biteback, p. 9.

19. Geoffrey Evans and Jonathan Mellon (2016), 'Social class: identity, awareness and political attitudes', *British Social Attitudes* 33, https:// www.bsa.natcen.ac.uk/media/39094/bsa33_social-class_v5.pdf.

20. Sam Friedman, Dave O'Brien and Ian McDonald (2021), 'Deflecting privilege: class identity and the intergenerational self', *Sociology* 55(4), pp. 716–33.

21. Oliver Heath (2015), 'Policy representation, social representation and class voting in Britain', *British Journal of Political Science* 45(1), pp. 173–93; G. Evans and J. Tilley (2017), *The New Politics of Class: The Political Exclusion of the British Working Class*, Oxford University Press; Geoff Evans and P. Langsaether (2021), 'The realignment of

class politics and class voting', *Oxford Research Encyclopaedia of Politics* 10, p. 1093.

22. Heath (2015), 'Policy representation'.

23. Evans and Tilley, *The New Politics of Class*.

24. YouGov/Channel 4 Megapoll, 2009, https://www.channel4.com/news/media/2009/06/day08/yougovpoll_080609.pdf.

25. Peter Kellner (2021), *From Red Walls to Red Bridges; Rebuilding Labour's Voter Coalition*, Tony Blair Institute.

26. Mattinson *Beyond the Red Wall*, pp. 125–6.

27. Ibid.

28. Mark Bovens and Anchrit Wille (2017), *Diploma Democracy: The Rise of Political Meritocracy*, Oxford University Press.

29. The percentage of Conservative MPs who went to fee-paying schools stayed above 70 per cent between 1979 and 1983, above 60 per cent between 1987 and 2005 and then dropped to 54 per cent in 2010 and 50 per cent in 2015. It later fell to 44 per cent in 2017 and then 44 per cent in 2019. The share who went to Oxbridge remained stable, above 40 per cent, until it fell to 34 per cent in 2010, 30 per cent in 2015, 34 per cent in 2017 and 29 per cent in 2019. 'Social backgrounds of MPs 1979–2019', House of Commons Library, https://researchbriefings.files.parliament.uk/documents/CBP-7483/CBP-7483.pdf.

30. Sutton Trust, 'The state school cabinet', 15 July 2016, https://www.suttontrust.com/news-opinion/all-news-opinion/the-state-school-cabinet/. Sutton Trust, 'Cabinet analysis 2021', https://www.suttontrust.com/our-research/sutton-trust-cabinet-analysis-2021/; Sutton Trust, 'Cabinet analysis 2022', 7 September 2022, https://www.suttontrust.com/our-research/sutton-trust-cabinet-analysis-2022/.

31. Daniel Tomlinson, 'Trade union membership has fallen further than ever before', Resolution Foundation, 31 May 2017, https://www.resolutionfoundation.org/comment/trade-union-membership-has-fallen-further-than-ever-before/.

32. Evans and Tilley, *The New Politics of Class*, p. 128.

33. 'Social background of Members of Parliament 1979–2010', House of Commons Library, February 2022, https://commonslibrary.parliament.uk/research-briefings/cbp-7483/.

34. Ibid.

35. Ibid.

36. 'The Establishment is dead. But something worse has replaced it', *Spectator*, 15 September 2007.

37. Richard S. Katz and Peter Mair (1995), 'Changing models of party organization and party democracy: the emergence of the cartel party', *Party Politics* 1(1), pp. 5–28.

38. Cited in Matthew Goodwin and Caitlin Milazzo (2016), *UKIP: Inside the Campaign to Redraw the Map of British Politics*, Oxford University Press.

39. Nick Vivyan, Markus Wagner, Konstantin Glinitzer and Jakob-Moritz Eberl (2020), 'Do humble beginnings help? How politician class roots shape voter evaluations', *Electoral Studies*, p. 63; Rosie Campbell and Philip Cowley (2014), 'Rich man, poor man, politician man: wealth effects in a candidate biography survey experiment', *British Journal of Politics and International Relations* 16(1), pp. 56–74; J. Robison, R. Stubager, M. Thau and J. Tilley (2020) 'Does class-based campaigning work? How working class appeals attract and polarize voters', *Comparative Political Studies* 54(5), pp. 723–52.

40. Rosie Campbell and Oliver Heath (2021), 'Fueling the populist divide: nativist and cosmopolitan preferences for representation at the elite and mass level', *Political Behaviour* 43(4), pp. 1707–28.

41. According to the Sutton Trust, in 2019, on average 44 per cent of people across Whitehall and public bodies attended an independent school and 39 per cent attended Oxbridge, far higher than the national average: https://assets.publishing.service.gov.uk/government/uploads/system/uploads/attachment_data/file/811045/Elitist_Britain_2019.pdf.

42. Bridge Group (2016), *Socio-Economic Diversity in the Fast Stream*, Cabinet Office.

43. Social Mobility Commission (2021), *Navigating the Labyrinth. Socio-economic Background and Career Progression within the Civil Service*. Social Mobility Commission.

44. L. Elsässer, S. Hense and A. Schäfer (2021), 'Not just money: unequal responsiveness in egalitarian democracies', *Journal of European Public Policy* 28(12), pp. 1890–1908.

45. Bovens and Wille, *Diploma Democracy*.

46. Ibid., p. 2.

47. N. Carnes (2018), *The Cash Ceiling*. Princeton University Press, pp. 2–3.

48. W. Schakel and D. van der Pas (2021), 'Degrees of influence: educational inequality in policy representation', *European Journal of Political Research* 60(2), pp. 418–37.

49. Ibid.

50. Elsässer et al., 'Not just money'; A. Hakhverdian (2015), 'Does it matter that most representatives are higher educated?', *Swiss Political Science Review* 21(2), pp. 237–45; L. Aaldering (2016), 'Political representation and educational attainment: evidence from the Netherlands (1994–2010)', *Political Studies* 65(1); C. Lesschaeve (2016), 'Naar een voorwaardelijk model van ongelijkheid in vertegenwoordiging: een onderzoek naar het moderatie-effect van beleidsdomeinen op ongelijkheid in beleidscongruentie', *Res Publica* 58(1), pp. 61–80.

51. D. Traber, M. Hänni, N. Giger and C. Breunig (2021), 'Social status, political priorities and unequal representation', *European Journal of Political Research* 61(2), pp. 351–73.

52. T. O'Grady, (2019), 'Careerists versus coal-miners: welfare reforms and the substantive representation of social groups in the British Labour party', *Comparative Political Studies* 52(4), pp. 544–78.

53. 'When Labour played the racist card', *New Statesman*, 22 January 1999.

54. British Election Study Candidate survey data.

55. Tim Bale, Sofia Vasilopoulou, Philip Cowley and Anand Menon (2016), 'Speaking for Britain? MPs broadly reflect the views of their supporters on Europe – but one side should worry a little more than the other', LSE Blogs, http://eprints.lse.ac.uk/73311/1/blogs.lse.ac.uk-Speaking%20for%20Britain%20MPs%20broadly%20reflect%20the%20views%20of%20their%20supporters%20on%20Europe%20%20but%20one%20side%20should.pdf.

56. 'EU vote. Where the cabinet and other MPs stand', *BBC News*, 22 June 2016, https://www.bbc.co.uk/news/uk-politics-eu-referendum-35616946.

57. A. Wager, T. Bale, P. Cowley and A. Menon (2021), 'The death of May's law: intra- and inter-party value differences in Britain's Labour and Conservative parties', *Political Studies*, vol. 70.

58. Ibid.

59. Tim Bale (2021), 'Ploughed under? Labour's grassroots post-Corbyn', *Political Quarterly* 92(2), pp. 220–28.

60. Wager et al., 'The death of May's law'.

61. 'Jack Straw: Labour made mistake letting Poles in early', *Guardian*, 13 November 2013.

62. Jonathan Rutherford, 'From Woodstock to Brexit: the tragedy of the liberal middle class, *Blue Labour*, 1 January 2020.

63. People from 'privileged backgrounds' are commonly thought to have at least one parent whose job was a higher or lower managerial,

administrative or professional occupation; Ofcom, 'Breaking the glass ceiling – social make-up of the TV industry revealed', 18 September 2019, https://www.ofcom.org.uk/about-ofcom/latest/media/media-releases/2019/breaking-the-class-ceiling-tv-industry-social-makeup-revealed; 'Channel 4 is Britain's poshest broadcaster, diversity study finds', *Guardian*, 22 August 2018; Sam Friedman and Daniel Laurison (2020), *The Class Ceiling: Why It Pays to Be Privileged*, University of Bristol; Sutton Trust (2019), 'Elitist Britain', https://www.suttontrust.com/our-research/elitist-britain-2019/.

64. Ofcom (2021), 'Five year review: diversity and equal opportunities in UK broadcasting', https://www.ofcom.org.uk/__data/assets/pdf_file/0029/225992/dib-five-years–2021.pdf.

65. H. Carey, R. Florisson, D. O'Brien and N. Lee (2020), 'Getting in and getting on: class, participation and job quality in the UK's creative industries', Multiple: Creative Industries Policy and Evidence Centre, University of Edinburgh and Work Advance, https://pec.ac.uk/research-reports/getting-in-and-getting-on-class-participation-and-job-quality-in-the-uks-creative-industries.

66. D. O'Brien, D. Laurison, A. Miles and S. Friedman (2016), 'Are the creative industries meritocratic? An analysis of the 2014 British Labour Force Survey', *Cultural Trends* 25(2), pp. 116–31.

67. O. Brook, D. O'Brien and M. Taylor, 'Panic! Social class, taste and inequalities in the creative industries', http://createlondon.org/wp-content/uploads/2018/04/Panic-Social-Class-Taste-and-Inequalities-in-the-Creative-Industries1.pdf.

68. O'Brien et al., 'Are the creative industries meritocratic?'.

69. Sutton Trust (2016), *Leading People 2016*, 24 February 2016, https://www.suttontrust.com/our-research/leading-people-2016-education-background/.

70. Sarah McNicol and Andrew McMillan, 'Britain's real working-class voices are not being heard – here's why', *The Conversation*, 24 August 2018,https://theconversation.com/britains-real-working-class-voices-are-not-being-heard-heres-why–101546.

71. Sutton Trust, *The Educational Backgrounds of Leading Journalists*, 1 June 2006, https://www.suttontrust.com/our-research/educational-backgrounds-leading-journalists/.

72. Sutton Trust (2016), *Leading People 2016*.

73. Ibid.

74. Neil Thurman, Alessio Cornia and Jessica Kunert (2016), *Journalists in the UK*, Reuters Institute for the Study of Journalism.

75. Sutton Trust, *Elitist Britain 2019*, 24 June 2019, https://www.sutton trust.com/our-research/elitist-britain-2019/.

76. Ibid, p. 41.

77. NCJT (2022), *Diversity in Journalism: An Update on the Characteristics of Journalists*, National Council for the Training of Journalists.

78. https://downloads.bbc.co.uk/aboutthebbc/reports/annualreport/2018–19.pdf; see also 'BBC/diversity: working class heroes are in the eye of the beholder', *Financial Times*, 10 April 2022.

79. Sutton Trust, *Elitist Britain 2019*.

80. While the corporation acknowledged the need briefly in the report to look at socio-economic diversity, this was not considered enough of a priority to be included in the 50:20:12 target: http://downloads. bbc.co.uk/aboutthebbc/reports/reports/creative-diversity-report–2020.pdf.

81. Justin Webb, 'Oxbridge is killing journalism', *UnHerd*, June 2021, https://unherd.com/2021/06/oxbridge-is-killing-journalism/.

82. Lewis Goodall. 'The BBC gender pay gap is bad – but its class gap is worse', *Sky News*, 23 July 2017, https://news.sky.com/story/the-bbc-pay-gap-is-bad-its-class-gap-is-worse-10957166.

83. Neil Thurman, Alessio Cornia and Jessica Kunert (2016), *Journalists in the UK*, Reuters Institute for the Study of Journalism.

84. B. Ungar-Sargon (2021), *Bad News: How Woke Media Is Undermining Democracy*, Encounter Books.

85. David Rozado, Musa al-Gharbi and Jamin Halberstadt, 'Use of sexist and racist in the *New York Times* increased over 400 per cent since 2012. Why?', *Guardian*, 26 February 2022; David Rozado, Musa al-Gharbi and Jamin Halberstadt (2021), 'Prevalence of prejudice-denoting words in news media discourse: a chronological analysis', *Social Science Computer Review*, 08944393211031452.

86. Rozado et al., 'Use of sexist and racist'; Rozado et al., 'Prevalence of Prejudice-Denoting Words'.

87. David Rozado and Eric Kaufmann (2022), 'The increasing frequency of terms denoting political extremism in U.S. and U.K. news media', *Social Sciences* 11(4).

88. Connor Ibbetson, 'Do people in the UK trust the media?', YouGov, 16 December 2019, https://yougov.co.uk/topics/politics/articles-reports/2019/12/16/do-britons-trust-press?utm_source=twitter&utm_medium=website_article&utm_campaign=trust_in_the_press.

89. Ibid. Aisha Majid, 'Almost seven in ten peole worry that they are being lied to by journalists according to latest Edelman trust survey', *Press Gazette*, 19 January 2022, https://pressgazette.co.uk/almost-seven-in-ten-people-worry-they-are-being-lied-to-by-journalists-according-to-latest-edelman-trust-survey/.

90. YouGov, 'Cancel culture: what views are Britons afraid to express?', 22 December 2021, https://yougov.co.uk/topics/politics/articles-reports/2021/12/22/cancel-culture-what-views-are-britons-afraid-expre.

91. YouGov and University of Cambridge Globalism Project 2020 (includes France, Germany, Sweden. Denmark, Spain, Italy, Greece, Hungary, Poland, Australia, America, Canada, Brazil, Mexico, Turkey, India, Japan, Indonesia, Thailand, Nigeria, South Africa), 30 July–24 August 2020, https://yougov.co.uk/topics/international/articles-reports/2020/11/12/globalism-project-2020-populist-beliefs-down-consp.

92. YouGov, 'Cancel culture'.

93. Albert H. Halsey (1992), *The Decline of Donnish Dominion: The British Academic Professions in the Twentieth Century*, Oxford University Press (see Chapter 11).

94. Chris Hanretty, 'Is the left over-represented within academia?', *Substack*, 9 March 2017; see also Remi Adekoya, Eric Kaufmann and Tom Simpson (2020), *Academic Freedom in the UK: Protecting Viewpoint Diversity*, Policy Exchange. Globally, meanwhile, one study by Pippa Norris at Harvard, published in 2021, found that 72 per cent of professors who teach politics identify as left-wing, with 14 per cent 'far left'. P. Norris (2021), 'Cancel culture: Myth or reality?', *Political Studies*, 00323217211037023, https://journals.sagepub.com/doi/10.1177/0032 3217211037023. My own research also found a sharp imbalance in elite universities around the world. More than three-quarters of academics, 76 per cent, identified on the political left, with 21 per cent identifying as 'far left'. Only 11 per cent put themselves on the right. Matthew Goodwin (2022), *Is Academic Freedom Under Threat?*, Legatum Institute.

95. CSPI (2021), *Academic Freedom in Crisis: Punishment, Political Discrimination and Self-Censorship*, Center for the Study of Partisanship and Ideology, Report No. 2.

96. Jonathan Grant and Kirstie Hewlett (2020), *Student Experience of Freedom of Expression in UK Universities*, The Policy Institute, Kings College London, https://www.kcl.ac.uk/policy-institute/assets/student-experience-freedom-of-expression.pdf.

97. Matthew Goodwin (2022), *Is Academic Freedom Under Threat?*, Legatum Institute.

98. Remi Adekoya, Eric Kaufmann and Tom Simpson (2020), *Academic Freedom in the UK: Protecting Viewpoint Diversity*, Policy Exchange.

99. 'Cambridge University rescinds Jordan Peterson invitation', *Guardian*, 20 March 2019; 'Cambridge college sacks researcher over links with far right', *Guardian*, 1 May 2019; '150 lecturers refuse to teach at Oxford's Oriel College in protest over refusal to remove Cecil Rhodes statue', *Independent*, 10 June 2021; 'Cambridge vice-chancellor admits list of "micro-aggressions" was a mistake', *Metro*, 28 May 2021; 'Edinburgh university donors desert after racism and trans rows', *The Times*, 2 November 2021; 'Race report chair slams honorary degree withdrawal', *BBC News*, 18 March 2022; 'Students at Durham University threaten to stop rent payments', *Northern Echo*, 13 December 2021.

100. Colleen Flaherty, 'Tracking attacks on scholars' speech', Inside Higher Ed, 31 August 2021, https://www.insidehighered.com/news/2021/08/31/fire-launches-new-database-tracking-attacks-speech.

101. Goodwin, *Is Academic Freedom Under Threat?*

102. Herbert Marcuse (1965), *Repressive Tolerance*.

103. For a summary of this evidence in the United States see CSPI (2021), *Academic Freedom in Crisis: Punishment, Political Discrimination, and Self-Censorship*, Centre for the Study of Partisanship and Ideology.

104. Jonathan Rauch, 'The constitution of knowledge', *National Affairs*, Winter 2022, https://nationalaffairs.com/publications/detail/the-constitution-of-knowledge.

105. Ibid.

106. Carroll Doherty and Jocelyn Kiley, 'Americans have become much less positive about tech companies' impact on the U.S.', Pew Research Center, 29 July 2019, https://www.pewresearch.org/fact-tank/2019/07/29/americans-have-become-much-less-positive-about-tech-companies-impact-on-the-u-s/.

107. Richard Hanania, 'Why is everything liberal?' Richard Hanania Substack, https://richardhanania.substack.com/p/why-is-everything-liberal.

108. Bovens and Wille, *Diploma Democracy*.

109. Hanania, 'Why is everything liberal?'.

CHAPTER 5: VIRTUE

1. H. J. Curzer (2012), *Aristotle and the Virtues*, Oxford University Press.
2. David Brooks (2016), *The Road to Character*, Penguin.
3. J. van Noord, B. Spruyt, T. Kuppens and R. Spears (2021), 'In the shadow of the schooled society: feelings of misrecognition and the education ladder', *Social Problems*, https://academic.oup.com/socpro/advance-article/doi/10.1093/socpro/spab034/6364787.
4. J. Goldthorpe (2012), 'Back to class and status: or why a sociological view of social inequality should be reasserted', *Revista Española de Investigaciones Sociológicas (REIS)* 137(1), 201–15; also T. Chan (2019), 'Understanding social status: a reply to Flemmen, Jarness and Rosenlund', *The British Journal of Sociology* 70(3), pp. 867–81.
5. David Goodhart (2020), *Head Hand Heart: The Struggle for Dignity and Status in the 21st Century*, Penguin, p. 189.
6. 'Gig economy workforce hits 4.5 million in England and Wales', *Financial Times*, 5 November 2021.
7. Matthew Goodwin, 'What's the point of the Labour Party?', *The Sunday Times*, 9 May 2021.
8. Department for Education, 'Post-18 review of education and funding: independent panel report', 2019, https://www.gov.uk/government/publications/post-18-review-of-education-and-funding-independent-panel-report.
9. Luke Sibieta, Imran Tahir and Ben Waltmann (2022), *Adult Education: the Past, Present and Future*, Institute for Fiscal Studies; Chris Belfield, Christine Farquharson and Luke Sibieta (2018), *2018 Annual Report on Education Spending in England*, Institute for Fiscal Studies; Institute for Fiscal Studies (2019), *2019 Annual Report on Education Spending in England*, Institute for Fiscal Studies. I exclude spending on apprenticeships.
10. Department for Education, 'Post-18 review of education and funding'.
11. 'Employed graduates in non-graduate roles, parts of the UK, 2015 to 2019'. Office for National Statistics, 16 November 2020, https://www.ons.gov.uk/employmentandlabourmarket/peopleinwork/employmentandemployeetypes/adhocs/12501employedgraduatesinnongraduaterolespartsoftheuk2015to2019; OECD (2018), 'Education at a glance: OECD indicators. Country note: United Kingdom', OECD; F. Green and G. Henseke (2016), 'Should governments of OECD countries worry about graduate underemployment?', *Oxford Review of Economic Policy*, 32(4).

12. Gianna Boero, Dan Cook, Tej Nathwani, Robin Naylor and Jeremy Smith (2020), 'How does the return to a degree vary by class of award?', Higher Education Statistics Agency, https://www.hesa.ac.uk/files/Return-to-degree-by-class–20200310.pdf; James Higgins, 'Graduate earnings premium suffers "precipitous fall"', University Business, 25 November 2021, https://universitybusiness.co.uk/students/graduate-earnings-premium-suffers-precipitous-fall/; see also Augar Review (2019), 'Review of post-18 education and funding', University and College Union, https://www.ucu.org.uk/media/10290/The-Augar-review—where-UCU-stands-Jun-19/pdf/The_Augar_Review___Where_UCU_stands.pdf.; YouGov, 'Are degrees from English universities good value for money?', February 2022, https://yougov.co.uk/topics/education/trackers/are-degrees-from-english-universities-good-value-for-money: 51 per cent said they are value for money – the standard of education and increased wages graduates earn mean it is worth the money, while 25 per cent said they are not value for money – the standard of education and the wages graduates earn are not enough to warrant the cost.

13. M. J. Sandel (2020), *The Tyranny of Merit: What's Become of the Common Good?*, Penguin.

14. Michael Young (1994 [1958]), *The Rise of the Meritocracy*, Routledge.

15. Sandel, *The Tyranny of Merit*.

16. E. Bukodi and J. H. Goldthorpe (2021), 'Meritocracy and populism – is there a connection?', Working Paper, https://ukandeu.ac.uk/wp-content/uploads/2021/02/Meritocracy-and-its-problems.pdf.

17. A. R. Hochschild (2016), *Strangers in Their Own Land*, New Press.

18. Ibid.

19. 'Study reveals mainly stupid people will vote Brexit', *The London Economic*, 20 June 2016; Suzanne Moore, 'We must respond to Brexit with more than yelling', *Guardian*, 4 February 2020.

20. J. van Noord, B. Spruyt, T. Kuppens and R. Spears (2021), 'In the shadow of the schooled society: feelings of misrecognition and the education ladder', *Social Problems*, https://academic.oup.com/socpro/advance-article/doi/10.1093/socpro/spab034/6364787.

21. N. Gidron and P. Hall (2020), 'Populism as a problem of social integration', *Comparative Political Studies* 53, pp. 1028–59; see also N. Gidron and P. Hall (2017), 'The politics of social status: economic and cultural roots of the populist right', *British Journal of Sociology*, 68, pp. S57–S81.

22. I refer here to the 'C2' skilled workers. The Conservatives emerged with an 18-point lead among the C2s, a 13-point lead among the 'DE'

social grade and, overall, a 15-point lead among 'C2DEs': https://you-gov.co.uk/topics/politics/articles-reports/2019/12/17/how-britain-voted-2019-general-election.

23. Bukodi and Goldthorpe, 'Meritocracy and populism'.

24. T. Kuppens, R. Spears, A. Manstead, B. Spruyt and M. Easterbrook (2018), 'Educationism and the irony of meritocracy: negative attitudes of higher educated people towards the less educated', *Journal of Experimental Social Psychology* 76, pp. 429–47.

25. D. Skelton (2021), *The New Snobbery*, Biteback.

26. Ibid.

27. L. Carella and R. Ford (2020), 'The status stratification of radical right support: reconsidering the occupational profile of UKIP's electorate', *Electoral Studies*, 67, 102214; T.-W. Chan, M. Henderson, M. Sironi and J. Kawalerowicz (2020), 'Understanding the social and cultural bases of Brexit', *British Journal of Sociology*, doi: 10.1111/1468-4446.12790.

28. Bukodi and Goldthorpe, 'Meritocracy and populism'.

29. E. Currid-Halkett (2017), *The Sum of Small Things*, Princeton University Press; though see also Max Weber (2018), *Class, Status, Party*, Routledge.

30. Rob Henderson (2019), 'Thorstein Veblen's theory of the leisure class – a status update', *Quillette*, https://quillette.com/2019/11/16/thorstein-veblens-theory-of-the-leisure-class-a-status-update/.

31. George Orwell (2017), *England Your England*, Penguin.

32. Daniel Bell (1972), 'The cultural contradictions of capitalism', *The Journal of Aesthetic Education*, 6(1/2), pp. 11–38.

33. One of the first intellectuals who noticed the growth of these ideas in 'high culture' was Daniel Bell. See ibid. For more recent books which document how they have gone mainstream in various sectors of society see: E. Kaufmann (2018), *Whiteshift: Populism, Immigration, and the Future of White Majorities*, Penguin; J. Haidt and G. Lukianoff (2018), *The Coddling of the American Mind: How Good Intentions and Bad Ideas Are Setting Up a Generation for Failure*, Penguin; J. McWhorter (2021), *Woke Racism: How a New Religion Has Betrayed Black America*, Swift Press; B. Cobley (2021), *The Tribe: The Liberal-Left and the System of Diversity* (vol. 63); T. Holland (2019), *Dominion: The Making of the Western Mind*, Hachette; H. Pluckrose and J. A. Lindsay (2020), *Cynical Theories: How Activist Scholarship Made Everything About Race, Gender, and Identity – and Why This Harms*

Everybody, Pitchstone Publishing; Batya Ungar-Sargon (2021), *Bad News: How Woke Media Is Undermining Democracy*, Encounter Books; V. Ramaswamy (2021), *Woke, Inc.: Inside Corporate America's Social Justice Scam*, Hachette; Bradley Campbell and Jason Manning (2018), *The Rise of Victimhood Culture*, Palgrave Macmillan; F. Fukuyama (2018), *Identity: Contemporary Identity Politics and the Struggle for Recognition*, Profile Books; M. Lilla (2018), *The Once and Future Liberal: After Identity Politics*, Oxford University Press.

34. Bradley Campbell and Jason Manning (2018), *The Rise of Victimhood Culture*, Palgrave Macmillan, p. 11.

35. Haidt and Lukianoff, *The Coddling of the American Mind*, p. 70.

36. More in Common, 'Britain's choice', https://www.britainschoice.uk/; Kings College London News Centre, 'UK "culture war" debate: public divide into four groups, not two', 18 June 2021, https://www.kcl.ac.uk/news/uk-culture-war-debate-public-divide-into-four-groups-not-two-warring-tribes.

37. YouGov, 'Defining woke', 26–8 February 2021, https://docs.cdn.yougov.com/xu2oj6jxzz/YouGov% 20-%20What%20is%.

38. Inspection of the American School in London, Ofsted, https://files.ofsted.gov.uk/v1/file/50178819.

39. Quillette, 'Thorstein Veblen's theory of the leisure class'.

40. McWhorter (2021), *Woke Racism*.

41. Ibid.

42. Paul Collier (2019), *The Future of Capitalism*, Penguin, pp. 3–4.

43. Cobley, *The Tribe*.

44. Ibid.

45. Ibid, p. 140.

46. Mark Lilla, 'The end of identity liberalism', *The New York Times*, 18 November 2016.

47. Ramaswamy, *Woke, Inc.*

48. https://twitter.com/sainsburys/status/1311672756010917889?s=20&t=2VrIWmX7Q3BtPmogCoospQ.

49. 'New Sainsbury's chief Mike Coupe invests in controversial tax avoidance scheme', *Independent*, 3 February 2014.

50. Quillette, 'Thorstein Veblen's theory of the leisure class'.

51. YouGov, 'What does the British public think is and is not racist?', 20 December 2018, https://yougov.co.uk/topics/politics/articles-reports/2018/12/20/what-does-british-public-think-and-not-racist.

52. Campbell and Manning, *The Rise of Victimhood Culture*, p. 16.

53. John McTernan (2013), 'The left has to get politically tough on Labour migration', http://www.policy-network.net/pno_detail.aspx?ID=4474& title=The+left+has+to+get+politically+tough+on+labour+migration; Nick Cohen, 'Take your country back from those who seek to destroy it', *Guardian*, 19 June 2016; Laurie Penny, 'I want my country back', *New Statesman*, 24 June 2016; Matthew D'Ancona, 'Let's be honest about what's really driving Brexit – bigotry', *Guardian*, 2 December 2018.

54. 'David Lammy says comparing ERG to Nazis "not strong enough"', *Guardian*, 14 April 2019; 'Britain's political and social fabric is under unusual strain', *The Economist*, 17 October 2020, https://www.econo mist.com/britain/2020/10/15/britains-political-and-social-fabric-is-under-unusual-strain.

55. 'Rural Britain is racist, says Countryfile presenter Ellie Harrison', *The Times*, 16 October 2020; 'UK Justice system is racist', *Independent*, 10 January 2017; 'Boris Johnson is "racist" says black MP who called out abuse', *Metro*, 16 October 2019; Fiona Dowling and Anne Flintoff (2018), 'A whitewashed curriculum? The construction of race in contemporary PE curriculum policy', *Sport, Education and Society* 23(1), pp. 1–13; 'Now PE is racist, says tax-payer funded study', *Mail on Sunday*, 18 March 2018; 'British schools are institutionally racist', *Guardian*, 24 March 2021; 'Church of England "deeply institutionally racist"', *Independent*, 11 February 2020; 'Ofcom to investigate Top Gear after accusation of casual racism', *Guardian*, 6 May 2014; 'Royal family "very much not racist" – William', *BBC News*, 11 March 2021; 'BBC defends Strictly Come Dancing as viewers are accused of racism', *Guardian*, 11 October 2016; 'Most British black people think the Tories are racist', *National*, 22 June 2020; 'Black scientists say UK research is institutionally racist', *BBC News*, 11 October 2021; 'British police "still institutionally racist", claims senior officer', *Politics Home*, 13 October 2018; 'Barbican staff say it is "institutionally racist" despite action plan', *Guardian*, 11 June 2021; 'Oxford and Cambridge universities accused of social apartheid', *Independent*, 20 October 2017; 'Rural racism in Dorset: why is our countryside 98 per cent white?', *BBC News*, 7 July 2021; 'England is "systematically racist", says report to UN', *Evening Standard*, 14 July 2021; 'Riba investigates architect's allegations of institutional racism', *Guardian*, 3 December 2015; 'British sport must examine its racist past', *Financial Times*, 24 July 2020.

56. P. Wintour, N. Watt and S. Carrell (2014), 'UKIP condemned by cross-party group for running "racist" campaign', *Guardian*, 28 April 2014;

H. Carter and M. Wainwright (2010), 'Gillian Duffy: a lifelong Labour voter who may bring down the PM', *Guardian*, 28 April 2010; 'Diane Abbott: Labour's controls on immigration mugs are shameful', *Guardian*, 29 March 2015; John Wight, 'Labour's immigration mug will be a collector's item for racists up and down the country', *Huffington Post*, 30 May 2015; 'To fix its problems now, Labour must face the racism of its past', *Guardian*, 8 March 2019; M. Hasan, 'Five questions for anyone who says "it's not racist to talk about immigration"', *New Statesman*, 13 November 2014; 'Is flying a George Cross flag an act of patriotism or a symbol of all that is bad about England?', *Independent*, 18 June 2018; C. Kimber, 'Standing up to UKIP's racism', *Socialist Worker*, 2 May 2014; M. Shaw, 'Vote Leave relied on racism', *Guardian*, 8 January 2019; J. Choonara, 'After the Leave vote: we can beat back racism and austerity', *Socialist Review*, 26 June 2016; Lisa Nandy, 'Putting Britain first is a classic nationalist dogwhistle', *The Canary*, 25 September 2020.

57. M. Sobolewska and R. Ford (2020), *Brexitland: Identity, Diversity and the Reshaping of British Politics*, Cambridge University Press.

58. Ingrid Storm, Maria Sobolewska and Robert Ford (2017), 'Is ethnic prejudice declining in Britain? Change in social distance attitudes among ethnic majority and minority Britons', *British Journal of Sociology* 68(3), pp. 410–34; see also Robert Ford (2008), 'Is racial prejudice declining in Britain?', *British Journal of Sociology* 59(4), pp. 609–36.

59. Ipsos MORI, 'Attitudes to race and inequality', June 2020, https://www.ipsos.com/en-uk/attitudes-race-and-inequality-great-britain.

60. Storm et al., 'Is ethnic prejudice declining in Britain?'; see also the EMBES survey data reported in the online appendix of Sobolewska and Ford, *Brexitland*.

61. Ipsos MORI, 'A review of survey research on Muslims in Britain', 21 March 2018, https://www.ipsos.com/en-uk/review-survey-research-muslims-britain-0; 'Half of all British Muslims think homosexuality should be illegal, poll finds', *Guardian*, 11 April 2016.

62. Cassilde Schwartz, Miranda Simon, David Hudson and Jennifer van-Heerde-Hudson (2021), 'A populist paradox? How Brexit softened anti-immigrant attitudes', *British Journal of Political Science* 51(3), pp. 1160–80.

63. For survey evidence on British public attitudes see, for example: You-Gov survey on British attitudes toward Afghan interpreters, 31 August 31 2021, https://yougov.co.uk/topics/politics/survey-results/daily/2021/

08/31/59493/1; British attitudes toward Ukraine refugees, March 2022, https://yougov.co.uk/topics/politics/articles-reports/2022/03/02/ support-taking-ukraine-refugees-rises–76; and British attitudes toward taking Hong Kongers July 2020 https://yougov.co.uk/topics/politics/ articles-reports/2020/07/01/support-helping-british-passport-holders-hong-kong.

64. A. F. Heath and V. Di Stasio (2019), 'Racial discrimination in Britain, 1969–2017: a meta-analysis of field experiments on racial discrimination in the British labour market', *The British Journal of Sociology* 70(5), pp. 1774–98; K. Auspurg, A. Schneck and T. Hinz (2019), 'Closed doors everywhere? A meta-analysis of field experiments on ethnic discrimination in rental housing markets', *Journal of Ethnic and Migration Studies* 45(1), pp. 95–114.

65. 'Key Stage 4 performance 2019 (revised)', www.gov.uk/government/ statistics/key-stage–4-performance-2019-revised; also Ethnicity Facts and Figures, 'Students getting 3 A grades or better at A level', 26 May 2022,https://www.ethnicity-facts-figures.service.gov.uk/education-skills-and-training/a-levels-apprenticeships-further-education/students-aged-16-to-18-achieving-3-a-grades-or-better-at-a-level/latest#:~:text= 28.9%25%20of%20all%20students%20got,out%20of%20all%20 ethnic%20groups. At A-levels, Indians, Chinese and mixed ethnic children are more likely than their white British peers to get three A grades at A-level, Asians are almost as likely as their white peers to do so while black Africans and black Caribbeans are less likely. Black African, Chinese, Indian and Asian children are more likely than their white peers to progress to university, and have been for thirty years, while white working-class children routinely trail every group, except their Irish Traveller and Gypsy peers. T. Modood (1993), 'The number of ethnic minority students in British higher education: some grounds for optimism', *Oxford Review of Education*, 19(2), pp. 167–82. On the relative performance of white working-class children see the evidence compiled in Education Committee (2021), 'The forgotten: how white working-class pupils have been let down, and how to change it', Education Committee Report, https://publications.parliament.uk/pa/cm5802/ cmselect/cmeduc/85/8502.htm. Shortly before the Covid-19 pandemic while 67 per cent of disadvantaged Chinese boys, 54 per cent of Indian boys, 53 per cent of Bangladeshi boys, 52 per cent of black African boys, 42 per cent of Pakistani boys, 24 per cent of black Caribbean boys and 24 per cent of boys of mixed ethnic heritage progressed into

higher education, less than 13 per cent of white working-class children did. See '"Free school meals, gender and ethnic group" from "Widening participation in higher education"', 8 March 2021, https://explore-education-statistics.service.gov.uk/data-tables/permalink/77f3aabf-1e21-4c2f-bb58-b5671c695307.

66. Ethnicity Facts and Figures, 'Entry rates into higher education', 9 March 2022, https://www.ethnicity-facts-figures.service.gov.uk/education-skills-and-training/higher-education/entry-rates-into-higher-education/latest. Between 2006 and 2021, black British children had the biggest entry rate increase of all groups, from 22 per cent to 49 per cent, while white pupils had the smallest increase.

67. On the historic under-representation of minorities in the most elite 'high tariff' universities see V. Boliver (2016), 'Exploring ethnic inequalities in admission to Russell Group universities', *Sociology* 50(2), pp. 247–66; on progress made since 2010 see Universities and Colleges Admissions Service UCAS (2021), '2020 entry UCAS undergraduate reports by sex, area background, and ethnic group', https://www.ucas.com/data-and-analysis/undergraduate-statistics-and-reports/ucas-undergraduate-end-cycle-data-resources-2020/2020-entry-ucas-undergraduate-reports-sex-area-background-and-ethnic-group.

68. 'Oxford shows continued progress on state school and ethnic minority student admissions', 4 February 2021, https://www.ox.ac.uk/news/2021-02-04-oxford-shows-continued-progress-state-school-and-ethnic-minority-student-admissions.

69. Office for National Statistics, 'Ethnic differences in life expectancy and mortality from selected causes, England, and Wales: 2011 to 2014', 26 July 2021, https://www.ons.gov.uk/peoplepopulationandcommunity/birthsdeathsandmarriages/lifeexpectancies/articles/ethnicdifferencesinlifeexpectancyandmortalityfromselectedcausesinenglandandwales/2011to2014; Office for National Statistics, 'Mortality from leading causes of death by ethnic group, England, and Wales: 2012 to 2019', 19 August 2021, https://www.ons.gov.uk/peoplepopulationandcommunity/birthsdeathsandmarriages/deaths/articles/mortalityfromleadingcausesofdeathbyethnicgroupenglandandwales/2012to2019#ethnic-group-breakdown-used-in-this-article.

70. On unemployment see Ethnicity Facts and Figures, 'Unemployment', 29 January 2021, https://www.ethnicity-facts-figures.service.gov.uk/work-pay-and-benefits/unemployment-and-economic-inactivity/unemployment/latest#by-ethnicity. In 2019, the median hourly pay for

white British was £12.49 compared to £17.55 for white Irish, £13.37 for white Asian, £14.43 for Indians, £10.55 for Pakistanis, £10.58 for Bangladeshis, £15.38 for Chinese, £12.03 for black Caribbeans and £11.50 for black Africans: Office for National Statistics, 'Ethnicity pay gap reference tables', 12 October 2020, https://www.ons.gov.uk/employmentandlabourmarket/peopleinwork/earningsandworkinghours/datasets/ethnicitypaygapreferencetables.

71. https://www.gov.uk/government/publications/the-report-of-the-commission-on-race-and-ethnic-disparities-supporting-research/the-social-mobility-of-ethnic-minorities-in-britain-in-the-last–50-years–1972–2019-by-professor-yaojun-li#main-results.

72. Ethnicity Facts and Figures, 'NHS workforce by ethnicity and grade (medical staff), source: NHS Workforce Statistics 2020', 26 January 2021, https://www.ethnicity-facts-figures.service.gov.uk/workforce-and-business/workforce-diversity/nhs-workforce/latest; Insititute for Government, 'Ethnicity in the Civil Service', 'https://www.institutefor government.org.uk/explainers/ethnicity-civil-service; Britain's most diverse parliament', *BBC News*, 17 December 2019, https://www.bbc.co.uk/news/election–2019–50808536; Diversity UK, 'Britain's most ethnically diverse Cabinet ever', 25 July 2019, https://diversityuk.org/britains-most-ethnically-diverse-cabinet-ever/; John Parker (2022), *Improving the Ethnic Diversity of UK Boards: An Update Report from the Parker Review*, https://assets.ey.com/content/dam/ey-sites/ey-com/en_uk/topics/diversity/ey-what-the-parker-review-tells-us-about-boardroom-diversity.pdf.

73. J. Gest (2016), *The New Minority: White Working Class Politics in an Age of Immigration and Inequality*, Oxford University Press.

74. J. Gest, T. Reny and J. Mayer (2018), 'Roots of the radical right: nostalgic deprivation in the United States and Britain', *Comparative Political Studies* 51(13), pp. 1694–719.

75. D. Mattinson (2020), *Beyond the Red Wall*, Biteback.

76. Ibid., originally cited in E. Bukodi and J. H. Goldthorpe (2021), 'Meritocracy and populism – is there a connection?', Working Paper, https://ukandeu.ac.uk/wp-content/uploads/2021/02/Meritocracy-and-its-problems.pdf.

77. Ben Cooper, 'A mature approach: how Labour can reconnect with older voters', Fabian Society, April 2022, https://fabians.org.uk/publication/a-mature-approach/; Deltapoll/Tony Blair Institute, 'Aligning Labour's voters', 26 November 2021, https://deltapoll.co.uk/polls/aligning-labours-voters.

78. Peter Kellner (2021), *From Red Walls to Red Bridges; Rebuilding Labour's Voter Coalition*, Tony Blair Institute.
79. Zach P. Grant and Geoffrey Evans (2022), 'A new dilemma of social democracy? The British Labour Party, the white working-class, and ethnic minority representation', working paper emailed to author.
80. Zach Goldberg, 'America's white saviors', *Tablet Magazine*, 6 June 2019; J. Weiler and M. Hetherington (2009), *Authoritarianism and Polarisation in American Politics*, Cambridge University Press.

CONCLUSION: COUNTER-REVOLUTION

1. YouGov, 'How Britain voted in the 2019 General Election', 17 December 2019, https://yougov.co.uk/topics/politics/articles-reports/2019/12/17/how-britain-voted–2019-general-election; https://www.ipsos.com/en-uk/how-britain-voted–2019-election.
2. https://www.standard.co.uk/news/politics/brexit-news-latest-deatherendum-site-which-counted-deaths-of-leave-voters-taken-down-after-horrific-abuse-a4042196.html.
3. Office for National Statistics, 'Living longer: how our population is changing and why it matters', August 2018, https://www.ons.gov.uk/releases/livinglongerhowourpopulationischangingandwhyitmatters.
4. YouGov, 'How Britain voted in the 2019 general election', 17 December 2019; see also Peter Kellner (2021), *From Red Walls to Red Bridges; Rebuilding Labour's Voter Coalition*, Tony Blair Institute.
5. Ben Cooper, 'A mature approach: how Labour can reconnect with older voters', Fabian Society, April 2022, https://fabians.org.uk/publication/a-mature-approach/.
6. Ibid; Deltapoll / Tony Blair Institute, 'Aligning Labour's voters', 26 November 2021, https://deltapoll.co.uk/polls/aligning-labours-voters; on immigration polling see YouGov, 'Do Brits think immigration has been too high or low in the last 10 years?', https://yougov.co.uk/topics/politics/trackers/do-brits-think-that-immigration-has-been-too-high-or-low-in-the-last-10-years.
7. British Election Study, 'Age and voting behaviour at the 2019 general election', 27 January 2021, https://www.britishelectionstudy.com/bes-findings/age-and-voting-behaviour-at-the-2019-general-election/#.YxC1d3bMJPY.
8. Laura Gardiner (2016), *Votey McVoteface: Understanding the Growing Turnout Gap between the Generations*, Resolution Foundation.

9. M. J. Goodwin and O. Heath (2016), 'The 2016 referendum, Brexit and the left behind: an aggregate-level analysis of the result', *Political Quarterly* 87(3), pp. 323–32.

10. Paula Surridge (2018), 'The fragmentation of the electoral left since 2010', *Renewal: A Journal of Social Democracy* 26(4), pp. 69–78.

11. Originally cited in Robert McKenzie and Allan Silver (1968), *Working Class Conservatives in Urban England*, University of Chicago Press, p. 14.

12. Peter Pulzer (1967), *Political Representation and Elections; Parties and Voting in Great Britain*, vol. 1, Praeger.

13. Peter Kellner (2021), *From Red Walls to Red Bridges; Rebuilding Labour's Voter Coalition*, Tony Blair Institute.

14. Geoffrey Evans and Kat Chzhen (2013), 'Explaining voters' defection from labour over the 2005–10 electoral cycle: leadership, economics and the rising importance of immigration', *Political Studies* 61, pp. 138–57; Geoffrey Evans (2002), 'European integration, party politics and voting in the 2001 election', *British Elections and Parties Review* 12(1), pp. 95–110.

15. Robert Ford and Matthew Goodwin (2014), *Revolt on the Right: Explaining Support for the Radical Right in Britain*, Routledge.

16. Ibid.; Matthew Goodwin and Caitlin Milazzo (2015), *UKIP: Inside the Campaign to Redraw the Map of British Politics*, Cambridge University Press. John Curtice, Stephen Fisher and Patrick English, 'The geography of a Brexit election: how constituency context and the electoral system shaped the outcome', in Robert Ford, Tim Bale, Paula Surridge and Will Jennings (2021), *The British General Election of 2019*, Palgrave Macmillan, pp. 461–94; Matthew Goodwin and Oliver Heath (2017), *The UK 2017 General Election Examined: Income, Poverty and Brexit*, Joseph Rowntree Foundation; Oliver Heath and Matthew Goodwin (2017), 'The 2017 General Election, Brexit and the return to two-party politics: An aggregate-level analysis of the result', *Political Quarterly* 88(3), pp. 345–58.

17. R. Ford and M. J. Goodwin (2010), 'Angry white men: individual and contextual predictors of support for the British National Party', *Political Studies* 58(1), pp. 1–25; R. Ford, M. J. Goodwin and D. Cutts (2012), 'Strategic Eurosceptics and polite xenophobes: support for the United Kingdom Independence Party (UKIP) in the 2009 European Parliament elections', *European Journal of Political Research* 51(2), pp. 204–34.

18. Kellner, *From Red Walls to Red Bridges*.
19. Data drawn from the British Election Study.
20. I draw here on British Election Study data; see also Geoffrey Evans and Jon Mellon (2020), 'The re-shaping of class voting', British Election Study, https://www.britishelectionstudy.com/bes-findings/the-re-shaping-of-class-voting-in-the-2019-election-by-geoffrey-evans-and-jonathan-mellon/#.YxC8IXbMJPY.
21. Ipsos, 'How Britain voted in the 2019 election', 20 December 2019, https://www.ipsos.com/en-uk/how-britain-voted-2019-election.
22. https://commonslibrary.parliament.uk/general-election-2019-voting-patterns-in-student-seats/.
23. Heath and Goodwin (2017), 'The 2017 general election, Brexit and the return to two-party politics'.
24. B. Duffy (2021), *Generations: Does When You're Born Shape Who You Are?*, Atlantic Books, p. 140; YouGov. 'Attitudes toward British Empire', 10–11 June 2019, https://docs.cdn.yougov.com/z7uxxk071z/YouGov%20-%20British%20empire%20attitudes.pdf.
25. 'National identity: exploring Britishness', *British Social Attitudes* 31, https://www.bsa.natcen.ac.uk/media/38984/bsa31_national_identity.pdf.
26. Zoomers were more than twice as likely as the average person to think the Royal Family is racist. Overall, 20 per cent said it is and 55 per cent said it is not (don't knows excluded), YouGov, 'Young Britons are turning their backs on the monarchy', 21 May 2021, https://yougov.co.uk/topics/politics/articles-reports/2021/05/21/young-britons-are-turning-their-backs-monarchy.
27. YouGov, 'How proud are you if at all to be British?', 25 June 2020, https://yougov.co.uk/topics/travel/survey-results/daily/2020/06/25/31f14/2; J. Tilley and A. Heath (2007), 'The decline of British national pride', *British Journal of Sociology* 58(4), pp. 661–78.
28. YouGov, 'How Britain voted in the 2019 General Election', 17 December 2019, https://yougov.co.uk/topics/politics/articles-reports/2019/12/17/how-britain-voted-2019-general-election.
29. There are different versions of this saying, but it is often traced to King Oscar II of Sweden, cited in 'The truth in its proper use', *Wall Street Journal*, 17 February 1923.
30. 'Voting: the 2017 election – new divides in British politics?', *British Social Attitudes* 35, https://www.bsa.natcen.ac.uk/media/39255/bsa35_voting.pdf; YouGov, 'How Britain voted in the 2019 General Election'.

31. Ibid.

32. On attitudes of British Muslims on these issues see Ipsos MORI, 'A review of survey research on Muslims in Britain', https://www.ipsos.com/sites/default/files/ct/publication/documents/2018-03/a-review-of-survey-research-on-muslims-in-great-britain-ipsos-mori_0.pdf; on support for intergroup relationships see I. Storm, M. Sobolewska and R. Ford (2017), 'Is ethnic prejudice declining in Britain? Change in social distance attitudes among ethnic majority and minority Britons', *British Journal of Sociology* 68(3), pp. 410–34.

33. A. Heath, S. Fisher, G. Rosenblatt, D. Sanders and M. Sobolewska (2013), *The Political Integration of Ethnic Minorities in Britain*, Oxford University Press.

34. J. Curtice, S. Fisher and R. Ford (2016), 'Appendix 2: the results analysed', in P. Cowley and D. Kavanagh (eds.), *The British General Election of 2015*, Palgrave Macmillan, pp. 387–431.

35. Nicole Martin (2019), 'Ethnic minority voters in the UK 2015 general election: a breakthrough for the Conservative Party?', *Electoral Studies*, 57, pp. 174–85.

36. Ipsos-MORI includes estimated breakdowns for minority ethnic voters: https://www.ipsos.com/en-uk/how-britain-voted–2019-election.

37. Farah Hussain, 'Can Labour fix its relationship with its Muslim voters before it's too late?', *The Conversation*, 27 August 2021, https://theconversation.com/can-labour-fix-its-relationship-with-its-muslim-voters-before-its-too-late–166766; on twenty-six constituencies see https://mcb.org.uk/wp-content/uploads/2019/11/MCB–2019-General-Election-Policy-Platform.pdf.

38. 'Culture wars: keeping the Brexit divide alive?', *British Social Attitudes* 39, https://www.bsa.natcen.ac.uk/media/39478/bsa39_culture-wars.pdf, p. 17.

39. Heath and Goodwin, 'The 2017 general election, Brexit and the return to two-party politics'.

40. Pew Research Center, 'Growing share of Americans say they want more spending on police in their area', 26 October 2021, https://www.pewresearch.org/fact-tank/2021/10/26/growing-share-of-americans-say-they-want-more-spending-on-police-in-their-area/.

41. Equis Research, 'Post-mortem: the American dream voter', 2020, https://static1.squarespace.com/static/5d30982b599bde00016db472/t/61b7e8e75c74f5558036268b/1639442667560/Post-Mortem+Part+Two+FINAL+Dec+13.pdf.

42. Andrew Gamble (2021), 'The remaking of Conservativism: Boris Johnson and the politics of Brexit', *Political Quarterly* 92(3), pp. 461–8.

43. Nick Timothy (2020), *Remaking One Nation: The Future of Conservatism*, Polity.

44. Nicholas Allen and Judith Bara (2019), 'Marching to the left? Programmatic competition and the 2017 party manifestos', *Political Quarterly* 90(1), pp. 124–33.

45. I take these points from voter responses to the British Election Study and British Social Attitudes surveys.

46. G. Evans, R. De Geus and J. Green (2021), 'Boris Johnson to the rescue? How the Conservatives won the radical-right vote in the 2019 General Election', *Political Studies*, https://journals.sagepub.com/doi/full/10.1177/00323217211051191.

47. Heath and Goodwin, 'The 2017 General Election, Brexit and the return to two-party politics'; David Cutts, Matthew Goodwin, Oliver Heath and Paula Surridge (2020), 'Brexit, the 2019 General Election and the realignment of British politics', *Political Quarterly* 91(1), pp. 7–23; see also 'The results analysed', in Cowley and Kavanagh, *The British General Election of 2017*.

48. Georgina Sturge (2022), *Migration Statistics*, House of Commons Library.

49. Home Office (2022), *Immigration Statistics Quarterly Release*, Home Office.

50. I draw these data from YouGov and Ipsos-MORI. See: https://yougov.co.uk/topics/politics/trackers/how-the-government-is-handling-the-issue-of-immigration-in-the-uk?crossBreak=conservative; https://yougov.co.uk/topics/politics/trackers/the-most-important-issues-facing-the-country?crossBreak=conservative; and also https://www.ipsos.com/sites/default/files/ct/news/documents/2022-03/attitudes-towards-immigration-british-future-ipsos-march–2022.pdf.

51. Richard Dawkins speaking on BBC *Newsnight* 'Viewsnight', https://www.youtube.com/watch?v=AaySOifpusg.

52. Jason Brennan (2016), *Against Democracy*, Princeton University Press.

53. Janan Ganesh, 'Democracy works better when there is less of it', *Financial Times*, 9 September 2020.

AFTERWORD

1. I draw on YouGov data here. YouGov/The Times January 24-26 2020 https://d25d2506sfb94s.cloudfront.net/cumulus_uploads/document/pvy6eonjjl/TheTimes_VI_Results_200127_w.pdf and YouGov/The Times November 29-30 2022 https://docs.cdn.yougov.com/eyyy9mimz1/_The Times_VI_221130_W.pdf.

2. John Curtice (2022) Taxation, Welfare and Inequality, British Social Attitudes 39. Available online: https://www.bsa.natcen.ac.uk/media/39481/bsa39_taxation-welfare-and-inequality.pdf.

3. Nigel Farage-led party could attract more than a quarter of voters, poll reveals, *The Telegraph* November 12 2022 https://www.telegraph.co.uk/politics/2022/11/12/nigel-farage-led-party-would-attract-quarter-voters-poll-reveals/.

Index

ALLEN LANE
an imprint of
PENGUIN BOOKS

Also Published

Ian Kershaw, *Personality and Power: Builders and Destroyers of Modern Europe*

Alison Bashford, *An Intimate History of Evolution: The Story of the Huxley Family*

Lawrence Freedman, *Command: The Politics of Military Operations from Korea to Ukraine*

Richard Niven, *Second City: Birmingham and the Forging of Modern Britain*

Hakim Adi, *African and Caribbean People in Britain: A History*

Jordan Peterson, *24 Rules For Life: The Box Set*

Gaia Vince, *Nomad Century: How to Survive the Climate Upheaval*

Keith Fisher, *A Pipeline Runs Through It: The Story of Oil from Ancient Times to the First World War*

Christoph Keller, *Every Cripple a Superhero*

Roberto Calasso, *The Tablet of Destinies*

Jennifer Jacquet, *The Playbook: How to Deny Science, Sell Lies, and Make a Killing in the Corporate World*

Frank Close, *Elusive: How Peter Higgs Solved the Mystery of Mass*

Edward Chancellor, *The Price of Time: The Real Story of Interest*

Antonio Padilla, *Fantastic Numbers and Where to Find Them: A Cosmic Quest from Zero to Infinity*

Henry Kissinger, *Leadership: Six Studies in World Strategy*

Chris Patten, *The Hong Kong Diaries*

Lindsey Fitzharris, *The Facemaker: One Surgeon's Battle to Mend the Disfigured Soldiers of World War 1*

George Monbiot, *Regenesis: Feeding the World without Devouring the Planet*

Caroline Knowles, *Serious Money: Walking Plutocratic London*

Serhii Plokhy, *Atoms and Ashes: From Bikini Atoll to Fukushima*

Dominic Lieven, *In the Shadow of the Gods: The Emperor in World History*

Scott Hershovitz, *Nasty, Brutish, and Short: Adventures in Philosophy with Kids*

Bill Gates, *How to Prevent the Next Pandemic*

Emma Smith, *Portable Magic: A History of Books and their Readers*

Kris Manjapra, *Black Ghost of Empire: The Long Death of Slavery and the Failure of Emancipation*

Andrew Scull, *Desperate Remedies: Psychiatry and the Mysteries of Mental Illness*

James Bridle, *Ways of Being: Beyond Human Intelligence*

Eugene Linden, *Fire and Flood: A People's History of Climate Change, from 1979 to the Present*

Cathy O'Neil, *The Shame Machine: Who Profits in the New Age of Humiliation*

Peter Hennessy, *A Duty of Care: Britain Before and After Covid*

Gerd Gigerenzer, *How to Stay Smart in a Smart World: Why Human Intelligence Still Beats Algorithms*

Halik Kochanski, *Resistance: The Undergroud War in Europe, 1939-1945*

Joseph Sassoon, *The Global Merchants: The Enterprise and Extravagance of the Sassoon Dynasty*

Clare Chambers, *Intact: A Defence of the Unmodified Body*

Nina Power, *What Do Men Want?: Masculinity and Its Discontents*

Ivan Jablonka, *A History of Masculinity: From Patriarchy to Gender Justice*

Thomas Halliday, *Otherlands: A World in the Making*

Sofi Thanhauser, *Worn: A People's History of Clothing*

Sebastian Mallaby, *The Power Law: Venture Capital and the Art of Disruption*

David J. Chalmers, *Reality+: Virtual Worlds and the Problems of Philosophy*

Jing Tsu, *Kingdom of Characters: A Tale of Language, Obsession and Genius in Modern China*

Lewis R. Gordon, *Fear of Black Consciousness*

Leonard Mlodinow, *Emotional: The New Thinking About Feelings*

Kevin Birmingham, *The Sinner and the Saint: Dostoevsky, a Crime and Its Punishment*

Roberto Calasso, *The Book of All Books*

Marit Kapla, *Osebol: Voices from a Swedish Village*

Malcolm Gaskill, *The Ruin of All Witches: Life and Death in the New World*

Mark Mazower, *The Greek Revolution: 1821 and the Making of Modern Europe*

Paul McCartney, *The Lyrics: 1956 to the Present*

Brendan Simms and Charlie Laderman, *Hitler's American Gamble: Pearl Harbor and the German March to Global War*

Lea Ypi, *Free: Coming of Age at the End of History*

David Graeber and David Wengrow, *The Dawn of Everything: A New History of Humanity*

Ananyo Bhattacharya, *The Man from the Future: The Visionary Life of John von Neumann*

Andrew Roberts, *George III: The Life and Reign of Britain's Most Misunderstood Monarch*

James Fox, *The World According to Colour: A Cultural History*

Clare Jackson, *Devil-Land: England Under Siege, 1588-1688*

Steven Pinker, *Rationality: Why It Is, Why It Seems Scarce, Why It Matters*

Volker Ullrich, *Eight Days in May: How Germany's War Ended*

Adam Tooze, *Shutdown: How Covide Shook the World's Economy*

Tristram Hunt, *The Radical Potter: Josiah Wedgwood and the Transformation of Britain*

Paul Davies, *What's Eating the Universe: And Other Cosmic Questions*

Shon Faye, *The Transgender Issue: An Argument for Justice*

Dennis Duncan, *Index, A History of the*

Richard Overy, *Blood and Ruins: The Great Imperial War, 1931-1945*

Paul Mason, *How to Stop Fascism: History, Ideology, Resistance*

Cass R. Sunstein and Richard H. Thaler, *Nudge: Improving Decisions About Health, Wealth and Happiness*

Lisa Miller, *The Awakened Brain: The Psychology of Spirituality and Our Search for Meaning*

Michael Pye, *Antwerp: The Glory Years*

Christopher Clark, *Prisoners of Time: Prussians, Germans and Other Humans*

Rupa Marya and Raj Patel, *Inflamed: Deep Medicine and the Anatomy of Injustice*

Richard Zenith, *Pessoa: An Experimental Life*

Michael Pollan, *This Is Your Mind On Plants: Opium—Caffeine—Mescaline*

Amartya Sen, *Home in the World: A Memoir*

Jan-Werner Müller, *Democracy Rules*

Robin DiAngelo, *Nice Racism: How Progressive White People Perpetuate Racial Harm*

Rosemary Hill, *Time's Witness: History in the Age of Romanticism*

Lawrence Wright, *The Plague Year: America in the Time of Covid*

Adrian Wooldridge, *The Aristocracy of Talent: How Meritocracy Made the Modern World*

Julian Hoppit, *The Dreadful Monster and its Poor Relations: Taxing, Spending and the United Kingdom, 1707-2021*

Jordan Ellenberg, *Shape: The Hidden Geometry of Absolutely Everything*

Duncan Campbell-Smith, *Crossing Continents: A History of Standard Chartered Bank*

Jemma Wadham, *Ice Rivers*

Niall Ferguson, *Doom: The Politics of Catastrophe*

Michael Lewis, *The Premonition: A Pandemic Story*

Chiara Marletto, *The Science of Can and Can't: A Physicist's Journey Through the Land of Counterfactuals*

Suzanne Simard, *Finding the Mother Tree: Uncovering the Wisdom and Intelligence of the Forest*

Giles Fraser, *Chosen: Lost and Found between Christianity and Judaism*

Malcolm Gladwell, *The Bomber Mafia: A Story Set in War*

Kate Darling, *The New Breed: How to Think About Robots*

Serhii Plokhy, *Nuclear Folly: A New History of the Cuban Missile Crisis*

Sean McMeekin, *Stalin's War*

Michio Kaku, *The God Equation: The Quest for a Theory of Everything*

Michael Barber, *Accomplishment: How to Achieve Ambitious and Challenging Things*

Charles Townshend, *The Partition: Ireland Divided, 1885-1925*

Hanif Abdurraqib, *A Little Devil in America: In Priase of Black Performance*

Carlo Rovelli, *Helgoland*

Herman Pontzer, *Burn: The Misunderstood Science of Metabolism*

Jordan B. Peterson, *Beyond Order: 12 More Rules for Life*

Bill Gates, *How to Avoid a Climate Disaster: The Solutions We Have and the Breakthroughs We Need*

Kehinde Andrews, *The New Age of Empire: How Racism and Colonialism Still Rule the World*

Veronica O'Keane, *The Rag and Bone Shop: How We Make Memories and Memories Make Us*

Robert Tombs, *This Sovereign Isle: Britain In and Out of Europe*

Mariana Mazzucato, *Mission Economy: A Moonshot Guide to Changing Capitalism*

Frank Wilczek, *Fundamentals: Ten Keys to Reality*

Milo Beckman, *Math Without Numbers*

John Sellars, *The Fourfold Remedy: Epicurus and the Art of Happiness*

T. G. Otte, *Statesman of Europe: A Life of Sir Edward Grey*

Alex Kerr, *Finding the Heart Sutra: Guided by a Magician, an Art Collector and Buddhist Sages from Tibet to Japan*

Edwin Gale, *The Species That Changed Itself: How Prosperity Reshaped Humanity*

Simon Baron-Cohen, *The Pattern Seekers: A New Theory of Human Invention*

Christopher Harding, *The Japanese: A History of Twenty Lives*

Carlo Rovelli, *There Are Places in the World Where Rules Are Less Important Than Kindness*

Ritchie Robertson, *The Enlightenment: The Pursuit of Happiness 1680-1790*

Ivan Krastev, *Is It Tomorrow Yet?: Paradoxes of the Pandemic*

Tim Harper, *Underground Asia: Global Revolutionaries and the Assault on Empire*

John Gray, *Feline Philosophy: Cats and the Meaning of Life*

Priya Satia, *Time's Monster: History, Conscience and Britain's Empire*

Fareed Zakaria, *Ten Lessons for a Post-Pandemic World*

David Sumpter, *The Ten Equations that Rule the World: And How You Can Use Them Too*

Richard J. Evans, *The Hitler Conspiracies: The Third Reich and the Paranoid Imagination*

Fernando Cervantes, *Conquistadores*

John Darwin, *Unlocking the World: Port Cities and Globalization in the Age of Steam, 1830-1930*

Michael Strevens, *The Knowledge Machine: How an Unreasonable Idea Created Modern Science*

Owen Jones, *This Land: The Story of a Movement*

Seb Falk, *The Light Ages: A Medieval Journey of Discovery*

Daniel Yergin, *The New Map: Energy, Climate, and the Clash of Nations*

Michael J. Sandel, *The Tyranny of Merit: What's Become of the Common Good?*

Joseph Henrich, *The Weirdest People in the World: How the West Became Psychologically Peculiar and Particularly Prosperous*

Leonard Mlodinow, *Stephen Hawking: A Memoir of Friendship and Physics*

David Goodhart, *Head Hand Heart: The Struggle for Dignity and Status in the 21st Century*

Claudia Rankine, *Just Us: An American Conversation*

James Rebanks, *English Pastoral: An Inheritance*

Robin Lane Fox, *The Invention of Medicine: From Homer to Hippocrates*

Daniel Lieberman, *Exercised: The Science of Physical Activity, Rest and Health*

Sudhir Hazareesingh, *Black Spartacus: The Epic Life of Touissaint Louverture*

Judith Herrin, *Ravenna: Capital of Empire, Crucible of Europe*

Samantha Cristoforetti, *Diary of an Apprentice Astronaut*

Neil Price, *The Children of Ash and Elm: A History of the Vikings*

George Dyson, *Analogia: The Entangled Destinies of Nature, Human Beings and Machines*

Wolfram Eilenberger, *Time of the Magicians: The Invention of Modern Thought, 1919-1929*

Kate Manne, *Entitled: How Male Privilege Hurts Women*

Christopher de Hamel, *The Book in the Cathedral: The Last Relic of Thomas Becket*

Isabel Wilkerson, *Caste: The International Bestseller*

Bradley Garrett, *Bunker: Building for the End Times*

Katie Mack, *The End of Everything: (Astrophysically Speaking)*

Jonathan C. Slaght, *Owls of the Eastern Ice: The Quest to Find and Save the World's Largest Owl*

Carl T. Bergstrom and Jevin D. West, *Calling Bullshit: The Art of Scepticism in a Data-Driven World*

Paul Collier and John Kay, *Greed Is Dead: Politics After Individualism*

Anne Applebaum, *Twilight of Democracy: The Failure of Politics and the Parting of Friends*

Sarah Stewart Johnson, *The Sirens of Mars: Searching for Life on Another World*

Martyn Rady, *The Habsburgs: The Rise and Fall of a World Power*

John Gooch, *Mussolini's War: Fascist Italy from Triumph to Collapse, 1935-1943*

Roger Scruton, *Wagner's Parsifal: The Music of Redemption*

Roberto Calasso, *The Celestial Hunter*